To Ellen Hostett
from Faculty - Staff of Western
Menn. School.

The Power of Christlike Living

The Power of Christlike Living

The Power
of Christlike Living

by
LESLIE B. FLYNN

ZONDERVAN PUBLISHING HOUSE
GRAND RAPIDS, MICHIGAN

To the young people of Grace Conservative
Baptist Church, Nanuet, New York, whose
interest in the theme of "following Christ"
prompted this Sunday evening series of sermons

Foreword

Exactly what is Christlikeness?

One of the best known attempts to answer this question is Charles Sheldon's *In His Steps* which, except for the Bible, has outsold all other books in the last century. This best-seller imagines how Jesus would act in a series of situations.

However, the kind of Christlikeness pictured in the New Testament does not spring from imaginative contemplation of Jesus' supposed deportment under certain circumstances. Rather, the New Testament singles out certain qualities in Jesus' character and bids us emulate Him in these particular temperaments.

Approximately a dozen such traits in the disposition of Christ are specifically mentioned as an example for us to follow. These virtues, explicitly spotlighted for us in the Master's conduct as a model for our own behavior, are discussed separately in the following chapters.

Five of these chapters have appeared in *Christian Life* magazine. The author expresses his appreciation to Editor Robert Walker, to whom he is already deeply indebted for his encouragement in the field of journalism, for permission to use these chapters in this book.

People today are striving after beauty of body, spending millions on the outer man. True beauty is the beauty of the soul — the culture of Christlikeness within.

Contents

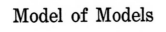

Model of Models

1

Model of Models

A FEW WEEKS BEFORE the Allied invasion of Nazi-held
Europe across the English Channel in 1944, an English officer
was assigned the unusual task of impersonating General Bernard
Montgomery. To enhance his natural resemblance to the general the officer drilled in numerous details, learning to grin,
salute, walk, eat and talk like Montgomery. After several days
of close study on the general's staff he mastered his role.

Whisked to Gibraltar, the new "Monty" leaked information
about a special plan to invade southern France. Clever Nazi
agents relayed the information to Hitler. On to Algiers and the
Middle East he let lurking informers overhear more snatches of
the same secret strategy. The officer played the role so well that
he not only fooled enemy intelligence but many high-ranking
English brass. As a result, Hitler deployed his forces toward the
south of France away from the English Channel, making it
easier for Allied soldiers to get a successful foothold on the
continent on D-Day.

God has a special assignment for every Christian. The ultimate aim of redemption is to make every believer resemble Jesus
Christ. Only, unlike the imitation of the officer, the Christian
outward conformity is strengthened by inward dynamic.

CHRISTLIKENESS — GOD'S PLAN

Originally God created man in His own image. Through
disobedience man scarred this image. To restore this marred
image God sent His Son who was the express image of His
Person. The Lord Jesus Christ lived a perfect example of ideal
manhood, then died on the cross to release the power to realize
this pattern in humans. He became like us that we might be
made like unto Him.

When a man is converted, immediately a far-reaching goal
confronts him. Not optional, but predetermined, the plan calls

13

for conformity to Christ's nature. "For whom he did foreknow, he also did predestinate to be conformed to the image of his Son, that he might be the firstborn among many brethren" (Romans 8:29). The Bible and the church exist mainly for the cultivation of Christlikeness. The Holy Spirit's task is to make men holy after the pattern of Christ.

Though redeemed sinners do not perfectly reflect the example of Christ in this life, some day every believer will fully bear the family resemblance, likeness to the Father and the Elder Brother. The example of Christ is not only a command of what we *should* be but a promise of what we *shall* be.

CHRISTLIKENESS — GOD'S PRECEPT

Christ is both Saviour and Example. The church hasn't always maintained relationship between these two truths. At times stress has been laid on imitation of the Master to the neglect or denial of the atonement. On the other hand, emphasis on pardon and peace through the blood of the cross has on occasion almost crowded out accent on conformity to the character of Christ. Liberals nullify the Gospel when they omit salvation through the blood. Evangelicals emasculate the truth when they fail to underscore the believer's responsibility to follow the model of Christ.

Admittedly, Christ is needed as Redeemer before He is to be imitated as Ideal. A man told a preacher after a sermon on the death of Christ, "I'd rather hear a talk on the example of Jesus!"

"Would you be willing to follow Him if I preach Christ as an example?" asked the minister.

When the man agreed, the preacher replied, "Let us take the first step." Then he explained, "After the Bible says that we should follow in Christ's step, it states in the next verse about Christ, 'Who knew no sin.' Can you take this step?"

The man looked confused. "No, I do sin and readily admit it."

"Well, then," said the preacher, "your first need of Christ is not as an example, but as a Saviour from your sins!"

Many try to walk in the steps of the Master who haven't taken the first step, which is to receive Him as personal Saviour. After that we may follow Him.

Both the Lord and the apostles clearly declare that Christ

came to be not only Saviour but supreme Model for human behavior. For instance, after washing His disciples' feet the Lord said, "I have given you an *example*, that ye should do as I have done to you" (John 13:15).

So indelible an impression was made on sword-swinging Peter by the Lord's non-retaliatory reaction in His final hours, that he wrote, "If, when ye do well, and suffer for it, ye take it patiently, this is acceptable with God. For even hereunto were ye called: because Christ also suffered for us, leaving us an *example*, that ye should follow his steps" (I Peter 2:20, 21).

In approximately a dozen areas the New Testament specifically points to the example of Christ as a pattern for us to follow. We need to look clearly and meditatively at each of these traits of the divine portrait. Not only will this exercise give a distinct impression of what God wants us to be, but by beholding the glory of the Lord, we will be changed into the same image. Since contemplation leads to transformation, consideration of His character will help conform us in Christlikeness.

John Owen, 17th century Vice-Chancellor of Oxford University, wrote, "If our future blessedness shall consist in being where He is and beholding His glory, what better preparation can there be for it than a constant previous contemplation of that glory as revealed in the gospel, that by a view of it we may be gradually transformed into the same glory?"

CHRISTLIKENESS — GOD'S PORTRAIT

Exactly what is Christlikeness?

It is not physical resemblance to Christ. Physically the Lord looked like other men, for on the night of the betrayal Judas had to arrange a sign so those arresting Jesus would know which one was He.

Nor is it a cultural similarity. If it were, then we would walk about in sandals, wear long-flowing robes, speak Aramaic, and men would have beards. Independent of culture, Christlikeness transcends the customs of time and place.

Nor is it following Him in every outward step and circumstance. If we imitated Him literally, we would be carpenters till age 30, then leave our secular work for three years of itinerant teaching, avoid marriage and family life, show little interest in art, science or national affairs, often sleep out-of-doors, and go about penniless. Many medieval Christians mistakenly thought that to fully follow Jesus they had to take the vows of celibacy and poverty.

Many think that Christlikeness is imagining what Jesus would do in every situation, then following His supposed course of action. Such contemplation can be provocative. However, major difficulty is that our conclusions are based on *imagining* what Jesus would do. Often our answer becomes the mere projection of our wishes and opinions. Some people think Jesus would attend a good movie; others are convinced He would watch no television. Some folks suppose Jesus would drink socially in moderation; others are just as sure He would be a total abstainer. The kind of Christlikeness the New Testament enjoins does not spring from fallible speculation on Jesus' hypothetical behavior under certain conditions.

Christlikeness is having the mind of Christ, to catch His spirit, to cultivate His qualities, then apply these attitudes to every situation. Detailed rules of universal moral application are impossible. The motive behind the act is much more important than the overt deed itself. Long prayers offered by Pharisees seem outwardly commendable, but when covering up an embezzlement of widows' property or parading religiosity, such petitions turn out to be sheer hypocrisy. The quality of a deed in isolation is much less significant than the quality of mind from which it springs.

Thus we are to follow Christ in certain inward qualities, temperaments of spirit, frames of mind. This explanation of Christlikeness may prove disappointing to those who like cut and dried rules. But if our inward disposition can become like Christ's, our outward behavior will reflect His likeness.

These qualities involved in Christlikeness, because timeless and changeless, belong to no particular age and culture but adapt to every period, place or situation. Even though Christ never married, His example can lift marriage to its highest level. In fact, the strongest command given to husbands refers to Christ's example. "Husbands, love your wives, even as Christ also loved the church, and gave himself for it" (Ephesians 5:25).

Significantly, Christlikeness resides not in the realm of doctrine, as necessary as orthodoxy may be, but in the area of disposition. It would be possible to contend for a correct creed with a contentious, un-Christlike bitterness. Both are needed — right belief and Christlike spirit.

Neither does Christlikeness relate to gross sins of the flesh but to the "refined" sins of the spirit.

Here are the qualities of Christlikeness specifically singled out in the New Testament for our emulation:

non-retaliation	(I Peter 2:21-23)
menial serving	(John 13:14, 15; Matthew 20:28)
humility	(Philippians 2:3-8)
gentleness	(II Corinthians 10:1)
self-denial	(Romans 15:1-3; Matthew 16:24)
patient under trial	(Hebrews 12:1, 2; I Peter 3:17, 18)
forgiving	(Colossians 3:13)
friendly to outsiders	(Romans 15:7)
joyful	(John 15:11; 17:13)
obedient	(I John 2:6; 3:2, 3; John 15:9-12)
loving	(Ephesians 5:2, 25; John 13:34; 16:12; I John 3:16)

Though "loving" is listed last, love is the all-comprehensive quality, embracing all others. Someone has said that the great love chapter in the Bible, I Corinthians 13, is really Jesus Christ sitting for His portrait. By substituting "Christ" for "love" note how many Christlike clauses are listed in the middle verses of that chapter.

"Christ suffereth long (non-retaliation), and is kind (menial service); Christ envieth not; Christ vaunteth not Himself, is not puffed up (humility), Doth not behave Himself unseemly (gentleness), seeketh not His own (self-denial), is not easily provoked (patient under trial), thinketh no evil (forgiving); Rejoiceth not in iniquity, but rejoiceth in the truth (joyful)."

Love is the principal ingredient in most of the qualities of Christlikeness. Because love permeates each characteristic handled in the following chapters, no separate treatment has been devoted to the theme of love.

How like the varieties of the fruit of the Spirit are the qualities of Christlikeness. "The fruit of the Spirit is love (loving), joy (joyful), peace, longsuffering (forgiving, non-retaliation), gentleness, goodness (menial service), faith (faithfulness, obedience), meekness (patience under trial), temperance (self-denial)."

Similarity between Christlikeness and the fruit of the Spirit is not surprising, for the work of the Holy Spirit is to produce the holy character of Christ within the believer.

CHRISTLIKENESS — GOD'S PROVISION

Christlikeness involves much more than mere outward imitation. To emulate the pattern of Christ in the outer life takes the power of Christ in the inner life. James Stalker who wrote an excellent treatise on *The Image of Christ* pointed out three defects in the otherwise excellent medieval classic on the same theme, *Imitation of Christ,* by Thomas a Kempis. He said the latter work is suited for residence in a monastery, not life in the outside world. Also, it fails to stress the need of forgiveness as a basis for imitation. Finally, it doesn't emphasize internal union with Christ as a source of exterior imitation.

Christlikeness is not laboriously achieved by external effort and vigorous self-discipline. Christlikeness unfolds from within, as we obey the indwelling Christ, inevitable expression of His unfolding life. For a non-Christian to live the Christian life is impossible. Mahatma Ghandi once asked for an impossibility, "I wish I could be Christlike without being a Christian."

The example of Christ by itself does not suffice, for after 19 centuries men are still immoral and avaricious. If the dramas of Shakespeare, or the paintings of Rembrandt, or the compositions of Beethoven were placed before you as examples from which you were to create similar masterpieces, you would fail because you lacked the inward genius of these men. The exterior example of Christ's matchless life cannot be reproduced unless an inward impulse is imparted.

A son often resembles his father in looks, tones, gestures, walk, almost laughably so. Why is this likeness so accurate? Partly because of his continuous opportunity to observe his father and thus unconsciously imitate. More than this, the boy at birth received his father's nature, so that something within is responsible as well as the father's example without. To live Christ we must be able to say with Paul, "Christ liveth in me."

The outliving of this Christ life is not automatic. The New Testament knows nothing of the workings of the Spirit of Christ in us apart from our own moral responses in faith and surrender. Watchfulness, prayer, conscious effort and intelligent cooperation in the program of God are requisites to progress in Christlikeness. Also, the New Testament demands a conscious and determined approximation to the example of Christ. To cultivate this resemblance to Christ's frame of mind, outlook, aims, spirit, qualities, attitudes and disposition, we are specifically commanded to observe the matchless portrait of Christ. But all this eager striving will be but useless beating of the air unless we have received inner grace.

Andrew Murray put it thus in *Like Christ*, "If Jesus Himself through His life union will work in me the life likeness, then my duty becomes plain, but glorious. I have, on the one side, to gaze on His example so as to know and follow it. On the other, to abide in Him, and open my heart to see the blessed workings of His life in me."

The Holy Spirit uses Christ before us to help reflect Christ within us.

The winsomeness of Christlikeness provides a powerful method of drawing people to the Christian faith. A wealthy family was scheduled to entertain a famous minister who was coming for a series of services in their town. The mistress sent the maid downtown to buy the finest cut of meat, adding, "I want the best for the minister."

In the butcher shop the maid sneered, "Some saint is coming to our town to speak, and my mistress is entertaining him. I must have the finest cut of meat. You would think that the Lord Himself is coming."

A few days later the maid returned to the butcher shop for more meat. She seemed subdued and quiet. The butcher asked how she was getting along with the saintly visitor.

Meekly the maid replied, "A few days ago I said you would think that the Lord Himself was coming. I want you to know I think I have seen the Lord this week!"

Do others see the Lord in you?

So, They Insulted You

2

So, They Insulted You
(I Peter 2:21-23)

BACK IN THE DAYS OF SLAVERY a plantation owner who suffered financial reverse was forced to sell Cuff who had served him faithfully. His new master was an atheist. "You'll find Cuff a good worker in every way except for one thing," he told the atheist.

"What's that?"

"He'll pray quite a bit and you can't break him of the habit. But that's his only fault."

"I'll soon whip that out of him," threatened the new master.

"I wouldn't advise you to try, for Cuff would rather die than give up," were the former master's parting words.

Cuff was faithful to his new master, obeying orders, sweating from morning to night. But he prayed. Word reached the master. Angrily he sent for him, "Cuff, you must not pray any more. Never let me hear any more such nonsense."

"O Massa, Ah loves to pray to Jesus, and when Ah prays Ah loves you and the Misses all the moh, and can work all the harder for you."

"I don't care. We don't want it here. If you pray again, you'll be taken out and flogged."

Despite the order Cuff prayed. The master heard of it and summoned him. "Why have you disobeyed me?"

"O Massa, Ah has to pray; Ah can't live without it."

The master flew into a temper, ordered Cuff tied to the whipping post and cracked the whip over his raw back five times. Then he kept on bringing the lash on the bleeding back. Cuff's wife ran out. He threatened to beat her. Finally out of exhaustion he stopped beating the slave, ordering salt rubbed into his wounds. Ordered back to work, Cuff went away singing,

23

"Mah sufferin' time will soon be o'er; When Ah shall sigh and weep no moh." He worked faithfully the rest of the day. That night the master couldn't sleep. He was convicted of his cruelty. He woke his wife and asked if she thought anyone on the plantation would pray with him. She suggested Cuff. "Do you think he would pray for me?" he asked.

"Yes, I think he would," his wife replied.

Cuff was summoned. When the messenger found Cuff, he was praying, and thought sure he was in for another beating. Brought into the master's presence he was amazed to hear him ask, "O Cuff, can you pray for me?"

"Bless the Lawd, Ah's been prayin' for you all night!" He spoke of the Saviour to the master who became a believer. Both of them toured the nearby vicinity telling the Gospel.

By his patient behavior Cuff obeyed Peter's command to slaves to follow the example of Christ. "For even hereunto were ye called: because Christ also suffered for us, leaving us an example, that ye should follow his steps: Who did no sin, neither was guile found in his mouth: Who, when he was reviled, reviled not again; when he suffered, he threatened not; but committed himself to him that judgeth righteously" (I Peter 2:21-23).

Our Lord's actions in connection with His crucifixion encourage a meek non-retaliation in the face of abuse and invective. In fact, we are specifically told that Christ's longsuffering without complaint or counterblast is a model for us to follow.

The word "example" refers to a schoolboy's copy-slate on which the writing-master wrote characters which were to be copied carefully. Likewise, penned for us in Sacred Writ are the indelible strokes that spell out the Saviour's silent suffering in the face of rankest, rudest mistreatment, which we are commanded to studiously imitate. The figure changes from copy-slate to a path along which we are urged to follow His steps of calm submission.

Though the sufferings of Christ were unique in regard to the atonement, for none of us can suffer as the Saviour and thus provide forgiveness for others, yet the sufferings of Christ with respect to reaction to scurrilous maltreatment provide a pattern for similar conduct by those who profess to be His followers.

He Reviled Not

The vendetta, in which obligation rests on relatives of a murdered or wounded man to take blood vengeance on the person who has caused death or injury, still prevails in some quarters, such as Corsica. But the Lord Jesus Christ never undertook a vendetta against those who conspired against His life or the life of His friends.

When growing up He learned of Herod the Great's attempt on His life which forced His family to flee to Egypt and which caused the slaughter of innocent babes, but He instituted no revenge against the descendants of wicked Herod. Nor did He seek vengeance on another Herod who beheaded His cousin, John the Baptist.

After preaching in His home town of Nazareth, He was rejected by His own townsfolk, who tried to throw Him over a precipice. His reaction was, "A prophet is without honor in his own house." Though He marveled at their unbelief and limited His miracle-working, He didn't revile.

The folk in Jairus' house laughed Him to scorn when He suggested Jairus' daughter was not dead. He didn't return the mockery by shouting, "I'll show you!" but restored her to her parents. He never sulked with nursed resentment.

The blasphemous accusation of being in league with the devil was hurled at Him by the Pharisees who said that He cast out demons by the prince of demons. The Lord didn't castigate them in reply, though He did show them the absurdity of their charge.

When ordered out of an area after healing demon-possessed men, He didn't say, "I'll go, but first let me tell you something," then proceed to give His hearers a piece of His mind, and later report, "I sure gave them an earful!"

To be called insane is not easy to take. Jesus' brothers made light of Him, suggesting He was out of His mind (Mark 3:21). No retaliatory remark escaped His lips.

When the Pharisees took counsel to slay Him He didn't call down twelve legions of angels but quietly withdrew from the area (Mark 3:6, 7). To the officers sent by the Pharisees to apprehend Him He spoke gently and graciously so that the soldiers returned to the chief priests empty-handed saying, "Never man spake like this man" (John 7:32-46). Repeatedly His enemies sought to arrest Him, but no man laid hands on

Him, because His hour was not yet come, neither is there a record of a nasty word hurled by our Lord at His would-be murderers (John 7:30; 8:20, 59; 10:31, 39).

Invectives against our Lord during His ministry were sporadic and scattered. During the final twenty-four hours of His life insults became concentrated and almost continuous. To the yelling mob who came to arrest Him in the garden He simply asked, "Whom seek ye?" When He told them, "I am He," they toppled backward to the ground through the majesty of His person but through no retaliatory blow by Jesus. Had He wished, He could have discharged thousands of angels to wipe out this band of Romans. He didn't revile Judas who was then committing one of the vilest acts of treachery in human history. Rather He allowed Judas to kiss Him and even called the traitor, "Comrade" (Matthew 26:50). When Peter drew his sword and cut off the ear of the high priest's servant, Jesus restored the ear.

Soviet Premier Khrushchev on a visit to a French Cathedral said, "There is much in Christ that is in common with us Communists, but I cannot agree with Him when He says when you are hit on the right cheek, turn the left cheek. I believe in another principle. If I am hit on the left cheek I hit back on the right cheek so hard that the head might fall off." How different from Christ! Few persons have ever been reviled like Jesus Christ. No one has reacted so magnificently. And we have been commanded to follow suit.

Before Caiaphas and the Sanhedrin false witnesses accused Jesus, but He was silent. Because non-retaliation makes a fight impossible, it was said, "He held His peace" (Mark 14:61). He did not fume back. Then the chief priests, scribes and elders mocked Him, buffeted Him, blindfolded Him and struck Him on the face with the palms of their hands sneering, "Prophesy, thou Christ, which one smote you." Many other blasphemies they threw in His face (Luke 22:63-65).

Accused before Pilate by the chief priests and elders, He answered nothing, which made the governor marvel. Sent to Herod because He came under His jurisdiction, Jesus was mocked by Herod, set at nought or made a zero, and dressed up in a gorgeous make-believe royal robe (Luke 23:9-11). He took it sweetly.

Pilate ordered Jesus scourged. The cruel whip lashed His

back, cutting deep and even swishing around to gash His front. The soldiers scoffingly placed a crown of thorns on His brow, outfitted Him in a kingly garment, put a reed in His hand as a make-believe sceptre, bowed as if to worship and saluted, "King of the Jews" (Matthew 27:27-31). Then they spat on His face, and with the spit dripping down His face and hanging from his beard they wrenched the reed from His hand, smote Him on the head, pulled off the robe and put His own raiment on. He never struck back by word or deed.

Historians report that when a man was about to be crucified he would invariably struggle against his executors as they tried to hold his arms so a nail could be hammered through his hand. The victim would squirm, scratch, kick, bite, scream, swear, spit at his tormentors until he had been securely hung up. Not so with Jesus. Instead of vile vituperation he prayed, "Father, forgive them; for they know not what they do" (Luke 23:34).

Lifted up for all to see He became an object of abject sarcasm. Passersby wagged their heads, "You said you could rebuild the temple in three days. Save yourself, if you are the Son of God. Come down from the cross." The rulers, chief priests, scribes and elders derided Him, "He saved others; Himself He cannot save. Come down from the cross and we will believe you." The soldiers jeered; both thieves at first cast the same scoffings in His face. "If thou be the Christ, save thyself and us." But all through the six hours of the cross, not a cry of revenge broke the stillness. Seven short sayings, uttered at an average of one per hour, revealed the anguish of His soul, words only of redemption, not retaliation. How humiliating for the Lord of glory to take such abuse from sinful, loathsome creatures. But Thomas a Kempis in his book, *Of the Imitation of Christ*, says, "He deserves not the name of patient who is only willing to suffer as much as he thinks proper, and from whom he pleases. The truly patient man asks not from whom he suffers, his superior, his equal, or his inferior; whether from a good and holy man, or one who is perverse and unworthy. But from whomsoever, how much soever, or how often soever wrong is done him, he accepts it all as from the hand of God, and counts it gain."

To stand on our rights, claim our privileges, return evil for evil and blow for blow, to demand our pound of flesh reflects not the Lord Jesus Christ who gave His back to the smiters and His cheek to those that plucked off His hair, who hid not His face from shame and spitting (Isaiah 50:6), and who as a sheep before her shearers is dumb opened not His mouth (Isaiah 53:7).

The cross of Christ stands not only as an act of unique atonement, but also as an example of patience under sufferings. In the hour of mistreatment our Lord does not expect to us to perform an act of redemption for sin, for this has been effected once-for-all by Christ's vicarious death, but He does require that we follow in His steps and bear the injustice without recrimination. Admittedly, this precept becomes complicated when interwoven with other duties such as the protection of others against violence, but when it involves only ourselves in a personal situation, the injunction remains clear.

HE RESTED IN DIVINE JUSTICE

The silence of Jesus in the face of injustice was not due to any failure on His part to recognize as evil the abusive treatment He was suffering. But His calm behavior evidenced deep faith in the moral government of the universe. Though evil wore a crown while good was nailed to a cross, He believed that His Father reigned on the throne and some day would make all things right, punishing wrong and rewarding right.

Hence He told His disciples that if they were rudely received in a city to shake off the dust from their feet as a symbol of future judgment when it would be more tolerable for Sodom than for that city. But judgment on that city was not their business but the Lord's responsibility. "Vengeance is mine, saith the Lord." Should a person speak vilely to us, he puts himself in danger of judgment (Matthew 5:22); but should we revile him in return, we likewise make ourselves possible candidates for judgment. Far better to commit the insult to the Judge above and thus follow the steps of Christ.

Non-reviling doesn't necessarily mean a person should not answer back. Before the Sanhedrin Jesus was asked if He were the Christ. He didn't keep silent at this point but affirmed that He was the Messiah, adding that they would "see the Son of man sitting on the right hand of power, and coming in the clouds of heaven" (Mark 14:62).

When an answer was needed to vindicate the truth, Jesus answered. When an answer was pointless, no reply was forthcoming. When reviling was in progress, an answer would only add fuel to the fire. But to the tempting Satan He replied, "It is written." He defended His association with publicans and sinners. He upheld the practice of corn-picking and healing on the Sabbath. He did not hesitate to correct error, "Ye have heard that it was said, but I say unto you." He defended Mary's expenditure of expensive ointment against the claim of waste. When the Pharisees charged Him with casting out demons by the devil, His reply made their accusation easily misfire. When criticized because His followers transgressed the tradition of the elders, He retorted by charging His accusers with violating the tradition of God. To the Pharisees who claimed He was bearing false record of Himself He answered kindly but firmly. In fact, many discourses in John's gospel are replies to disbelief and false charges. When the Pharisees and Sadducees tried to trap Him with trick questions, He answered, and answered so well He left them gasping. So, non-retaliation doesn't rule out defense.

Nor does a non-reviling attitude forbid rebuking. He rebuked His disciples for their little faith and hardness of heart. He reproved Martha for over-agitation on mundane matters. He scolded Peter, "Get thee behind me, Satan: thou art an offence unto me: for thou savourest not the things that be of God, but those that be of men" (Matthew 16:23). He warned against the doctrine of the Pharisees. He called them to their face, "a wicked and adulterous generation" (Matthew 12:39). He rebuked but never reviled.

He even became angry at times, pronouncing in righteous indignation woes on the hypocritical Pharisees, castigating the money-changers in the temple. Jesus' scathing scorn was never the result of personal vindictiveness but stemmed from love of righteous principles. A magazine article asked, "Do You Act — or React?" Too often we let other people's remarks and actions determine what our responses will be. Better for us to so possess the life of Christ within, that snubs, criticisms and harsh accusations do not disturb our inner serenity. Intemperate reaction indicates that we are controlled by the situation, rather than in control.

So often in our heated remarks we are egged on by pride and self-defense. When an object is thrust near our face our eye closes in self-defense. When an object moves in our direction, we automatically raise a hand to ward off the blow. Likewise a sense of proud honor jumps to defend any slight or insult against our person, egging us on to return evil for evil. Christ's anger was objective, impersonal, without malice. So much of ours is subjective, personal and spiteful. Many arguments around the home would never occur if we yielded to Christ's power within and His pattern without.

The Son cared not for His own honor, only the Father's honor, which He defended by reply, rebuke and sometimes righteous wrath. The Son knew that the Father would care for the Son's honor ultimately, thus entrusted all revilings to the Father who someday will judge righteously.

A preacher confided in a friend, "I'm going to resign. I've been mistreated by members of my church!"

The other asked, "Have they crowned you with thorns yet? Or did they spit on you? Have they nailed you to a tree?"

The preacher saw the point and continued his pastorate.

He Returned Good for Evil

Not only did our Lord refrain from reviling when reviled, but more than that, He returned good for evil and blessing for cursing. At His arrest He restored the ear of the high priest's servant. At the crucifixion He did not rail at His tormentors but instead prayed, "Father, forgive them, for they know not what they do." To the repentant thief who had previously joined his voice in mocking Him, Jesus promised, "This day shalt thou be with me in paradise." The first two of the seven cries from the cross were words of blessing in return for reviling. Even while being blasphemed, He was in the process of earning redemption for those calling Him names.

This kind of conduct astounded His viewers. Governor Pilate earlier had marveled at His silences (Matthew 27:14). The centurion in charge of the crucifixion was moved by such behavior to exclaim, "Truly this was the Son of God" (Matthew 27:54). Fifty days later 3,000 people changed their mind about Him, calling Him their Saviour and Lord, many of whom, if not the majority, probably insulted Him during His sufferings. To remain silent under provocation is so unnatural that it helps people to believe in the Supernatural. When the first martyr, Stephen, was being stoned with bricks and rocks that were battering his body into a bruised and broken mass of human pulp, he never picked up a single stone to throw back. Instead, following Jesus' example he prayed, "Lay not this sin to their charge" (Acts 7:60). Not long after this a young man who guarded the clothes of those who stoned Stephen, and who was the leading opponent of the early Christians, capitulated to Christ on the Damascus road. One of the pricks that goaded him toward Christ was the memory of Stephen's deportment.

Vituperation, insulting abuse and invectives will not persuade the non-Christian to trust in Christ. A lady went to her pastor to request him to speak to her husband about becoming a Christian. The pastor did and was told that the wife had a terrible temper. "If this is what Christianity does to a person, I want nothing of it," the husband replied. The pastor relayed the husband's complaint to the wife. She was shocked but realized that the charge was true. She fell before the Lord in penitent prayer. Next week when the husband entered the living room after a fishing trip his protruding pole accidentally knocked over his wife's prize lamp. Crash! The husband put his hands over his ears to drown out the next expected crash, his wife's scorching rebuke. But no crash. After momentary silence, he heard her say, "Don't worry about that lamp, dear. What's a lamp? We can always replace it!" He could scarcely believe her reaction. A few weeks later he made a profession of faith in Christ, whose beauty had been seen in his wife's life, as she followed His example.

When two prize chickens wandered into a neighbor's vegetable patch, the neighbor wrung their necks and tossed them over the fence whence they had come. The lady next door seeing her chickens fly over her fence and land with a thump on her lawn, ran out to the still flapping birds. Her children wondered what mother's reaction would be: angry denunciation of the ill-tempered neighbor, tears, or crying on father's shoulder when he came home. To their amazement she heated a big kettle of water and proceeded to make two delicious chicken pies, one of which she took to the neigbor with an apology for the damage her chickens had done to the vegetable patch. The children hid behind a bush to see the neighbor's expression. He who never lacked words to express his anger stood speechless and ashamed.

A soft answer not only stops anger, but stirs up amazement. Turning the other cheek, walking the two-mile way, helping those who hate us, and praying for our persecutors, are among the most potent ways of advertising the Gospel. Thereby is Christ seen in all His majestic strength of character.

A Spanish evangelist in Latin America was eating dinner in a restaurant before the evening service. Fastidious about his appearance, he was impeccably dressed in a white linen suit. Suddenly the waiter slipped and spilled soup all over the evangelist's coat and trousers. With profuse apologies he cringed before the evangelist, for waiters had been known to lose their jobs through such carelessness. But the evangelist who was slightly burned jumped to his feet and quickly reassured the waiter and the manager that all was well, even though he knew it meant preaching in soiled clothing. Next night the evangelist returned to the same restaurant. About to leave he saw the waiter beckon. He followed him to a side room where the waiter begged him to tell how he could have acted so kindly instead of letting loose with a string of oaths. The evangelist told him of Christ who when reviled, reviled not again.

To behave like that requires the power of Christ within. Only then can we follow the pattern of Christ without. A nurse complained to a preacher that she had been rudely treated by some of the patients. "Thank God," replied the preacher.

"What do you mean?"

"Why," said the minister, "if you are carrying a dish and someone bumps you, you can only spill out of the dish what's inside. Since you have Christ within, Christ will spill over." To trace in daily life the model of Christ in Holy Writ we need the might of Christ in our heart.

When Walter "Happy Mac" MacDonald, well-known evangelist, became a Christian in 1925 in the Pacific Garden Mission in Chicago, the old crony who ridiculed him the loudest was "Doc." Though he never learned Doc's last name, MacDonald made his acquaintance while he was in big-time vaudeville in Chicago and Doc was a barker for a dive where standing out on the sidewalk he would chant with a big, gravel voice, "You're just in time for the next show." MacDonald used to take several barkers into speakeasies during Prohibition and treat them to a drink. Doc, a big-boned, middle-aged six-footer with heavily lined face, hated the Pacific Garden Mission which was located just a few doors from his dive. The other barkers hated it, too, for many a star performer was lost to these joints through finding Christ in the mission. "It's unhealthy for our business to have that mission right in the same block," Doc would often say. But MacDonald didn't have the same dislike for the mission, for unknown to his friends he had been attending meetings there for weeks. He always made sure his friends never saw him go in or come out for he wanted to save face with his barker friends.

But came the night when MacDonald was saved. His life changed from hard-drinking, much-dancing, big-time comedian to one of real joy. Thrilled to know the reality of sins forgiven he soon became songleader at the mission but he wondered what his old pals would say when they found out, so avoided them for a week. But knowing he had to face them sooner or later he started down State Street one night. An old pal spotted him, "You louse! We ain't got no use for you! Beat it!"

Nearing Doc's place he heard his voice ring out, "The geereatest and biggest show in all Chicago!" He broke off, "Well, if it ain't little Reverend Happy Mac. Happy, say it's a lie. Say it ain't true that them Mission heads got my old pal."

"No, Doc, it isn't a lie. I've become a Christian. I'm through with the old life."

Doc wanted no more of it. He warned, "I might bring some of the boys and drop in on you at the service some night!"

Sure enough, next night, Doc and another barker stood outside while Mac led the singing, all the time flapping their arms and mimicking him. Says Mac, "The fact I didn't lose my temper but kept on singing was proof I had new life."

The climax came when eight friends met MacDonald on the street one night, lined up, four on each side. As he walked between them and spoke, they chanted, "One, two, three, ptoo!" They spit on his new tan suit and shoes. Unlike his old self, Mac responded, "Your aim is excellent, Doc. Caught my new trouser leg and my shoe."

Doc growled back, "That all you got to say?"

"Not quite, Doc. There's this. When you get to know Jesus Christ the way I do, you'll be able to unclench your fists. You'll let a guy spit on you, and it'll be all right!"

MacDonald didn't see Doc for three weeks until one night he showed up in the mission, on the front row. As the invitation was given, MacDonald slipped beside him. "You're not mad at me, Mac?" Doc asked.

"The Lord won't let me get mad anymore."

"Mac, you been a Christian long enough to know how to lead a guy to Jesus?"

"Yes, Doc."

"Then, I'm your customer." That night Doc accepted Christ. Then he showed Mac a letter that had been the reason for his coming to the mission. His mother was dying and he was preparing to go to her bedside. He had promised her years before he would become a Christian but had never come within miles of keeping his word.

Two weeks later Doc was back in Chicago. He had spent just three hours with his mother before she passed away, overjoyed at her son's decision. Doc still continued as a barker on the street, only this time inviting people into the Pacific Garden Mission. One day two weeks later he dropped dead on the sidewalk. Says MacDonald, "I thank God from the bottom of my heart for the day old Doc spit on my tan shoes and trousers."

An old Spanish proverb says, "To return evil for good is devilish; to return good for good is human; to return good for evil is God-like." We would make a slight change, "To return good for evil is Christ-like."

Service With a Capital "S"

3

Service With a Capital "S"

(John 13:13-16)

FAMED OPERA SINGER Jerome Hines walked unheralded into
the Union Gospel Mission in Chattanooga, Tenn., one evening
recently to sing for society's unfortunates. Fresh from successful
appearances at the Metropolitan Opera in New York and the
famed La Scala in Milan, Italy, he had come to the city for
a concert in Memorial Auditorium. He sang hymns and testified that for years he had stumbled around as a spiritual pan-
handler till the Lord found him. When several men responded
to the invitation, the physically imposing 6-foot 7-inch singer,
who commands thousands of dollars for concert appearances,
left the platform to kneel beside a man to pray with him.

In stooping to lowly service this giant singer is following the
example of Him who though greater than all condescended
to menial tasks. The Creator and Sustainer of the universe
became not only man but servant, tending the needs of His
creatures. He gave us a pattern of humble ministry which He
commanded us to follow. He taught that true greatness doesn't
consist in attaining first place to be served by others, but in
willingness to drop to an obscure spot to serve even a little
child for the sake of Christ (Mark 9:34-37).

Often the disciples argued among themselves who would
be chief in the coming kingdom. Once their ambition-laden
dispute incongruously followed the Lord's disclosure of His
coming deliverance and death. Another time James and John
aspired through their mother's intervention to the two top seats
in the kingdom. The Lord answered that ambition in heathen
circles sought to land number one position so as to wield
power. But in Christ's circles it was to be the opposite. "Who-
soever will be great among you, shall be your minister: And who-
soever of you will be the chiefest, shall be servant of all." Then

to offset the lofty attitude of His disciples He introduced the
example of His own lowly service, adding, "For even the Son
of man came not to be ministered unto, but to minister, and to
give his life a ransom for many" (Mark 10:43-45).

Most graphic of all occasions when the disciples fought
over future leadership was when the Lord not only taught lowly
service but followed with an indelible demonstration.

During the Paschal supper, with the Saviour's cross less than
24 hours away, the reclining disciples inappropriately fought
among themselves which should rank the highest. Again our
Lord patiently advised, "He that is greatest among you, let him
be as the younger; and he that is chief, as he that doth serve."

Then He asked, "Whether is greater, he that sitteth at meat,
or he that serveth? is not he that sitteth at meat?"

The fillip came when the Lord declared that He was the
waiter, "I am among you as he that serveth" (Luke 22:26, 27).

At this point, according to some scholars, Jesus rose from
His place to do a servant's chore. Common courtesy demanded
that a host should at the arrival of guests wash their feet
soiled by treading dusty streets. Because the upper room was
borrowed no person was present to take care of the usual ablu-
tions. But basin and towel had been thoughtfully provided.
Who would do the honors? With the atmosphere charged with
feverish ambition no aspiring leader would abdicate his throne
of ambition to kneel before his subjects. Looking away from
the towel and basin with studied indifference each regarded
this task too menial for his dignity.

Then something amazing happened. Jesus rose from His
place and picked up the basin and towel. The Lord of Glory
at whose beckon legions of angels were ready to serve with in-
stantaneous response, with full consciousness of His divine
glory, chose the servant's place, taking the soiled feet in His
own hands.

When He had gone the rounds He stated in language which
must have fallen with thunder-like intensity that they were to
follow His model.

"If I then, your Lord and Master, have washed your feet;
ye also ought to wash one another's feet. For I have given you
an example, that ye should do as I have done to you" (John
13:14, 15).

Although a majority of believers do not believe the Lord

meant that we should establish a foot-washing ordinance, none of us can escape the clear injunction to serve others in need, even those on a lower social scale.

Late one night during a conference at Moody Bible Institute, the famed evangelist was walking around the halls to see that all was in order. Turning a corner he came upon the guest rooms where some visiting English preachers were sleeping. Outside each door was a pair of shoes.

Moody remembered the English practice which called for placing one's shoes outside the door on retiring so the host could polish them before morning.

Spotting several students he said, "These ministers are following the custom of their country where they always put their shoes out to be cleaned at night. Would you fellows get a piece of chalk from a class room, put the number of the room on the soles of the shoes, then shine them nicely."

One student protested, "Mr. Moody, I didn't come to this institution to clean shoes. I came here to study for the ministry." The others said the same.

"Very well," said Moody, "you may go back to your rooms."

Then Moody himself collected the shoes, took them to his room, polished them nicely and put them back in place.

An interesting sidelight in the career of the distinguished apologist and seminary professor, the late Dr. J. Gresham Machen, occurred during World War I. Applying for service with the overseas YMCA, he was first assigned the lowly task of manufacturing and selling hot chocolate drink in quarters in a French village. The involved process consisted in shaving up large bars of sweet chocolate, adding a fixed quantity of boiled water, then adding a larger quantity of water, all the time mixing the chocolate in, bringing the whole to a boil, adding condensed milk and then ending with a final boiling. To open the canteen at 7 A.M. meant rising much earlier to prepare the hot drink and postponing his own breakfast till after 9 A.M. Though he wished for heavier responsibility especially in Christian service, this ordained and scholarly professor was content with the opportunity to perform such menial service.

Meanness of work never lowers a person. Rather, the spiritual law of rank says the higher you wish to stand the lower you must stoop to serve. Exalting office comes through abasing service.

The Lord served in various ways, such as teaching, preaching and healing. It was He who broke the bread and distributed it in twelve baskets to His disciples. He it was who replenished the refreshments at the wedding at Cana. He arranged for the Upper Room, broke the bread and distributed the wine at the Last Supper. The Lord of Glory served!

In the Emmaus home after the resurrection He who was guest became host for again He broke bread. On the seashore in the third post-resurrection appearance to all the disciples He prepared the fire, had fish and bread laid thereon, then used the fish the disciples caught, issuing the invitation, "Come and dine." He appeared to be the cook.

Peter described Him as one "who went about doing good, and healing all that were oppressed of the devil" (Acts 10:38). All the time He was Master He was also Servant, answering the call for help and ministering to the needy.

How brimfull of activity our Lord's days must have been. In his *Harmony of the Gospels* A. T. Robertson terms the events recorded in Mark 3:19 - 5:21 a "busy day," just one of many such in the Master's ministry. In the morning He teaches a crowded audience. He is insulted. Later His mother and brothers try to take Him away as mentally deranged. In the afternoon He relates an unusual group of parables, some of which He privately interprets in a home. Toward night He crosses the lake by boat, so tired that he sleeps soundly amid the howling storm. On the other side He heals the Gadarene demoniacs, then returns the same night. What a toilsome day!

The supreme service He performed was the giving of Himself in redemption. This work is listed as a separate ministry. He came to minister "and to give his life a ransom for many." Even while giving His life on the cross He ministered to the spiritual cry of the dying thief and took care of His mother.

So strongly does the example of Christ's service dominate early Christian thinking that the titles given leaders in the early church signify service. A minister is simply one who ministers or serves — a servant. The word *deacon* comes from a verb which means to *minister* or *serve*. A pastor is a servant-shepherd of the flock. A bishop is an overseeing servant. Church leaders are not bosses but servants, as are all Christians.

Though heaven cannot be earned by works, the concept of service stands prominent in the gospels and epistles, not only in spiritual tasks like witnessing and giving, but in physical ministrations. Some positive applications of the law of service include relieving illness and pain, helping the mentally distressed, hospitality to strangers, visiting the aged, comforting the sorrowing, befriending the outcasts and feeding the hungry.

During World War II the vice-president of a bank on Wall Street found himself weighed down with extra work imposed by the war. Yet he found time four nights each week, after a hard day's work in the city and a weary commuter's ride to his New Jersey community, to act as volunteer orderly in the nearby veterans' hospital. He fed, washed and readied for bed warshocked soldiers.

Pure religion involves not only separation from worldliness but visitation of the fatherless and widows in their affliction (James 1:27).

Even the insignificant favor of a cup of cold water in Jesus' name will not go unrewarded — and even when offered to a despised person or child.

The parable of the Good Samaritan teaches that service must be extended to anyone in need that crosses our path, regardless of color or creed.

Americans live in a land blessed beyond measure materially. The rest of the world is not so fortunate. More people on our globe go to bed hungry each night than have sufficient food.

More people live in huts of mud and straw than in any other kind of shelter.

More people have a life expectancy of 35 years of age than of any higher figure.

More people travel by walking or on the backs of small animals than in any other way.

More mothers see half their children die than raise all their children to maturity.

More people live and die without the help of any doctor than enjoy even elementary medical care. Are not these unfortunate folks, so needy of service, our responsibility?

The Lord taught that in the day of judgment sheep will be separated from goats. The division will be based on the performance or neglect of simple ministrations. Those on the King's right hand will hear Him say, "Come, ye blessed of my Father, . . . For I was an hungred, and ye gave me meat: I was thirsty and ye gave me drink: I was a stranger, and ye took me in: Naked, and ye clothed me: I was sick, and ye visited me: I was in prison, and ye came unto me" (Matthew 25:34-36).

Because these displayed kindness to God's people they inherited the kingdom. Neglect of simple mercies sent others into everlasting punishment. Destiny hinges on man's response to the needs of others.

If our eternal destination rests on whether or not we have fed, visited, clothed and helped the needy, does this not contradict the Gospel of grace which says salvation comes through faith and not by works? Faith without works is dead. If we have genuinely experienced the mercy of Christ through faith, then we cannot help but be merciful to others in need. Failure to do good to the less fortunate may indicate that we have not truly experienced the mercy of Christ.

Significantly our Lord told the disciples to wash each other's feet because He had done the same to them (John 13:15). Because Christ stooped in lowliness to us, we should stoop to lowly deeds for others. Consciousness of personal relationship to Christ motivates kindness in our dealings with others. He served me, so I should serve. If I serve not, perhaps I've not been served by Christ.

The Pharisees bound heavy burdens on men's shoulders, but did not move them with one of their fingers (Matthew 23:4). How unlike Christ, the great Burden-bearer! Lack of sensitiveness to the loads of others indicated they had never been relieved of their load of sin.

A man was praying with great fervor in a prayer meeting for a family whose father had suddenly died.

"Oh God, do send someone to bring comfort to that sorrowing family. . . ."

Suddenly his voice faded. Quietly he left the meeting. Before the service closed, he returned.

Asked why he had so abruptly finished his prayer and left, he replied, "As I asked God to touch that grief-stricken family, He seemed to tell me that I was to go and touch them for Him."

Our whole duty to our fellow-man was reduced by our Lord to "love to neighbor" (Matthew 22:39). This duty Paul restates in this fashion, "By love serve one another" (Galatians 5:13, 14).

When Sir Bartle Frere, great English philanthropist and one time governor of Cape Colony, wrote his wife in London that he was coming home, she called the new coachman, "I want you to go to the station to meet your master." She told him the time of arrival. He politely bowed. "A moment, your ladyship. I have never seen Sir Bartle. How shall I recognize him at the station?"

She thought for a moment, then proudly replied, "Look for a great big man helping somebody. That will be my husband."

At the station cabs and carriages crowded the area. The coachman looked up and down the platform and saw a great many big men. Then he saw a woman trying to get out one of the train doors, but was wedged in with a big box and suitcase. Suddenly a tall man, morning-coated, came and raised his silk hat politely.

"Madam, may I help you?" Relieving her of all her bundles he asked, "Where are you going?"

She said, "I wish a cab, sir."

He took her across the platform, hailed a cab, then put her in, giving the cabbie directions.

As the cab drove off the coachman stood there. He saluted, "Is this Sir Bartle Frere, sir?"

"Why yes, who are you?"

"I am your coachman, sir."

"Oh yes, I remember. My wife told me the other man had left. And so you are my new coachman."

He was about to climb into the coach when he stopped, "By the way, how did you know me?"

"Please sir, her ladyship said I was to look for a big man helping somebody."

This isn't a bad definition of Christlikeness. Someone helping someone else because he has first been helped by the Greatest of all helpers. Sir Bartle Frere delighted to carry other people's burdens because Jesus had carried his.

Our sense of debt to Christ should urge us to faithful, unpretentious service. Out of gratitude for His grace that redeemed us from our guilt we should gladly minister to those in distress. With the pattern of Christ without, and with the power of Christ within, we should go about doing good, as He did. Even at best, we shall still be unprofitable servants.

You Aim to Please — But Whom?

4

You Aim to Please — But Whom?
(Romans 15:1-3)

A MARRIED COUPLE with no children was asked by the transportation committee of a church if they would pick up two brothers from a disinterested family and bring them to Sunday school each week.

As the only church members living in that area, the couple thought over the assignment. It would mean rising earlier every Sunday, driving several blocks out of their way, perhaps getting the car dirty from wet feet on rainy mornings. And it might hamper their frequent Sunday trips. They said "no" to the transportation committee.

But this is not the scriptural way. Christians are told not to please self but to please one's neighbor.

This command is reinforced by reference to Christ's example. "For even Christ pleased not himself; but, as it is written, The reproaches of them that reproached thee fell on me" (Romans 15:1-3).

We do no irreverence to our Lord to assume that He would have found it much more pleasant to remain where He could enjoy the privileges of heaven than to suffer the privations of earth. Had He selfishly pleased Himself we would not know the joys of redemption.

He temporarily abdicated His residence, reputation, riches, rest, even life itself. These comforts He voluntarily surrendered that we might enjoy the conveniences of salvation. Christlikeness demands denial of self for the upbuilding of others.

RESIDENCE

The Lord gave up His heavenly home to come to earth. To a would-be follower, Jesus pointed out that though the birds

47

had nests and the foxes had dens, He had no place to pillow His head (Matthew 8:19, 20).

At the end of a busy teaching day in the temple His hearers retired to the relaxation of their homes. But Jesus kept walking through the streets of Jerusalem, passed through the gate and climbed the mount of Olives, doubtless His frequent sanctuary for sleep and prayer. "And every man went unto his own house . . . Jesus went unto the mount of Olives" (John 7:53; 8:1).

In His final hours He said, "In my Father's house are many mansions" (John 14:2). No one knew better than He the mansions He had left behind.

In leaving His heavenly residence Christ left the immediate, intimate fellowship of His Father in glory, though He communed with Him in ceaseless prayer. With full consistency He could say to a potential disciple who wanted to take care of a dying father, "Follow me; and let the dead bury their dead" (Matthew 8:22). Or, "He that loveth father or mother more than me is not worthy of me" (Matthew 10:37).

When Jesus asked James and John to move out from under their father Zebedee's roof, He had already practiced what He preached, for He had left His Father's residence.

Christlikeness demands willingness to relinquish family ties despite the anguish it may cause. Self-indulgent church members little realize the torn hearts of missionaries as they leave their young children at schools on the field for months at a time, or at school in the homeland not to see them for five years.

About to return to their field in Argentina one couple wrote, "As sailing date approaches, we know the Lord will continue to be sufficient as we leave our son and daughter behind at school, and say what may well be our final good-bys to our aged parents until we meet on eternity's shores."

Are you willing to deny yourself your TV to attend Sunday evening service? Or the warmth of your fireplace to join the prayer meeting? Or the comfort of an easy chair to go out on visitation for the church?

RICHES

A well educated skeptic was trying to tell a humble believer that the Bible nowhere stated that Jesus Christ had any existence before He came into the world. They were standing on a train platform. The believer said he was sure the Scriptures were full of verses on the pre-existence of Christ but wasn't making much progress in the argument. Then an informed preacher appeared. Both men turned to him, "What do you think about the question?"

"One verse settles that for me," he said

"What verse?" asked the skeptic.

"Second Corinthians eight nine. 'For ye know the grace of our Lord Jesus Christ, that, though he was rich, yet for your sakes he became poor, that ye through his poverty might be rich.'"

"Well," retorted the skeptic, "how does that prove the question?"

"Tell me," replied the preacher, "when was He rich? Was He rich when He was born in a stable and cradled in a manger? Was He rich when He worked at the carpenter's bench in Nazareth? Was He rich when He had to say, 'The foxes have holes and the birds of the air have nests, but the Son of Man hath not where to lay His head'?"

The humble believer's face lit up, "I know when He was rich."

The preacher's train pulled in at that moment. As he stepped on board he heard the believer pressing the question to the skeptic, "Tell me, tell me, when was He rich?"

The pre-incarnate Christ possessed inestimable wealth. Though He owned the cattle on a thousand hills, He subjected Himself to poverty. As an incentive to some early believers to give generously, Paul introduced the example of Christ. "Though He was rich, yet for your sakes He became poor, that ye through His poverty might be rich" (II Corinthians 8:9). Because Christ denied Himself riches which were rightfully His, we should give sacrificially.

That Joseph and Mary lacked earthly goods is revealed in the offering they brought to the temple at the dedication of their baby Jesus. Proper offering was a lamb and a pigeon or dove (Leviticus 12:6). But the poor were permitted to bring a second dove or pigeon instead of the costly lamb (Leviticus 12:8). Joseph and Mary offered the alternative sacrifice (Luke 2:2, 3).

When the Lord began His public ministry He depended partly on the financial support of women-followers (Luke 8: 2, 3). The disciples pooled what little money they had in a common bag with Judas as treasurer. When the disciples plucked corn on the sabbath, it was because they were hungry. The practice of picking standing corn was permitted the wayfaring and the hungry, part of a Jewish program for the poor.

When the Herodians subtly asked Jesus if tax money should be paid Caesar, the Lord asked for a penny. He probably had none.

When tax-collectors asked Peter for his Master's tax the Lord provided the tax money by having Peter hook a fish in whose mouth was found a coin.

For many important events of His final week He had not the wherewithal. He used someone else's donkey for the so-called triumphal entry. When the disciples asked where they should prepare the passover, He gave directions to a borrowed room. Most people make provisions for their final resting-place by purchasing a plot in advance. He was laid away in someone else's sepulchre. At His death He had no possessions except those on His back, five items of clothing which were divided in front of His dying eyes.

Such an example gives sharp emphasis to His warnings against covetousness. It also explains why early believers sold their property to help their needy brothers.

Christlikeness does not require believers to take a vow of poverty. But it does demand self-denial in the midst of crass materialism.

How little sacrifice is known today! One Sunday school class decided that at Christmas they would not accept gifts from their teacher, but would together, students and teacher alike, bring an offering for an Alaskan orphanage.

A couple about to spend a lavish sum on a non-essential pondered Christ's refusal to indulge self and gave the money to their church's missionary fund.

What if every professing follower of the rich One who became poor began immediately by denying himself the purchase of some prospective luxury, and instead gave the money to the less fortunate?

REST

Some men in public life cannot step out on the street without recognition and crowd-adulation. Hence they eat their meals in hotel rooms, travel with bodyguards, use private elevators and keep their whereabouts secret. Yet from the beginning days of His public ministry the Lord's fame catapulted Him into the limelight which robbed Him of His privacy. Crowds thronged Him, bombarding Him with requests for service.

When four men brought a palsied fellow for healing, the crowd so blocked the door that they had to let the victim down through the roof (Mark 2:4). He once ordered a boat readied lest the mob crush Him (Mark 3:9). So great was the pushing multitude on some occasions that He and the disciples could not eat (Mark 3:20; 6:31). Another time the crowd was so large He had to preach from a boat (Mark 4:1). One day He was so tired that He fell asleep in the back part of a boat in the midst of a violent storm so great that seasoned sailors despaired of safety as wind and waves almost submerged their pitching craft.

No political campaigner ever hit the road harder than Christ, nor endured greater rigors.

He often rose early to find a solitary place to pray (Mark 1:35). He prayed all night before choosing the twelve (Luke 6:12). Would you deny yourself sleep to show up at an early morning prayer session?

When the Samaritan woman neared Jesus, who was sitting down because He was weary, He could have rationalized, "I'm too tired to talk to her." But He didn't please self. Despite weariness He proceeded to lead her to trust in Him.

How willing are we today to answer a call for service which may mean getting dressed up, leaving a favorite pastime or book, taking time and energy to go somewhere out of the way? Jesus repeatedly surrendered whatever plans He may have had to meet the problems of others.

A Sunday school teacher was invited to a picnic on Saturday afternoon. Though his family went, he felt he should make some visits. Though he frankly wished he was sitting in a nice cool spot under the shade of an apple tree, he ploddingly made his calls. One was the home of a little boy recently brought to Sunday school by a neighbor. Though the mother did not let him in, she later invited him back. As a result both parents were later won to Christ.

Had Jesus remained in heaven His peaceful existence would not have been interrupted. But He chose to give up the tranquility of glory for the turbulence of earth. To be like Him calls for relinquishment of rest, ease and comforts to help others who are restless, uneasy and in discomfort.

RIGHTS

Though the incarnate Christ did not abandon His deity on coming to earth, He did forego some of the rights of deity. Though He was the omnipresent One, He became subject to the limits of space. Though omnipotent, He learned like other children. He temporarily relinquished the rights to ubiquity, power and knowledge.

Christians are sometimes called on to surrender, for a while, certain rights to help weak Christians grow stronger. In the church at Rome some weak believers had scruples against eating meat and against non-observance of Sabbaths. Strong Christians, like Paul, knew that eating meat did not defile nor was it necessary to observe days. But to keep over-scrupulous believers from stumbling Paul suggested a surrender of rightful liberties (Romans 14:21). He sums up his argument thus, "We then that are strong ought to bear the infirmities of the weak, and not to please ourselves. Let every one of us please his neighbor for his good to edification." At this point he supports his argument by the example of Christ, who "pleased not himself" (Romans 15:1-3).

Insistence on our Christian freedoms may sometimes bring disaster to weaker saints. Had Christ insisted on His, no church would exist today. One man said, "Since Christ gave up His rights, I willingly deny myself the liberty of imbibing strong drink lest my influence drag others into the whirlpool of alcoholism."

LIFE

Not only did Christ give up for us His residence, reputation, riches, rest, rights, but even His very life. Paradoxically, He who was the author of life and called Himself the *Life* permitted Himself to be cut off out of the land of the living. No man took His life but He laid it down of Himself (John 10:18). He parted from life that we might partake of it.

Most believers can quote the well-known John 3:16 about God so loving the world that He gave His only begotten Son. But few can quote the other John 3:16, specifically known as I John 3:16, "Hereby perceive we the love of God, because He laid down His life for us: and we ought to lay down our lives for the brethren."

Christlikeness may call for the supreme sacrifice of dying for others. Jim Elliot, one of the five young men martyred by the Auca Indians, wrote, "We have bargained with Him who bore a Cross, whose emphasis was upon sacrifice. Let nothing turn us from the truth that God has determined that we become strong under fire, after the pattern of the Son." He also wrote, "He is no fool who gives what he cannot keep to gain what he cannot lose."

The non-Christian attitude seeks to please self at the expense of others, whereas self-denying love seeks to please others at the expense of self. Both priest and Levite failed to inconvenience self in any way as they passed by their wounded countryman. But the Good Samaritan put self-pleasure to the background, interrupted his travel schedule, expended time, energy and money to help the unfortunate Jew.

A prisoner at Rome, Paul wrote the Philippians that only Timothy had a genuine interest in them. Not one of Paul's other fellow helpers was sufficiently selfless to make the trip to Philippi. They were too occupied with the promotion of their own affairs. Their love of ease, family and comfort made them unwilling to sacrifice their own quiet security. This indicated to Paul that they hadn't yet learned very deeply the self-denying service of Christ (Philippians 2:20, 21).

An official of a church was asked why he hadn't supported a week of special meetings in his church. He replied that he couldn't shut down his business even one night in the week an hour earlier. But the following month he shut down his business, not just an hour earlier, but closed up entirely for a whole week to take a hunting trip.

A pastor called on a young man several times to persuade him to teach some teen-age boys in Sunday school. After many refusals his wife exclaimed, "Why don't you tell the preacher why you're refusing?"

He confessed it was because he played golf through the week and on Sunday morning, some of which he would have to give up for lesson preparation and teaching. The pastor pressed the challenge. The young man renounced his golf and took the class. A few months later he walked down the church aisle during an evangelistic campaign with the sixth and last boy to become converted in a class of thirteen.

Later the pastor asked, "Has giving up golf been worth-while?"

Tears flooded the young man's eyes as he jubilantly replied, "This is the greatest day of my life. Now I'd far rather spend my time telling others about Christ. I'm only sorry I didn't begin to teach years ago instead of wasting my time on less important things."

Self-renunciation is the essence of following Christ. Jesus gave of Himself. Do you yield to the Spirit of Christ within so that like Christ you can say, "Thy will, not mine be done in my life! Thy pleasure, not mine!"?

Outsiders Welcome!

5

Outsiders Welcome!

(Romans 15:7)

IN THE BOOK, *In His Steps*, author Charles M. Sheldon movingly portrays how a young lady from the upper register of society takes an outcast, alcoholic girl into her fashionable home to live, against the wishes of her horrified, aristocratic grandmother.

Driving in a carriage with several members of her smart set through the slum section of their city, Virginia is startled when the door of a notorious saloon suddenly opens and out reels a young woman singing in a drunken sob. When the girl leers up at the carriage rolling by, Virginia recognizes the girl as the one she had prayed with after an evangelistic meeting a few nights previously. Virginia, who recently has taken the pledge to live as Jesus would live, has felt it her duty to sing the Gospel in some services in the slums though she lived in a mansion on the boulevard and her voice often graced the concert stage.

"Stop," cries Virginia to the driver. In a flash Virginia leaps to the drunken girl's side, puts her arm around her, and calls her by name, "Loreen!" The girls in the carriage are smitten with astonishment. "Drive on," Virginia calls, "I'm going to see my friend home." The girls in the carriage gasp at the word "friend."

The carriage moves on and Virginia is alone with Loreen, except for some derelicts from the slums who look on with little expression. "Where does she live?" When no one answers, it dawns on Virginia that this wreck of humanity has no home. Then the thought flashes across her mind, "What's to hinder me from taking Loreen home? Why shouldn't this homeless wretch, reeking with liquor fumes, dirty and ragged, be cared for in my own home instead of being assigned to strangers in some hospital or place of charity? What would Jesus do?" Her decision made, she takes Loreen by the arm and steers her toward the trolley-stop at the corner.

Virginia painfully notes the stare of passengers on the crowded trolley. But her concern now centers on the approaching scene with her wealthy grandmother. What will Madam Page say?

As they leave the street-car and walk up the avenue with its lovely mansions, Loreen lurches heavily against Virginia time and time again, which makes people curiously turn and gaze at them. When they mount the steps of her handsome house Virginia breathes a sigh of relief even in the face of the interview with Grandmother Page.

As Loreen stares blankly at the magnificent furniture, Virginia says to her grandmother who had entered the hallway, "I have brought one of my friends home. She's in trouble, has no home and I'm going to take care of her here for a while."

Gulping in amazement, Grandmother Page asks, "Did you say she is one of your friends?"

"Yes," Virginia affirms in a clear voice, recalling a verse in the Bible which speaks of Jesus as a friend of sinners.

With a cold, cutting, sneering tone, the grandmother replies, "Do you know what this girl is?"

"I know she is an outcast. She is drunk at this minute. But I saw her kneel at the altar in the services the other night and ask to be forgiven. And I also see the devil reaching out to lure her back into her old life. By the grace of Christ I feel the least I can do is to give her a home for a little while to help keep her from slipping back. So I have brought her here and I shall keep her. After all, this house belongs to me!"

Madam Page clenches her fists, glares at Virginia, "We'll lose standing in society. This is so contrary to our social code. How can you be familiar with the scum of the streets?" Virginia puts her arm more tightly around Loreen. The grandmother stamps her foot and threatens emphatically, "I shall not stay in this house!" In a few hours she packs and leaves.

Whether she knew it or not, Virginia was obeying Paul's command, "Receive ye one another, as Christ also received us" (Romans 15:7). Also, she was following the example of Christ who in His dealings on earth with teeming humanity welcomed outcasts, outsiders and outlaws. If the exalted Lord

Jesus Christ received us in our unlovely status, should we not likewise welcome the unacceptable?

> Did you ever stop to think
> How lonely God would be
> If the only folks He loved
> Were those as good as He?

During His ministry He rubbed shoulders with rich rulers and poor widows. He accepted invitations to dinner at the home of the self-righteous Pharisee Simon and the penitent publican Matthew. He fellowshiped with adults but took babies and children in His arms. Multitudes moved Him to compassion but He had time for interviews with the individual. A large share of His energies were devoted to the sick, while still directing much effort toward the healthy. He paid attention to both white-collared lawyers and menial fishermen. His wide receptivity was foreshadowed in His infancy when poor shepherds and rich Magi came to adore Him.

Human nature often fawns before the ruler, the rich, the righteous, the mature, the robust and the respectable, at the same time slighting those on a lower social rung. Though receiving both types the Lord never hesitated to rebuke the so-called higher levels. While a guest in a Pharisee's home, He permitted a woman known to be a sinner in the city to anoint His feet, and chided His host for his self-righteousness. He warned of the leaven of the Pharisees and Sadducees, pronouncing a seven-fold woe on the religious leaders, even calling them, "Hypocrites, wicked and blind leaders of the blind." His failure to scrape before celebrities earned Him the reputation of fairness. His opponents said to Him, "Neither acceptest thou the person of any" (Luke 20:21). Literally, "You do not receive the face." Our Saviour was not a face-receiver, looking on the outer status and welcoming people because they were important or rich. He was not guilty of discrimination or snobbery. Let us follow Him in His welcome for the socially stigmatized, the Samaritans and the sinners.

WELCOME FOR THE SOCIALLY STIGMATIZED

1. Women

Though not exactly stigmatized, women and children were considered inferior to men on the social scale. Regard for them as mere chattel still prevails in many eastern countries. Before World War II a Westerner noted an eastern man riding on an animal while his wife walked several feet behind. After World War II he asked the native if the war had made any difference in the treatment of women. "Oh, yes," he replied, "I still ride on the animal, but my wife walks several feet in front of me." When pressed for a reason he explained, "That's in case there are any land-mines that haven't exploded!"

From the beginning Jesus welcomed a feminine following including such names as Mary, Martha, Mary Magdalene, Joanna, Salome and Susanna, who not only listened to His teachings but ministered to His material needs. Even women ostracized by society were recognized by Him. Women followed Him on His last journey from Galilee to Jerusalem, aided Him on the way to the cross, watched His burial, prepared spices for His interment, were first at the tomb on the resurrection morn and were the first to announce His rising from the dead. Certainly womanhood was lifted to a status before unknown in the history of their sex by the Lord's attitude toward them.

2. Children

In some areas missionaries must not say anything nice about a child. Some pagans believe that the gods are jealous of children. So as not to excite their jealousy they call their children by terrible names. Should a missionary admiringly exclaim, "What a lovely baby," the mother would be frightened lest the gods in jealousy snatch this little life from her. So unlike these envious gods, the Lord Jesus Christ lifted childhood to a new level of honor by His loving actions and remarks. When His disciples tried to keep mothers from bringing their babies to Him, thinking these infants-in-arms a nuisance to Him, Jesus sternly rebuked the disciples and said, "Allow the babies to come to me. They're no bother. Don't stop them, for of such is the kingdom of heaven." Then He took the infants in His arms and offered a blessing.

He upgraded childhood by putting a child on stage and pointing to it as an example of humility. Childlikeness, not childishness, is a requisite for entrance into God's family.

We tend to disparage child conversions. "Oh, it's just a child responding to the invitation to accept Christ," someone slightingly remarks. D. L. Moody once reported that he had had 2½ conversions the night before. "You mean — two adults and one child?" "No," said Moody, "two children and one adult. The adult only has half a life to live."

3. The Sick

Some healthy people find sick people a burden and do not wish to be bothered with them. A little boy who limped found himself left out of sports by playmates who didn't want to adapt their games in any way to his handicap. A blind lady found few people who would read to her or take her for a drive. Some persons feel squeamishly self-conscious if seen in the presence of the disfigured or deformed.

Not so with Jesus. He received all the sick brought to Him. Descending from a mount, He met a leper. Others were repulsed by the sight of a man full of leprosy and hurried away. Today viewers of missionary movies that vividly picture ulcerous sores of lepers often close their eyes or even become nauseated. But Jesus touched him! Once He healed ten lepers, men who were forced to cry "unclean" and live outside the towns and villages.

A blind man sat at a table at a Bible conference. Some Christians studiously avoided that table. In addition to the inconvenience of guiding his hand to his fork, knife, and spoon, was the gnawing embarrassment of sitting in the company of a blind person. But Jesus received many blind people. One man He took by the hand and led him along the road to the edge of town and healed him (Mark 8:22-26). More than once He put His fingers on what may well have been most "unsightly" eyes. When blind Bartimaeus persisted in calling out to Jesus as He walked along the highway, Jesus didn't pretend not to hear but welcomed him. If we are like Jesus supernatural receptiveness will overcome natural repulsiveness.

Some people mock the blind and make fun of the deaf and dumb. A little girl suffered a speech impediment. Another lassie who attended Sunday school and should have known better kept asking her questions just to hear her stammer and make other children laugh at her. Jesus received a man who was both deaf and impeded in speech, and healed him, even touching his tongue (Mark 7:32-37).

The demon-possessed presented unlovely sights. Two wild, fierce men, naked, living outdoors in the wilderness, able to break off any chains bound on them, were visited by Jesus who cast out the demons. Though demon-possession seems not too prevalent in our culture, many are mentally retarded or emotionally ill. A harmless mentally retarded boy, big for his age, was rejected by other children and mistreated by other parents who continually hollered at him, "Get off our porch. Go away from here." Paul says we should receive one another, even as Christ received us.

After World War II a radio announcement near Christmas urged relatives of veterans who were hospitalized with mental illness to visit them during the holiday season. It stated that one-quarter of 50,000 mental inmates had not received a visit from a relative for a year or longer.

Every state hospital has a list of patients who have been pronounced well and who could leave the institution immediately if only there were homes to receive them.

Our Lord received all types of sick folks. Seeing the multitudes He was moved with compassion on them, healing their diseases (Matthew 14:14). He welcomed the lame, the dumb, the tormented, the man with the withered hand, the palsied, the fevered, the impotent man who had been an invalid for 38 years, the woman with an issue of blood 12 years, the woman bowed and bent for 18 years, the epileptic.

A few miles north of New York City, Camp Joy, operated by the Rev. Mr. Win Ruelke of the Children's Bible Fellowship, runs several weeks of camping for mentally retarded and handicapped children. The loving reception given these afflicted boys and girls reflects the welcome Jesus always gave the sick.

4. *The Poor*

A young lady who dedicated her life to live as the Lord Jesus would have her live was walking up the main street of her city one morning. Just in front of her she noticed a woman carrying two big black bundles and tagging along, two untidy little children. She was a foreigner who had just come in from the east on the morning express. Her clothes were mussed and her head was covered by a dirty handkerchief. The Christian girl says, "I felt a strong impression to speak to her and offer help, but with it came a feeling of repulsion. What would people on the street think? They might take her for my mother and these filthy children for my sisters. I tried to get rid of the thought that it would be like Jesus to help her, but just as I was passing her, she turned and asked if I could give her directions to the bus terminal. I was going right by there myself, so now couldn't doubt that God wanted me to help her. What a struggle for a moment, but His grace enabled me to reply, 'Yes, I'm going right there and will show you the way. Let me take one of those bundles for you.' I took the bundle for Jesus' sake, although I felt as if a fire raged at the roots of my hair. It seemed everyone was staring at me and laughing. To make things worse, one of the children began to bawl loudly. Then I was sure everyone was looking at us. But I marched on for Jesus' sake, even taking the other bundle so the mother could carry the weary baby. When I put the bundles on the seat in the bus station waiting room I had to turn aside and weep, for the blessing of God came on my soul." She knew the joy of Jesus in receiving the poor and needy.

The poor had a large place in the Saviour's heart. When John the Baptist asked proof of Jesus' Messiahship, Jesus replied, "Tell him that the poor have the gospel preached to them."

5. *The laboring class*

In some circles people, perhaps unwittingly, give greater honor to the white-collared, professional man than to the fellow who works in overalls. Yet, for His first four disciples, our Lord called fishermen, not executives sitting behind glass-topped desks. None of us has anything to say about our birth, but our pre-existent Lord consented to be born in a carpenter's home, of a peasant maiden of low estate, in a run-of-the-mill family. He Himself became a carpenter at the bench, working with tools. No wonder He invited to come to Him, "All ye that labor and are heavy laden" (Matthew 11:28), those toiling and bearing difficult burdens.

He received the commoners of this world. A young lady who moved in society circles had a maid help her now and again. She made the domestic eat all her meals by herself, even when just the family was eating. Quite often she shared the maid with her mother, who was a Christian. Whenever the maid ate at the mother's she was invited to eat with the rest of the family as an equal. The Lord received many who were considered last down here but who in divine judgment may well someday be considered first.

6. *Those with some record of shame*

The dying thief was pardoned by the Lord. A man with a prison record found a welcome from the Saviour. One class of persons in modern society who sometimes have a strike or two against them are ex-convicts trying to go straight. It may well be that too harsh treatment has been dealt those who have run afoul of the law and paid their debt. A young man who had been in jail secured a job he liked very much, night clerk in a downtown hotel. After three weeks of faithful work, he was spotted at his desk one night by a detective. The detective then told the manager that he had an ex-convict working for him. The manager fired the man. The ex-convict later got in more trouble and ended up behind bars.

Our Lord spoke of visiting those in prison as well as the stranger, sick, ill-clad and hungry. His welcome extends to all outcasts including the broken-hearted and the bruised, and all who are socially "different." At a summer Bible conference a speaker approached the snack shop after the evening service. It was his custom to eat with the other speakers and distinguished conference leaders. As he entered the dining-room he spotted a queer-looking fellow sitting alone at a table, while most other tables were filled with conversation and gaiety. The hostess mentioned that this fellow had asked for company. The speaker went to that table and spent the next half-hour in conversation with this lonely Christian man who had driven 100 miles to attend the conference over the weekend. Would not Christ have done this? If Christ were to welcome us as we receive others, perhaps He would have to leave us out.

WELCOME FOR THE SAMARITANS

The Samaritans were outsiders, second-class citizens, in the mind of the Jews of Jesus' day. But our Lord welcomed the Samaritans equally with His own people. Early in the gospel record we read, "And he must needs go through Samaria" (John 4:4). The Jews usually deliberately avoided Samaria on their trips from Galilee to Jerusalem. On that trip Jesus joined in conversation with a Samaritan woman.

His lack of prejudice constantly asserted itself. When asked for a definition of a neighbor, He replied with a story commonly called the parable of "the Good Samaritan," which tells how a Jew, who was seriously beaten by thieves and deliberately by-passed by a Jewish Levite and priest, was mercifully doctored and provided for by a Samaritan. Our neighbor is everyone in need regardless of race, nationality or color.

An optometrist had just set up his office in his home in a new neighborhood in Los Angeles, when his first customer walked in to have her glasses fixed. After examining them the optometrist said he could find nothing wrong. The patient confessed, "I know they're all right. It was just an excuse to come in and get acquainted and make you feel welcome." This experience made the optometrist's heart glow, for his was the only Japanese-American family in the neighborhood.

During Christ's ministry the Jews were the chosen people. The Samaritans and the Gentiles were the outsiders. By His welcome of these outside groups Christ stood against anti-Gentilism. Today the tables are reversed. The church is composed chiefly of Gentiles; the Jews are the outsiders. The example of Christ's welcome to all is given to urge Gentiles and Jews to receive each other in the church at Rome (Romans 15:7). Some of the converted Jews wishing to join the church at Rome still held to sabbath-keeping and kosher meats. Paul urges the Gentiles to receive these on confession of faith (Romans 14:1). The group without scruples and the group with scruples should not judge or condemn each other but live its Christian life in good conscience before God. To both groups Paul exhorts, "Receive ye one another, as Christ also received us."

No Christian should be guilty of anti-Semitism. If Christ received those beyond the pale of Judaism, we should welcome those beyond the borders of Gentilism. Anti-Semitism which recently expressed itself in the extermination of six million Jews by Nazi Germany in a systematic, scientific, business-like way, is so unnatural, inhuman and irrational.

Some Americans speak disparagingly or think condescendingly of immigrants from other countries. Perhaps our prejudices take in more groups than we realize. During World War II, a lady phoned a USO Committee, "I'll be glad to have three soldiers for dinner next Sunday at one o'clock," then added, "I don't want Jews." Her doorbell rang at one o'clock sharp on Sunday. Answering the door she found three Negro soldiers standing there. One spoke up, "I understand, lady, that you want three soldiers for dinner today." Taken by surprise she replied, "I think some mistake has been made." The Negro smiled, "I don't think Sergeant Cohen made a mistake."

Someone has said that "the most segregated hour of the week is still 11 o'clock Sunday morning." Though people tend to gravitate in their social and church life along nationalistic and ethnic lines, is it Christlike to shut the door and exclude anyone because of his nationality or color, especially after the Sunday school has taught the boys and girls to sing, "Red and yellow, black and white; They are precious in His sight; Jesus loves the little children, All the children of the world"? Since 1952 all of Billy Graham's crusades have been nonsegregated. Though campaigns have been held in every southern state except three, sometimes with one-third the audience Negroes, not a single unpleasant incident has occurred.

The story is told of a Sunday morning service in a fashionable church in Richmond, Virginia, shortly after the Civil War. When communion was being served, a Negro who had entered the service walked down the aisle and knelt at the altar. Resentment rustled through the congregation. Suddenly a distinguished layman stood up, stepped forward and knelt beside the Negro. Captured by his magnanimous action the entire congregation followed suit. The layman was Robert E. Lee.

WELCOME FOR THE SINNERS

A major problem of Brazil is public prostitution. In a small Brazilian town some girls involved in this immoral practice came to the Presbyterian mission hospital for treatment. After medical care a fine Christian doctor witnessed to them of the Gospel of Christ, then invited them to the local church. A few weeks later half a dozen of them hesitantly walked into the morning service and sat timidly by themselves. At the end, when nobody spoke to them, they left hurriedly. They returned the next Sunday. Soon there was an uproar. The righteous ladies of the congregation were up in arms. They didn't want those women to dare to come in the church. Word indirectly reached the girls who never came back.

Christ's pattern would show the attitude of the church ladies to be un-Christlike. When on earth, the Lord accepted the woman of Samaria who had had five previous husbands and was at that time living with a man who was not her husband. Rather than withdraw from this stained soul, He led her to believe on Himself as the Water of Life so that she became a flaming witness to her own townsfolk who knew her unsavory reputation well. Jesus said on one occasion to the religious but self-righteous leaders, "That the publicans and the harlots go into the kingdom before you" (Matthew 21:31). When a woman caught in the very act of adultery was dragged before Him, He forgave her repentant soul.

No wonder the hymn writer penned,

> Sinners Jesus will receive;
> Sound this word of grace to all
> Who the heavenly pathway leave,
> All who linger, all who fall.

We speak of our receiving Christ, but we receive Him because He first received us. Careful scrutiny of Christ's genealogy in Matthew reveals a foreshadowing of His willingness to be linked with the socially inferior, the racial outsider, and sinners. He consented to be born into a line that specifically mentioned four women, at that time considered low on the social scale, two of whom at least were Gentiles, and another two of whom were guilty of adultery.

Because Christ came to save the lost, how fitting that He spent much time in the company of sinners. The occupation of tax-collector was held in deep disdain and linked with the lowest of the low. Hence the expression, "publicans and sinners." Yet our Lord called a publican to be one of His disciples and led him to author the first gospel, Matthew. After his call to service Matthew threw a big dinner to which he invited a large number of publicans and sinners and Jesus, for Mark says, "there were many, and they followed him" (Mark 2:15). And Jesus accepted the invitation. As a result He was criticized because He ate and drank "with publicans and sinners" (Mark 2:16).

If an alcoholic persists in seeking help in the fellowship of some evangelical churches, he might find something less than a welcome. Before long he might find himself shoved off to the Salvation Army, the waterfront mission or Alcoholics Anonymous. Yet Jesus so received sinners that He earned the reputation of a man "gluttonous, and a winebibber," as well as "a friend of publicans and sinners" (Matthew 11:19). He did not participate in drunken revellings which Peter forbids believers to indulge in (I Peter 4:3), but He did so associate with the intemperate that He was known as their companion and friend. Does the average Christian today let himself get very close to or involved with unsavory characters, or does he not rather pull his skirts of self-righteous separation about him and keep such sinful folks at proper distance? Much more Christlike was the gesture of Deputy Inspector Conrad Jensen of the New York City police who one night was told by Jim Vaus, worker among East Harlem delinquents, that a gang leader by the name of Shane had accepted Christ that evening. Policeman Jensen who knew Shane well, for he had often been in trouble with the law, put his arm around Shane and said, "That makes us brothers now."

Moody Monthly magazine carried the "Confession of a Pharisee" who along with two other church members lived in a lovely neighborhood where the only moral blot was Ada, a woman married to her second husband with whom she violently fought. The family brawls with their abusive language were caused by constant drinking. The three church members, all of whom lived across, next to or around the corner from Ada and all of whom were Sunday school teachers or members of the Ladies Society, were ashamed to meet Ada on the street or in a store, for fear with reeking alcoholic breath or loud voice she would introduce them as her friends. Not one of the ladies called on her. Then rumors began to circulate of Ada's serious illness. They planned to go over some time or ask her to lunch, and tell her about Christ and invite her to church. But one day a hearse drew up to Ada's house. Ada had tried to quit liquor but couldn't. The confession ends, "The silent witness of that body on the stretcher will haunt us for a long time. Can one of us honestly say we cared for Ada's soul? That's why I say we three are Pharisees."

Since our Lord came to die for sinners, including thieves, how fitting He should die between thieves. Most people would not like their picture taken with a thief on either side. But people are proud to have their picture snapped with some celebrity. Yet every time the three crosses are depicted, Christ hangs between robbers.

James has a paragraph pertinent to the subject of welcoming people into God's house. In modern parlance it reads, "My brothers, don't hold the faith and be guilty of snobbery. If there come to the door of your church a man with a gold ring, well-dressed, and there also enters a poor man in patched clothing, and you shower attention on the well-dressed man and say, 'Here's a front seat for you,' but you shove the shabby fellow back in the corner, are you not then guilty of partiality?" (James 2:1-4). James, whether he was half-brother or disciple of Jesus, knew full well that such discrimination was far removed from His Master's example.

Because the Lord Jesus Christ extended a loving welcome to outcasts, outsiders and outlaws, every Christian is debtor to the lowest, the least, the last and the lost.

"I'll Forgive, But I Won't Forget"

6

"I'll Forgive, But I Won't Forget"
(Colossians 3:13)

THE MURDER OF FIVE YOUNG American missionaries by Auca Indians on a river-bed deep in Ecuador's rain forest a few years ago startled the civilized world. Not so well known — since then Mrs. Betty Elliot, widow of one of the missionaries, and Rachel Saint, sister of another, have moved into Auca territory to live unharmed among the very Indians who took the missionaries' lives.

All five of the killers who are still living have asked the Lord for pardon. Also, they have taken hours of Christian instruction. In surprise some may ask, "How could Mrs. Elliot ever forgive these Aucas for killing her husband? How could Rachel Saint sit down day after day to patiently teach these savages who were her brother's murderers?"

The answer is found in the teachings and example of the Lord Jesus Christ. Not only did He emphasize forgiveness, but He practised it both during His ministry, and through His redemptive work on the cross. Sacred writ exhorts the Christian to "meekness, longsuffering; forbearing one another, and forgiving one another, if any man have a quarrel against any." Then to buttress this virtue, the inspired record points to the example of the Master. "Even as Christ forgave you, so also do ye" (Colossians 3:12, 13). Christlikeness calls for a forgiving spirit.

CHRIST FORGAVE

The good news of the Gospel boils down to one word — forgiveness. Christ came to forgive. To the man sick with palsy He uttered these cheering words, "Thy sins be forgiven thee." He led the woman of Samaria who had had five husbands to joyful heart-cleansing. He absolved the woman

71

taken in adultery, "Neither do I condemn thee; go, and sin no more" (John 8:11). He forgave Zaccheus his greed for gold and fraudulent practices saying, "This day is salvation come to this house" (Luke 19:9).

CHRIST FORGAVE MUCH AND MANY

Not only did Christ forgive but He forgave repeatedly and magnanimously. He taught unlimited forgiveness. Peter once asked the Lord, "How oft shall my brother sin against me, and I forgive him?" Without waiting for an answer Peter generously suggested "seven times," a number far in excess of the rabbinical teaching of three times. He scarcely could have anticipated the celestial arithmetic of forgiveness contained in Jesus' answer, "until seventy times seven."

We find it hard to forgive someone who hasn't listened to our instructions carefully the first time. When we scold, "Listen this time, for I won't repeat it," we virtually declare our willingness to forgive inattention no more than once. Or we say, "I'll forgive you this once, but don't let it happen again!" But Jesus declared we should forgive 490 times, if necessary.

He once commanded the disciples to forgive the same person seven times in the same day, if requested. No wonder they responded, "Increase our faith" (Luke 17:4, 5)!

To His disciples who repeatedly argued as to who would be greatest in the kingdom He exercised forgiving patience. Each time He tolerantly taught the same lesson of humility, finally demonstrating the lesson by washing their feet the night before He went to the cross.

About to be betrayed, denied and forsaken, He prayed in the garden for those who would prove so unfaithful.

When He mentioned at the table, "One of you shall betray me," He spoke not only prophetically but also wooingly toward Judas, letting him know his dastardly deed was not concealed, yet magnificently keeping his identity secret.

Even while Judas was in the very act of trickery Jesus called the betrayer "friend" and let him smirch His holy cheek with a pretended kiss. The divine arms were still open to bestow forgiveness should Judas have repented.

Would you feel kindly toward someone who fell asleep after you had specifically asked him to keep vigil with you during a critical situation? Would not your patience almost reach its limit if he dropped off to sleep a second time? In Gethsemane, Peter, James and John fell asleep three times after Jesus had asked them to keep watch. Yet Jesus' remark, "Sleep on now, and take your rest" (Mark 14:41), if taken ironically is at most a mild rebuke, indicating forgiveness. If taken literally, an interval of time elapsed before the arrest during which Jesus Himself watched over the drowsy disciples, who were too sleepy to watch over Him.

For the Pharisees, Sadducees and Herodians who persistently opposed Him and plotted against His life, He reserved His invectives till the last week of His life. Always He answered their questions and kindly. Even to the end He pled, taught, persuaded.

He held no malice against those arresting Him in the garden. Availability of full forgiveness for a whole gang was symbolized in His restoration of Malchus' ear chopped off by impetuous Peter.

Against His rejectors He bore no grudge. Rejected but not resentful, He would gladly have received His disclaimers under His wings as a hen gathereth her chicks, had they been willing.

His first two words from the cross were cries of forgiveness. For those involved in His death He asked, "Father, forgive them, for they know not what they do." Above the babel of wicked voices came the sweet music of mercy. This plea was the only word from the cross that was repeated. He kept saying, "Father, forgive." Hitherto quiet before His accusers, He now opens His mouth, not to curse, but to bless.

Not only did all participating in that dastardly deed receive temporary stay of execution from divine wrath, but thousands found forgiveness. The centurion a few hours later acknowledged Jesus as the Son of God. On the day of Pentecost, three thousand believed, many of whom had joined in that chorus of mockery "Crucify Him," 50 days before. Later a great company of priests also became obedient to the faith.

But first of all to be forgiven was the repentant thief. Sweeter words of remission never fell on erring ears, "Today shalt thou be with me in paradise." The second utterance from the cross was likewise a word of forgiveness.

How often the Lord forgave Peter for his wavering ways. When the cock crowed twice after Peter's third denial, the Lord looked so pityingly at Peter that the denier's heart broke bitterly. In love the Lord sought a private interview with Peter on the resurrection day. Later on the shore the Lord in forgiving Peter for the three public denials had him make three public affirmations of love.

At a camp meeting altar a Christian man threw his arms around a non-Christian who had just come forward, and falling to his knees wept with the repentant man. What made the scene unusual was the fact that the Christian's wife had been taken from him by this non-Christian penitent. Far more normal response would have been for the offended man to punch the wife-stealer rather than embrace him. Yet for Christ's sake, because Christ had forgiven him much, he forgave much.

CHRIST TOOK THE INITIATIVE IN FORGIVENESS

Christ took the initiative in the matter of forgiveness. Amidst the cruelty of the crucifixion Christ offered forgiveness even in the absence of any specific request for pardon. Well before others sought remission He showed willingness to forgive.

He had taught that the injured party should take the first step toward reconciliation. "If thy brother shall trespass against thee, go and tell him his fault between thee and him alone; if he shall hear thee, thou hast gained thy brother" (Matthew 18:15). If the injured party rebukes his trespasser seven times in one day, and the guilty culprit repents all seven times, the injured person must forgive him all seven times (Luke 17:3, 4).

One reason Christ showed by pattern and precept that the offended party should take the initiative was to prevent resentment. Most persons if mistreated with a fraction of the indignity Christ suffered would rankle with bitterness toward their tormentors. Sometimes hurt feelings carry high price tags. Scowling moods often backfire, causing indigestion, fatigue, insomnia or carelessness resulting in highway accidents or industrial mishaps. Someone has said, "What we eat may not harm us as much as what may be eating us."

So that grudges would not have time to be nursed into sulky self-pity or vengeful spite Christ instructed His followers to air their grievances immediately. The sun should not go down upon our wrath. Christlikeness does not stand on its dignity, making the other fellow come to us, but gets its complaint out of its system right away.

If an offending believer will not hear our rebuke, we are to approach him a second time with witnesses. If he remains adamant we are to tell it to the church who will excommunicate him as a heathen (Matthew 18:15-17).

Naturally we cannot forgive if forgiveness is not sought. But we can be willing to forgive. Though the Lord pronounced judgment on the cities of Galilee which rejected His presence, He held out the offer of pardon. So willing was He to forgive Jerusalem that not only did He weep over it, but He delayed its destruction forty years, giving its inhabitants a chance to repent.

A Christian lady told her doctor she was suffering from severe headaches. Noting her tenseness he asked a few routine questions. He discovered that her non-Christian husband made fun of her faith. He often brought trashy magazines into the living room to irritate her. Through wise counsel her Christian physician led her to see the harm of resentment. He pointed out the example of Christ who prayed for forgiveness for His tormentors. Pondering the pattern of Christ and permitting His indwelling presence to live out through her, she developed a forgiving spirit. Her headaches disappeared. Her husband mellowed toward the Gospel.

Christ Put Forgiveness Central

Christ placed forgiveness central. The reason He came was not to condemn but to forgive. The elements of the Lord's Supper picture a body broken and blood shed for the forgiveness of sins. The Great Commission commands announcement of this good news of available forgiveness.

Christ delighted to forgive penitent publicans and sinners. The Pharisees who murmured at Jesus' welcome to outcasts missed the main purpose of His mission by failing to grasp the all-important attribute of pardoning love. Like the elder brother, self-righteous, cold and hard like steel, they were out of tune with fatherly forgiveness.

A person who refuses to forgive those who offend him reveals he has not experienced forgiveness. The only section of the Lord's prayer elaborated on was the clause on forgiveness. Immediately after the "amen," Jesus explained, "For if ye forgive men their trespasses, your heavenly Father will also forgive you: But if ye forgive not men their trespasses, neither will your

Father forgive your trespasses" (Matthew 6:14, 15). Neither legalistic nor reserved for some future golden age, this comment points out that a forgiving spirit is evidence of the Father's forgiveness. Failure to forgive indicates we have never received divine remission, else we would be merciful.

Three days before He died, in the shadow of His forgiving cross, Christ warned, "When ye stand praying, forgive, if ye have ought against any: that your Father also which is in heaven may forgive you your trespasses. But if ye do not forgive, neither will your Father which is in heaven forgive your trespasses" (Mark 11:25, 26).

In His parable of the merciless servant the Lord used humorous exaggeration to drive home the indispensability of a forgiving spirit. A servant who owed his master a staggering debt, roughly equivalent to ten million dollars, about to be tossed into prison, begged for mercy and received it. But then the forgiven servant on his release refused a plea for mercy from a fellow servant who owed him the tiny debt of $10 and threw him into jail. On hearing the story the master who had at first remitted the ten-million-dollar debt reversed his initial cancellation of debt and threw the merciless servant into prison. Jesus ended the story, "So likewise shall my heavenly Father do also unto you, if ye from your hearts forgive not every one his brother their trespasses" (Matthew 18:35).

Refusal of the merciless servant to exercise mercy revealed his failure to realize the enormity of his debt and the vastness of the mercy extended him.

Our trespasses against Christ cannot be computed but stagger us with their magnitude. Our wrongs against Him are a million times greater than the wrong any human may do us. If we genuinely ask forgiveness of Christ for our million-size debt against Him, how can we refuse mercy to a fellow creature for his tiny-in-comparison harm against us? "Even as Christ forgave you, so also do ye." Refusal to forgive betrays a lack of comprehension of Christ's grace. An unforgiving spirit reveals an unforgiven spirit. But he who is forgiven much loveth much.

A man retorted, "I'll forgive him this time but never again!" What if Christ said the same to the forgiver, "I'll forgive you this time but never again"?

A lady said to her pastor, "I'll forgive Mrs. X but I won't

have anything to do with her. I don't want to see her again. I won't let her in my house!" The pastor replied, "Suppose Christ treats you the same way, wants nothing to do with you, won't let you into His presence or heavenly home?"

How often people react, "I'll forgive, but I won't forget." Christ hath both forgiven and remembered our sins no more. To remember a grievance betrays lack of full forgiveness. If we forgive, we must forget.

Sometimes tragedy makes people see the folly of holding resentment. During the San Francisco earthquake of 1906, a man running out on Market Street where buildings reeled for forty-eight seconds met and shook hands with a man he had refused to speak to for ten years.

Two missionaries, one German and one French, in an Asian country when World War II broke out between Germany and France, forgot their years of happy friendship. With dead prejudices revived the two men became enemies, raising a wall of hostility. One afternoon they came to the mission chapel at the same moment to ring the bell for vespers. Reaching for the bell rope, their hands touched. Looking upward, they both gazed at the cross on top of the mission. Then they threw their arms around each other, asking forgiveness. The love of Christ symbolized by the cross had broken down the barriers.

An American airman was shot down by a Japanese pilot. Somehow the parents of the American youth discovered who the Japanese pilot was. They gave several thousand dollars to bring the Japanese youth to the U.S. and paid several thousands of dollars they had saved for their son's education to send this lad to a Pennsylvania university.

A shamefaced employee was summoned to the president's office. The least he expected was angry dismissal. At most, years in prison for embezzling company funds. The old president asked, "Are you guilty?"

The clerk lowered his head, admitted his guilt and added how sorry he was.

"I shall not press charges that might send you to prison. If I take you back, can I trust you?"

Surprised but melted, the clerk gave assurance of absolute honesty.

The old clerk spoke slowly. "You're the second man who fell

and was pardoned. I was the first. The mercy you just received I received. May God have mercy on us both."

Vengeance is the natural human attitude toward those who mistreat us. But Christ's example overturned such thinking. Contemplation of the cross where He forgave us so fully and freely should dislodge any grudges we have toward others. We can't receive His forgiveness and keep our feet on our brother's neck and our hand at his throat.

Humility of Heaven

7

Humility of Heaven

(Philippians 2:3-8)

PRIME MINISTER JOHN DIEFENBAKER of Canada arrived unheralded at an empty, decrepit railroad freight station on the outskirts of a large Canadian city a few months ago. Then after chatting with nearby workmen, he took a cross-city taxi ride with a driver who thought he was just another fare. Downtown he strolled around the streets, humbly maintaining his anonymity. None of the local people recognized this important dignitary.

Infinitely greater condescension was displayed by the Prime Minister of heaven in His coming to earth 1900 years ago. The all-resplendent Christ surrendered His glory. He who was Deity became man. Master became servant. The Pre-eminent One of heaven became a nobody on earth. He who was Life suffered death. He who was spotlessly honorable suffered the shame of death on a Roman gibbet.

Humility is an elusive virtue. When we think we have it we've lost it! One religious order boasted, "Other groups may excel us in almsgiving, self-denial or scholarship, but when it comes to humility, we're tops!"

The prayer, "Lord, *keep* us humble," betrays a haughty assumption. In all modesty it should be, "Lord, *make* us humble." We must never be proud of our humility.

Because self-assertive pride was the cause of disunity in the Philippian church Paul urged the first century group to do nothing through strife or vainglory. The cure for disharmony was humility. To vividly illustrate the lowliness of mind for which he was appealing the apostle could point to no more majestic model than the Lord Jesus Christ, "who, being in the form of God, thought it not robbery to be equal with God;

81

but made himself of no reputation, . . . took upon him the form of a servant, . . . was made in the likeness of men: . . . humbled himself, and became obedient unto death, even the death of the cross" (Philippians 2:6-8).

Christ exhibited incomparable humility in His comedown from the highest to the lowest. From the throne of God He descended to the grave of man. From the glory of deity to the wounds of a corpse.

This series of classic clauses on the humiliation of Christ was not penned to prove subtle theological dogmas or teach minute mysteries, rather to demonstrate a Christian duty. Contemplation of Christ's condescension should help us pour contempt on all our pride. Similar frame of mind in us would undercut dissension and create kind regard for others.

HE DIDN'T GRASP AFTER GLORY

A wealthy woman generously offered to foot the bill for ice cream at a Sunday school picnic. When little children's hands were eagerly reaching for the ice cream after supper, the woman became angry because no one announced that she was giving the money and petulantly refused to pay.

Instead of grabbing for vainglory this woman should have gazed on One who didn't grasp after true glory. Christ didn't esteem the honor of equality with God, which was rightfully His, a prize to be held at all cost.

Most men in high office like to be known as president of the company or chairman of the board. The flesh is easily irked when others fail to recognize our honorable position or when we aren't the center of attraction. People enjoy posing for a picture with prominent persons, or readily assert friendship with notable figures. But Christ didn't count the prestige of equality with God such a fascination that it had to be tenaciously retained and conspicuously spotlighted. Willingly He gave it up to save us.

Though Christ laid aside the *expression* of His deity, He kept *possession* of it. He was always God even when He didn't look like God to others. His glory was concealed, not lessened. Had He wished, He could have moved around Judea and Galilee with dazzling glory which would have felled people as it did the three disciples on the mount of transfiguration, the apostle Paul on the Damascus road, and John on the Isle of Patmos.

But He chose to conceal His glory for thirty-three years. How quickly we should renounce vain show and conceited egotism, causes of so much dissension and meanness.

HE WHO WAS GOD BECAME MAN

He who was God became man. What happened at Christmas was the reverse of what happened in the rise of many dictators and emperors. The Caesars ordered emperor-worship. Until World War II the Japanese emperor was revered as a man who became a god. Many dictators have mistaken themselves for a god, ranting and raving with supposed absolute power. In gross self-inflation these puny men proudly lifted themselves to what they were not.

But at Christmas we have, not a man becoming God, but God in humility becoming man. Still retaining His deity the Lord Jesus Christ took on Him real human nature. He was born a baby. As a helpless infant he was carried by His parents in flight into Egypt.

His humility was reflected in His inglorious associations with outcasts, outsiders and outlaws. He touched lepers, talked with demon-possessed, preached to the poor, ate with publicans and sinners, and died between thieves.

As a man He suffered the entire gamut of infirmities known to the race apart from sin. Though the Bread of Life, He knew what it was to be hungry. Though the Water of Life, He experienced thirst. He who invited the heavy-laden to come to Him for rest became weary. He was lonely, despised, forsaken, mocked, lost a loved one in death and passed through the valley of the shadow of death.

If the Creator of all left His exalted position to become a creature on earth, how quickly should we who are but creatures of dust come down off our haughty thrones.

HE WHO WAS MASTER BECAME SERVANT

A newly appointed board chairman of a large company visited a branch factory in a distant city. Applying incognito for a job, he donned working clothes and performed regular tasks along with the men in the factory. Though still top man in the corporation he took orders as an employee among employees.

The Master of the universe, whose slightest bidding was immediately executed by myriads of angelic ministers, became a servant in His own creation. What a humiliating contrast for one accustomed to giving orders to take orders. It was as if the Queen of England should don overalls to sweep the street. Or a general stoop to K.P. duty. Or an admiral go below deck to stoke.

Last fall members of the Indian Parliament gave a tea party for their servants at a New Delhi hotel. Sitting with the Prime Minister were a sweeper, a butler, a gardener and a watchman. Caste barriers were fractured as members of parliament served tea to the servants. Christ vividly illustrated His servanthood when He, the Lord of creation, removed His outer garments and stooped to wash His disciples' feet, a job usually performed by menial help.

HE WHO WAS LIFE DIED

Death is humiliating. Eyelids close. Ears no longer hear. Mouth no longer speaks, nor hands do, nor feet walk. A corpse is an abject example of the utter weakness of human existence. How mortifying for the Lord of Life to die!

All things were made by Him, Giver and Sustainer of breath. As Resurrection and Life He raised the dead on at least three occasions. Then He permitted Himself to die.

Pondering Christ's obedience to death should spur us to crucify our self life, especially pride. An important Christian leader dropped into a church service where an outstanding Bible teacher was preaching. The speaker spotted the church dignitary and meant to acknowledge his presence before the end of the meeting. But in the enthusiasm of preaching he forgot, so sent a telegram later to the leader, who wired back, "Dead. Didn't even notice it."

Gladys Aylward, known as the "Small Woman," said in an address to college students, "Are you thinking of going to the mission field for thrilling and romantic experiences? If so, don't come! They aren't there. It's following Jesus, step by step, from the graveyard of selfish ambitions into the life of God." The place to begin is at the cross where contemplation of His death leads to mortification of conceit.

In listing the downward steps of Christ's voluntary humiliation, Paul lingers on His death. How astonishing that God the Son should die! But all the more amazing that He should die the way He did! "Even the death of the *cross!*" Execution by crucifixion was reserved for the lowest of the low, slaves, criminals, outcasts, never for a Roman citizen. The Jews regarded it as an accursed death.

All the indignities heaped on Christ on His way to the cross compounded the ignominy. How abasing for the King of kings to be questioned by earthly governors as to His authority for His actions, to be made sport of, spit on, betrayed, stripped of His clothes three times, hear the people vote for the release of public enemy number one in preference to Himself, stumble under the weight of the cross, crucified naked in public between criminals, wrapped in burial clothes, and laid in a sepulchre sealed by Roman authority.

HE WHO WAS SOMEBODY BECAME NOBODY

His lowliness of mind is aptly summed up in this descriptive statement, "He made Himself of no reputation."

During graduation exercises at a well-known eastern university the large audience sat dutifully through the monotonous proceedings of degree-conferring. Suddenly, the crowd jolted to attention, as if an electric shock had jarred everyone in the building. Walking down the aisle from a seat near the back, as his name was called, marched an erect five-star general of the army to receive an honorary degree. This top brass with all the dignity of his position commanded the rapt interest of all. But had he been dressed as a civilian and named without title, many would not have noticed.

Our Saviour, far above the five-star generalship of heaven, came to earth without His insignia showing. Assuming the garb of humanity He walked about on earth without people knowing who He was. Had you lived in Palestine you might have passed Him on a dusty road without the slightest inkling of His real person. A great artist paints a beautiful picture and is honored. Christ painted sunsets and scenes no human artist can begin to rival, yet as He walked around no one knew Him as the great Artist. A musician composes an oratorio and becomes famous; Christ made the music of the spheres and all music possible, yet as He moved from home to home, no one knew Him as the great Musician. Most school children know who discovered electricty; but He who made the suns was unsung. He knew all things, yet boasted no degrees after His name. He made Himself of no reputation.

When President Kennedy's son was born just before his

inauguration, the communication systems around the world proclaimed the news to all. When the Christ-child was born midst the stable stench of an animal's feeding trough, no fireworks nor fanfare blared out His coming. An angelic message announced this stupendous news to a mere handful of humble herdsmen. The circumstances of His birth doubtless made Him the butt of scandalous gossip.

His own brothers thought him insane. His opponents accused Him of possession by demons or partnership with the devil. He walked the paths of Palestine unknown by people.

John D. Rockefeller, Jr., used to walk around Rockefeller Center when the tall building was in the process of construction. Farsighted, he could observe most everything from the sidewalk. Once a watchman accosted him. "Move along, buddy," he growled. "You can't stand loafing here." He quietly withdrew, unrecognized.

Jesus Christ, the great Somebody, made Himself a Nobody. It was said of Him, "There standeth one among you, whom ye know not." Even when those He healed wished to broadcast His exploits He ordered them to tell no one. Most people would have likely greased their publicity machine into high gear.

He came to His own but His own received Him not. Shoved like a chess piece back and forth across a board, He became a pawn between governors Pilate and Herod. His final rejection, climaxed by His degrading death, He termed as being "set at nought" (Mark 9:12). He became a nothing. Feature the Infinite lowered to a zero. No wonder Andrew Murray once termed humility the secret of redemption.

The depth of Christ's descent contrasted violently with the vainglorious Pharisees who to show off before men prayed on street corners, trumpeted before giving and disfigured their faces when fasting. Humility, not hypocrisy, should characterize our lives.

A rider on horseback during the Revolutionary War came across a squad of soldiers trying to move a heavy piece of timber. A corporal stood by with a self-important air, giving lordly orders to "heave." But the piece of timber was a trifle too heavy for the squad.

"Why don't you help them?" asked the quiet man on the horse, addressing the officious corporal.

"Me? Why, I'm a corporal, sir!"

Dismounting, the stranger carefully took his place with the soldiers. "Now, all together, boys, heave," he exclaimed. And the big piece of timber slid into place.

The stranger mounted his horse. Then turning to the corporal he said, "Next time you have a piece of timber for your men to handle, corporal, send for the commander-in-chief." The horseman was George Washington!

Love of applause, vain show and the pride of life rear their haughty heads in modern life. Church members in our day have been hurt when their deeds failed to receive public acknowledgment, or their names weren't printed in the church annual for some special service. A worshiper readied a dollar bill in his hand at offering time in a fashionable church. When he noted that the usher coming down the aisle was an important business acquaintance, he replaced the dollar in his pocket and removed a $20 bill, waving it as he dropped it on the plate.

Usually far more money is promised during network telethons for charitable causes than ever is finally contributed. People like to hear their names mentioned over TV. Some employees have pretended patriotism by purchasing war bonds at work, then almost immediately quietly sold them. Some folks always want to be president, or running the show, or sitting at the head table.

Humility was never an admired virtue in the ancient world. In a day that stressed self-assertiveness, humility was usually regarded as the despised opposite of courage. For a person to fail to stand up for his rights betrayed weakness to the secular mind. But Christ by His supreme example of self-abasement reversed this mood. He established humility as a lofty virtue, and condemned pride along with murder and adultery.

If we would have the self-effacing mind of Christ we must ponder often His example of self-effacement which made Him leave the ivory palaces to sink to this world of woe. Possession of this mental disposition led one church member to give to a new church edifice with this instruction, "Use this gift in unseen parts of the building. You can find enough people who want to give their money for parts that can be seen."

Jesus, the Gentleman

8

Jesus, the Gentleman
(II Corinthians 10:1)

A LADY WHO WAS EXPECTING A BABY any day moved to a new area where her husband worked nights. Her only neighbor assured her, "My husband will drive you to the hospital should you have to go in the middle of the night."

After midnight on a windy night the expectant mother rang her neighbor's bell to arouse them. The wife opened the door. "Oh, I'm sorry but my husband can't take you to the hospital. But come in while I call a cab!"

Not till after the safe arrival of the baby did the new mother learn what had happened. Her husband brought her a note he had found at his front door on returning from work at dawn. It read, "I'm sorry my husband was not here to drive your wife to the hospital. He passed away of a heart attack yesterday. I did not want to tell your wife as I was afraid it would upset her."

Despite the grief tearing at her heart the bereft wife displayed kind consideration. The prominent trait in Christ's personality was His gentleness. So tender was He that a dove fluttered down on Him at His baptism. He was called the *Lamb* of God. Not only was He King of kings and Lord of lords, but Gentleman of gentlemen.

Because the apostle Paul did not bully nor browbeat but conducted himself meekly and considerately, his enemies accused him of weakness and contemptible speech. In defense of his mild manners Paul pointed to the example of Jesus, "Now I Paul myself beseech you by the meekness and gentleness of Christ" (II Corinthians 10:1). His appeal to this quality not only explained his seeming timorous behavior but indirectly urges Christians today to meek and gentle conduct.

Meekness is not weakness, nor is it Milquetoast timidity.

Rather it is strength grown gentle. The stevedore who after tossing huge crates around the wharf goes home to handle his five-month-old baby so tenderly, not like freight, has not become weak. He has toned down his strength to gentleness.

The gentleness of Jesus was all the more remarkable when etched against His strength. Despite the impression of paintings which make Him effeminate, insipid, sentimental and on the verge of tears, He was vigorous and strong. His manliness attracted robust and rough Galilean sailors. His courageous scorn made Him dangerous enough to be crucified.

Because His righteous anger flashed out against Pharisaical injustice, His gentleness was never soft nor flabby but lined with steel. Against the background of His scathing indignation at the Pharisees who in hardness of heart did not want to see a man healed on the sabbath, stood out His tenderness to the unfortunate fellow with the withered hand. Someone has said, "He was gentle as only the fiercest can be gentle." The essence of gentleness lies in the curbing of strength to avoid injury to the weak. This our Lord did with a tenderness that was never weak and with courage never brutal.

Many people picture a gentleman as an aristocrat with a monocle, stovepipe hat, striped trousers, cane and Victorian manners. But the New Testament word for *gentleness* can be rendered *forbearance, consideration, sweet reasonableness,* or *mildness.* Two drivers, a man and a woman, tried to be first away on a green light. The man was heading straight, while the woman wanted to make a left turn across his lane. It was a tie with bumpers barely touching. But neither would back up, both insistent on right of way. Cars jammed up for five blocks in four directions from the intersection. When police arrived, both drivers were sitting silently but stubbornly behind their respective wheels. Had gentleness prevailed, each driver should have sweetly, mildly and reasonably yielded right of way to the other.

So gentle was the Lord that it was declared, "A bruised reed shall he not break, and smoking flax shall he not quench, till he send forth judgment unto victory" (Matthew 12:20).

A reed, a frail plant so unlike the firm oak, though already bruised and broken with vitality sapped, He would not finish breaking. Those bowed down with penitent unworthiness and bruised feeble by the blows of life, the tender Christ would not injure more nor destroy, but would rather strengthen their delicate life.

When a lamp wick began to burn dimly and smoke thickly, the tendency was to quickly extinguish it. But when the flame flickered in the hearts of those on the verge of spiritual extinction, the mild Christ would not blow even so softly lest He snuff out the dying flame. He never broke anyone's spirit.

TENDER IN DEED

A woman with a city-wide reputation as a sinner came unbidden into Simon the Pharisee's house where Jesus was a dinner guest and began to wash His feet with her tears and wipe them with her hair. The emotional warmth must have been embarrassing. But not only did He treat her kindly, but also defended her against Simon's cynicism (Luke 7:37-40).

The woman dragged to the feet of Jesus by the Pharisees who seized her in the very act of adultery must have stung under their accusations. How gently Jesus relieved her shame. After challenging those without sin to cast the first stone, He stooped to write something in the sand. His action turned attention away from the humiliated woman and permitted the convicted Pharisees to slip away one by one (John 8:6).

Many were the occasions when He set Himself between public sinners and the accusing finger of society, or came to the defense of the vulnerable.

How courteous He was to Judas, hiding his identity as traitor almost to the end. Most of us would have frankly named him but Jesus spared his feelings. At the arrest Jesus even called him "Comrade" and permitted the betrayer to kiss Him.

When helpless mothers with infants in arms were turned away from Jesus by gruff disciples, He rebuked the disciples and took the babies in His arms. Ruskin once observed that there were no children in Greek art, but that Christian art abounds with children. The prophet had declared that He would "gather lambs with his arm and carry them in his bosom and shall gently lead those that are with young" (Isaiah 40:11).

His first miracle relieved the predicament of a young couple at whose wedding refreshments ran out. How embarrassing if word got round, "Not enough drink for the wedding. Why, they couldn't really afford to get married!" Perhaps extra guests had come in from the country. The Lord graciously performed the miracle secretly so that even the host was surprised. The only people who knew about the miracle were the servants who also knew about the problem.

Mary was accused of waste by the disciples for anointing Jesus with a considerable quantity of expensive ointment. Knowing she had done this with keen insight as advance burial ministration, the Lord defended her action. Some clergymen might have given a sermon against the misuse of money, a far cry from Jesus' gentle approval.

Major temptation of the strong is impatience with the weak, and of righteous contempt of the erring. But the strong Son of God extended His most gracious love to the frailest sinner who turned in His direction.

Accommodating consideration was shown the timid Nicodemus who came by night for an interview.

How gentle the Lord was in pointing out to the Samaritan woman that she had had five husbands. Some personal workers would have immediately begun the conversation with "You're a wicked woman!" But the Lord started with the request for a drink of water, then gently swung into her past. So kind was His approach she didn't mind that He told her all things ever she did (John 4:29).

As Jesus walked with Zaccheus toward his home after inviting Himself for dinner, the stunned crowd murmured that He was gone to be guest with a notorious sinner. As the murmuring buzzed more loudly it became embarrassing not only to the crooked tax-collector but to Jesus whose reputation was in danger of sully by association with a seemingly unrepentant publican. Some of us would have been tempted sternly to lecture Zaccheus on his need for restitution and charity, but Jesus patiently gave him a chance to express himself. His moderate treatment paid off as Zaccheus announced his intent to make amends.

Frankness can be unnecessarily and brutally blunt at times. But the Lord combined mildness with His firmness.

Too often we react with fire against the slow-thinking and skeptical. But to weeping Mary in the garden He feelingly spoke her name. With the discouraged Emmaus disciples He sparred in genial conversation, patiently leading them to renewed faith in Himself. To doubting Thomas He extended an invitation to put his finger in the nailprints, willing to submit to Thomas' pre-stated test.

Many of His physical gestures revealed gentleness. How often He tenderly touched the sick as He healed.

In cleansing the temple He whipped out the money-changers, sheep, oxen, dumped out the changers' money and overturned the tables. But He didn't drive out the doves. Rather He said to those selling doves, "Take these things hence" (John 2:16), rather than harass those sensitive birds.

When He healed a man with a speech impediment, He may have taken the victim aside from the crowd so as to spare his feelings by providing privacy for his first attemps to speak plainly (Mark 7:32, 33).

MILD IN SPEECH

Gentleness controlled Christ's speech. Do you ever yell at your children or your students? Do you ever shout at clerks or the driver who cuts you off? Ever raise your voice at your husband or your employees? Ever hear people loud in conversation?

Though on rare occasions the Lord did shout some important truth (John 12:44), His voice was usually conversational. Isaiah had predicted His soft-spokenness, "He shall not strive, nor cry; neither shall any man hear his voice in the streets" (Matthew 12:19). He was patient with His disciples, permissive with those undecided, and polite to His enemies.

His forbearance must often have been tested by the slowness of His disciples to learn. Yet He didn't fume at them, but kindly asked, "Do ye not yet understand?" Then He would meekly repeat His instruction.

How easy in trying to persuade others to our way of thinking to become argumentative, harsh and authoritarian. But the Lord never strove but was gentle unto all men, meekly and patiently instructing those that opposed the truth. His invitations to conversion and consecration were always permissive. Though grieved when the rich young ruler turned away, He didn't pressure him into remaining.

Christlikeness in speech demands courtesy and kindness. This is why Paul referred the proudly assertive false teachers at Corinth to the meekness and gentleness of Christ.

Compassionate in Heart

Christ's gentleness in deeds and words stemmed from His tenderness of heart. Able to share another's brokenness, the compassion of Christ radiated in every direction, toward those in pain, the poor, the plaintive and the potentially penitent.

Our emotions are often jaded. A couple about to be married in a radio serial received loads of presents delivered by truck after truck to station headquarters in New York. Yet some real couples about to be married in real life, living around the corner from some donors, would receive nothing. We weep over imaginary characters and their plight in fiction plots, but steel our cold and calloused hearts against people in real-life distress who live in our neighborhood. Christlikeness produces concern over lost souls.

A preacher was visiting in another church. A man remarked, "Our people are a most united church." When the preacher replied, "Praise the Lord for that," the man warned, "Just a minute before you praise any more till you hear the kind of unity we have. Our members are frozen together!" Some thought Jesus was Jeremiah, the weeping prophet. If others are to see Jesus in us, our attitude will have to be possessed by His compassionate gentleness.

Several times the gospel writers specifically mention Christ's compassion for the ill. He was intensely moved by the sufferings of invalids, the palsied, the lame, the leprous, the maimed, the deaf, the dumb, the blind.

Though He had great power at His disposal He never used it for His own safety or comfort. More than two thirds of His miracles were performed for the relief of those sick in body or mind.

He was keenly sensitive to the plight of widows, the poor, and the needy. Because He had compassion on the hungry He fed the multitude. He didn't scold the crowd about their lack of foresight in following Him around without sufficient provisions, nor did He accept the disciples' suggestion to send them away. Rather, in sympathy He fed them.

The sorrows of others always touched the Saviour's heart. When the Lord raised the dead it wasn't for the sake of the deceased, for they were far better off in heaven than back on earth. Compassion for the bereaved led Him to restore life.

When He raised Jairus' daughter and the widow of Nain's son, His pity was doubtless intensified in each case by the child's status as an only daughter and an only son. How often He was moved by the implorings of a parent for a child, sometimes an only child (Luke 9:38).

Loss over the death of Lazarus plus sympathy for Mary and Martha caused Him to weep at the grave (John 11:35). Even though He knew He was about to exercise the power of His deity by calling Lazarus forth from the tomb, the tears of His gentle humanity trickled down His holy cheeks.

When we see vast crowds of people hurrying by some busy intersection, how do we react? Our Lord saw the multitudes as scattered sheep without a shepherd, lost, astray. He was moved with compassion over them (Matthew 9:36).

During His ministry He lamented over Jerusalem. "How often would I have gathered thy children together, as a hen doth gather her brood under her wings, and ye would not!" (Luke 13:34).

Less than a week before He died, on His so-called triumphal entry into Jerusalem, He shed profuse tears over its blindness and fate (Luke 19:41).

A man who fractured a bone in his foot found it necessary to hobble around with a cane for several days. People helped him into buses, opened doors for him, and made room for him in elevators. But when he recovered sufficiently to leave the cane at home people returned to their old jostling selves. Who knows how many folks are walking the streets every day who have frail emotional bones that have been broken and who need gentle treatment from others?

The healthy should picture what life is like looking out from the walls of a sick room. The successful should ask how it feels to be underprivileged and underfed. The mature should remember that once they were young and filled with misgivings. Youth should put themselves in the place of the aged shut-in and disillusioned. Those blessed with brains should imagine what it would be like going through life with dull thinking. The moral should visualize life as an outcast prodigal in the bowery.

Recently a Christian young man went to collect the rent from a couple who lived in a house he owned. He found the husband dying of an incurable disease and in such bad shape the young man would not take the rent money. Rather, he went home and wept because of the man's desperate condition. Then he notified the church where the man was a member so they could help him.

Are you brusque in your dealings with people? Do you run roughshod over their feelings?

Christlikeness should make us gentle as doves.

In the Hour of Trial

9

In the Hour of Trial
(Hebrews 12:1-3)

JESUS PROMISED PERSECUTION to His followers. He warned that they would be betrayed by relatives, hated of all men, delivered to councils, scourged in public, tried before governors and kings and even put to death (John 16:1-4; Matthew 10: 17 ff). In fact, those who hounded His followers would think they were doing God a favor. No wonder Jesus foretold, "In the world ye shall have tribulation" (John 16:33).

Most of the apostles died a violent martyr's death. Paul's sufferings in behalf of Christ are catalogued in detail (II Corinthians 11:20-29). In the extracanonical letter of the Smyrneans, a church for whom severe affliction had been predicted (Revelation 2:10), a tribute is paid to the noble and patient loyalty of their martyrs. Then a brief description follows, "seeing that when they were so torn by lashes that the mechanism of their flesh was visible even as far as the inward veins and arteries, they endured patiently, so that the very bystanders had pity and wept." Then follows a detailed account of the death of the aged Polycarp, Bishop of Smyrna, who burning at the stake praised Christ midst the flames.

Well known are the afflictions of the saints at Rome who were beheaded, fed to beasts in the arena, or used as human torches to light the way for the infamous Nero to ride to the coliseum.

Through the centuries Christians have met cruel treatment. *Foxe's Book of Martyrs* contains voluminous records of the final agonies of harassed saints under brutal and inhuman torture.

Modern times have witnessed widespread martyrdom. One religious publication stated that there were more martyrs in the nineteenth century than in all previous centuries put together. No one knows the complete toll in Russia, Korea, China and Colombia.

An eye witness gives the account of a pastor's martyrdom in Colombia, South America, a few years ago. "A machete cut opened his face from ear to ear. The victim let out no sound. His only expression was in his eyes, and the police, conscious of the fact, pierced them until they fell out. The saint continued on his knees, on a great pillow of blood. Other police intervened and beat him with their belt buckles. The saint fell to the ground and the detectives and policemen began to jump on him. No one knew when he died; only that when they crucified him it could be seen that blood no longer flowed from his wounds."

The same witness goes on, "If you could have seen the fervor with which all those Christians died who were burned alive, tied to the trees with wires and wet down with gasoline, you would realize that the Lord did not abandon them in those moments. Although the pain must have been tremendous, you heard no blasphemy."

Conservative estimates list 75 Christians martyred in Colombia, South America, between 1948 and 1956, also 46 churches fired or dynamited.

Reports from China tell of how Christians were seized, their noses stopped and water poured into their mouths. Every time the Christians breathed they swallowed water. When their stomachs became distended, their tormentors would stomp on their stomachs.

Most American Christians know little or nothing of persecution. Perhaps ridicule, mockery, charges of obscurantism or puritanism have been leveled at us, but not bodily harm. Perhaps the day will come when Christians, even in America, will have to stand up firmly and be counted in the face of possible persecution.

If persecution comes, we have a supreme example of how to bear it. Martyrs of all ages have been strengthened by the perfect pattern of faith in the hour of trial, the Lord Jesus Christ. We are told to look to Him who for the joy set before Him endured the cross and despised the shame (Hebrews 12:1-3).

Caution should be exercised to make sure that opposition from others is not our fault. We should neither court opposition nor develop persecution complexes. Some people excuse their poorly attended church services on the ground that their church preaches the Gospel. Or we can't get news releases in the papers about our Sunday school because we preach the Bible and papers don't like the Bible. True — there is an offense of the Gospel, but there is no need to be offensive in its presentation. Though some will be repulsed by the Gospel, we need not be repulsive in our manners. We are to be as winsome as possible, not carrying a chip on our shoulders. A young person who carries a Bible to school, but who cheats on tests, fools his teachers and laughs with others at his cleverness, or skips classes and signs his parent's name on a note of excuse, will cause others to ridicule him. Their mockery is not at the Gospel but at the young Christian's inconsistency. We are to be wise as serpents and harmless as doves. We are to make sure that persecution that comes our way is for the Gospel's sake, not for our lack of tact, poor manners or queerness.

The Lord Jesus Suffered

The epistle of Hebrews was written to Jews who had made a profession of Christ but who were in danger of faltering back to Judaism. What was slowing them down was affliction, reproach, the spoiling of their property (Hebrews 10:32-34). To encourage them the writer points to characters who through faith weathered obstacles to win major victories. These historical personages are catalogued in the famous gallery of heroes in Hebrews 11. But the supreme example of faith in the face of opposition is Jesus Christ with whom the writer begins the twelfth chapter of Hebrews. The Lord Jesus Christ is the leader of faith over all other examples of faith. We are to consider Him, who endured the cross, despised the shame, keeping in view the heavenly reward which He now permanently enjoys (Hebrews 12:1-3).

The Lord Jesus Christ suffered the contradiction of sinners, the cross and contempt.

Contradiction of Sinners

A university president whose job demanded the procurement of large gifts for the school, radiated charm and affability. Because a new young professor often blurted out the truth rather bluntly, the president diplomatically invited the young professor to a chapel service. The president spoke on the theme of how Jesus found common ground with His hearers to win them to His way. After the service the young professor thanked the president. "I shall try to profit by your address. But one thing bothers me. If Jesus was so beautifully tactful and diplomatic, how did He manage to get Himself crucified?"

Christ's claims were defiantly rejected from the beginning. His home town folks tried to push Him over a cliff (Luke 4: 27-30). He was accused of blasphemy because He made Himself equal with God (John 10:33). He was accused of insanity (Mark 3:21) and of partnership with Beelzebub. He was sneered at for never having learned (Matthew 12:24). His brothers disbelieved Him (John 7:3-5).

He was criticized because His disciples plucked corn (Matthew 12:1-9), and because He healed on the sabbath (Luke 13:14). He was derided by covetous Pharisees (Luke 16:14). Continually the Pharisees tried to entangle Him in His talk. The Sadducees asked Him one of their trick questions. A lawyer tested Him with a question. The Herodians tried to trap Him. He was charged with letting the disciples trangress the tradition of the elders. His authority was questioned. He was murmured at because of His association with publicans and sinners (Luke 15:1).

The opposition became vehement (Luke 23:10). It culminated in His arrest and trial, where He was mocked as a make-believe king with crown of thorns, reed, and gorgeous robe. In loud chorus the chief priests and scribes cried out, "Away with this man. Crucify Him!" A hail of mockery was hurled at Him in His final agonies. He was betrayed by one of the twelve, denied by another, and forsaken by all.

Cross

Painful indeed were the sufferings of crucifixion. These were preceded by the cruel scourge, a whip with leather pieces or bits of metal which would bite deeply into the flesh. Brought down brutally on the bare back, this whip would often lash around to dig into the face.

Physical taunts added to the pain, as soldiers smote Him, asking Him to prophesy who it was that did the striking. They also spat on Him.

The victim was often nailed to the cross flat against the ground. Soldiers would hold one hand, then the other, while a spike was driven through the palm, spurting blood. Lifted up into a hole in the ground, the victim would be jarred and jolted in every bone in His body. Then would follow hours of the excruciating, complex tortures of crucifixion.

Because He was omniscient, the Lord suffered from the anticipation of this ordeal all during His ministry. He repeatedly foretold His sufferings. How great would our anticipatory knowledge torment us if we knew that in six months we would be impaled on a tree.

Shame

Added to the cruelty was shame. His kind of death was reserved for criminals and slaves — the death of the cross. His sufferings were compounded by disgrace.

Today we honor the emblem of the cross. But in His day wearing a cross would have been the equivalent of wearing a gallows, electric chair or a gas chamber in our day. The Romans would have laughed had someone said that the cross would be an ornament some day. Christ's glorious sufferings have transformed the shame into glory.

The Lord Jesus Endured His Sufferings

The Lord's sufferings did not cause Him to falter or turn back. Rather He endured them. In this He is an example to us. If He bore such great opposition, pain and shame, we should follow suit, especially since our sufferings can never be so intense. For we have not resisted to the point of giving our life's blood. In the face of Calvary our tribulations should appear light. He is the supreme Exemplar of affliction-enduring faith. The Captain of our salvation never wavered.

He Endured the Contradiction

In the face of unwarranted hostility He sometimes was silent; often He gave a defense of His position. On the cross when urged to save Himself, He was quiet. Yet He spake so boldly to the high priest at His trial, that He was struck by an officer. But Jesus never apologized. Paul urges Timothy to fight the good fight of faith in view of the good confession which Christ witnessed before Pilate (I Timothy 6:13). How often He defended Himself before the verbal onslaughts of His enemies, routing them completely.

He Endured the Cross

What suffering He bore, unjust suffering. The cross meant physical and spiritual pain to Christ. Yet He patiently underwent it. His example should animate us. "For it is better, if the will of God be so, that ye suffer for well doing, than for evil doing. For Christ also hath once suffered for sins, the just for the unjust, that He might bring us to God" (I Peter 3:17, 18).

> Lord, should my path through suffering lie,
> Forbid it I should e'er repine,
> Still let me turn to Calvary,
> Remembering thine.

He Esteemed the Shame As Nothing

He despised the shame. He regarded the ridicule as nothing in view of the glorious outcome.

Harassed believers are urged to look unto Jesus, turning away from all other things to make Christ the object of reflection (Hebrews 12:2). The next verse again tells believers to consider Christ (vs. 3). Analyze Him. Enter into His spirit. As He acted, we are to act. Contemplation of Him should dispel a fainting spirit.

We are to look unto Him not only as the perfecter of our faith but as the captain of our faith, leading us to imitate Him in this contest. We are to follow the leader. He didn't quit the race but stayed through every obstacle. If discouraged, a reminder of Him, the grandest portrait in the gallery of faith's heroes, should help us persist through bitter anguish to win the prize.

News out of China tells how in one area where Christian leaders were suspected of loyalty to the Gospel, thirty pastors were called together. All who promised never to preach the Gospel again were asked to stand to one side. Two forsook the faith, but the other twenty-eight stood firm. Then these twenty-eight were taken out and shot.

A letter to someone in Hong Kong came out of Red China from a Christian. On one side of the envelope was the address, but on the other side was John 3:16 written out in Chinese. Two stamps were affixed, one on each side, so that those who had to check the stamps could not escape seeing John 3:16. The Christian inside Red China was giving a testimony to his faith in a way which risked his life. He was enduring.

A recent news report captioned, "It's not easy to be a Christain in East Berlin," related how in East Germany the government is bringing more and more pressure on Christian families to send their children to Communist youth dedication ceremonies instead of having them confirmed in the church. If the child goes to confirmation, he is barred from further education in the state-controlled schools. Sometimes the father is fired from his job on some flimsy pretext. Many give in to such pressure, but those who remain true do not sneak into services, but walk proudly down the main street Sunday morning, carrying Bible and hymnbook conspicuously.

A new school teacher in a suburban New York school gave a testimony how three years ago he was a non-Christian living in Colombia. His conversion stemmed from seeing the steadfastness of an evangelical pastor who had been beaten up for preaching the Gospel in a remote area. The pastor's face was beaten black on one side, yet he rejoiced that he could suffer for Christ. He never registered a complaint. That started the young teacher thinking. Later he became a Christian. His family turned against him. To leave Colombia for America he had to sell his books.

Not only should the Christian in persecution not retaliate, but he should joyfully and patiently endure. A commander in the U.S. Navy joined the outskirts of a crowd when General Eisenhower came to Paris a few years ago. A mob of Communists was demonstrating against the coming of the American president as well as against NATO. Police arrested a large group of these demonstrators, including the commander. He spent three hours in jail before he could explain he was an American curiously looking on, and not a Communist. While in jail a significant thing happened. He said these Communists began to sing and shout and were absolutely thrilled that they had the privilege of suffering for Communism. We need the same devotion to Christ, like Paul and Silas who sang praises at midnight.

THE LORD JESUS WAS REWARDED

Incentive to endure criticism, the cross and the shame was the joy of reward held before Him. He "for the joy that was set before him endured the cross" (Hebrews 12:2).

He knew He would be raised from the dead, exalted to the Father's right hand (vs. 3), dispense salvation to those who would believe on Him, ultimately ruling and reigning, defeating Satan. The joy of triumphant outcome gave Him courage.

The joy of future reward, if an incentive to Christ, is certainly a legitimate, though not the chief motive for us to endure tribulations. The eternal glory makes the present trial seem but for a moment.

Paul knew that if deliverance did not come sometime from beating or imprisonment that there would be an ultimate, final deliverance through resurrection from the dead. He knew that when the executioner's sword fell, there would be yet another chapter. He would be raised some day. So knew all the apostles. This is why Peter could sleep the night before his scheduled execution. Jesus promised great reward to those who suffered for righteousness' sake (Matthew 5:11, 12).

An adventure story involves complication, then climax. Obstacles appear which are overcome in a grand and glorious solution. A little girl used to ask her daddy to tell a story, "What's got trouble in it but the trouble comes out all right." For the Christian there may be trouble, but some day it will be overcome.

The chorus says,

> It will be worth it all when we see Jesus;
> Life's trials will soon be o'er, when we see Him;
> One glimpse of His dear face, all sorrows will erase;
> So run the race, till we see Him.

A famous preacher used to tell the story of two boys. One, known to be very bad, used to throw mud at the moon. The other, a very good boy, took a basin of water and tried to wash it off. What was the moon doing all the while? It just kept shining! When troubles come our way, whether or not anyone comes to our defense, just keep enduring and shining.

Joyful Jesus

10

Joyful Jesus
(John 15:11)

SUPPOSE JESUS WERE TO ENTER A ROOM and find a group of people laughing — what would happen? Many would answer, "Either the people would stop laughing or Jesus would give them a lecture against levity."

Sometimes a solemn person in a home where youthful members begin to indulge in merriment will retreat to a gloomy corner. The peals of laughter that ring out from happy youth will be punctuated by melancholy sighs from that dark corner.

Severe persons point out that Jesus never laughed. At least no such record exists. But He did weep on at least three occasions. He was a man of sorrows and acquainted with grief. Thus, mirth must be avoided in our lives, so they conclude.

But they fail to recognize that a large proportion of the four gospels is devoted to the last week of Jesus' life. Almost one-third of the eighty-nine chapters in Matthew, Mark, Luke and John deal with the tragic events of those final days. Increasing animosity, betrayal, arrest, trial, scourging, crucifixion, and burial create a solemnity of spirit for a large segment of the gospel record. They also forget that the Lord lived thirty-three years before that climactic week, three years of which are covered by the four writers. In contrast to the serious atmosphere of the passion week stands out the lighthearted gladness so evident in His public ministry. Before the sad days were sunny years.

The gospel record begins with joy: announcement of the gladness to Zacharias, songs of Elizabeth and Mary, messages of angels, happy shepherds, praise by Simeon and Anna, and the delight of the wise men at the reappearance of the star. The gospel story ends with the disciples returning to Jerusalem with great joy after the ascension where they continually blessed

God in the temple. In between we have the delineation of One who was sociable, friendly, sunny, optimistic, cheerful, serene, self-possessed, peaceful, poised, calm, content, thankful, praiseful, who for the joy that set before Him despised the cross. The Lord Jesus Christ was as much a man of joy as a man of sorrows.

This joy He wanted His followers to have. On the way to Gethsemane He said to His disciples, "These things have I spoken unto you, that my joy might remain in you, and that your joy might be full" (John 15:11). In the garden He prayed, "And now come I to thee; and these things I speak in the world, that they might have my joy fulfilled in themselves" (John 17:13). He referred to Himself as a model of joy. He wanted His followers to experience this same joy to the full. Since joy is listed second in the catalog of the fruit of the Spirit, right after love, and since Christ had the Spirit without measure, He must have been a joyful man. One commentator referring to these verses said, "Joy is attainable by careful imitation of His example. He revealed to His disciples by precept and example that the path of duty is the only path of joy. After obedience comes joy." The person who obeys the voice of Christ within will radiate His joy without.

HE WAS SOCIABLE WITH EVERYONE

Jesus has been described as the most popular dinner guest in Jerusalem and Galilee. The newly-converted Matthew threw a feast for publicans and sinners to which he invited Jesus. When Pharisees invited Jesus for dinner, He accepted their hospitality (Luke 7:36 and 11:37). Some of His instruction was given when a guest at dinners (Luke 14:1-24). He readily entered into the common joys of dining with people and the enjoyable relaxation such fellowship provides. In fact, His happy nature, wholesome enjoyment and exuberant participation earned him the reputation among His enemies of "a man gluttonous, and a winebibber" (Matthew 11:19). Though not intemperate He was a delight to have around. He was sociable, not ascetic. His initial miracle was performed at a wedding in Cana. Had He been as solemn as some people make Him out to be, on hearing of the shortage of refreshments He might have austerely replied, "We've had enough merriment for one day. A few months ago I was hungry in the wilderness for forty days. It would be better if we all practiced self-discipline. We wish the couple a prosperous life. Now let us all go home!" But He performed a miracle to keep the party going.

Jesus was criticized by the Pharisees because He and His disciples didn't look gloomy enough, especially when John the Baptist and his followers had been so solemn (Luke 5:33). His reply was that His presence required joy just as when a bridegroom joins a wedding party (Luke 5:34). The Lord forbade pretentious solemnity (Matthew 6:16). What a contrast must have been evident between the long faces of the legalistic Pharisees and the cheerful countenance of the relaxed Christ.

So often in teaching, the Lord represented gospel blessings under the figure of a dinner. In the parable of the wise and foolish virgins the kingdom of heaven was likened to a marriage feast (Matthew 25:1-13). A famous painting portraying our Lord with the twelve is called "The Last Supper." Jesus' final invitation in the four gospels is "Come and dine" (John 21:12). One of the two church ordinances is known as "The Lord's Supper." The delights of saints united with Christ in heaven is termed "the marriage of the Lamb" (Revelation 19:7), and fulfills Christ's promise to His disciples to eat and drink at His table in His kingdom (Luke 22:30). Likeness of the Gospel to a supper conveys the idea of joyful fellowship, not melancholy. It was the elder brother who remained outside the merriment of the feast given in ecstasy over the return of the prodigal, which showed that the elder brother was out of tune with his father's joy and was the real prodigal.

No monk, far from shunning the society of men or condemning the common joys of life, the Lord had a zest for life which made Him take note of the beauty of landscapes, flowers, storms, birds, lakes, mountains, sunrise, the play of children, the beauty of the temple, the work of farmers, fishermen, vinedressers, judges and servants.

His lighthearted friendliness attracted people from all ranks of life, from the top of the social ladder to the bottom. From the upper levels there were Nicodemus, the wife of Herod's treasurer, and later Joseph of Arimathea; from the middle class fishermen, soldiers, lawyers; from the lower rungs lepers, publicans, sinners and the Samaritans who strongly desired Him to stay in their area (John 4:40). What a spectacle to see this motley group trailing Jesus through the streets and countryside!

A certain radiant, magnetic buoyancy must have emanated from His person to draw disciples so readily. Children ran to Him easily. Lower classes did not feel uneasy in His presence. Those who squirmed were hypocritical leaders with entrenched privilege. Crowds who lost Him temporarily but found Him again received Him gladly. His friends enjoyed every minute of His stay in their homes. He must have often been a guest in the home of Mary, Martha and Lazarus. Most evenings during His final week He retired to their Bethany home to fortify Himself for the intolerable burdens of the morrow.

A religious leader decided not to ask the blessing at dinner because just before and after grace his family would be laughing and merrily talking of trivia. Prayer in the midst of such conversation he felt sacrilegious. But is not God pleased with the uplifting of the heart when folks are happy? By such prayer the laughter before and after is exalted to a higher plane and presented to the Lord. The social camaraderie of Jesus exhaled no cold, freezing dignity but warm gaiety. In complete sympathy He both wept with those that wept and rejoiced with those that rejoiced. Laughter did not stop when He crossed the threshold. Not only was He a man of sorrows and acquainted with grief but "a man of joy and acquainted with fellowship."

HE WAS SUNNY, SPREADING CHEER TO THE DISCOURAGED

Optimistically the Lord saw the bright side of things. He told His disciples He would die, but He added that He would rise again. When He informed them that in a little while they would not see Him, He made sure to promise that a little while later they would see Him again (John 16:16). When He ate the last supper with them, He promised they would sup again in the Father's kingdom.

His sunny disposition shed cheer wherever He went. What joy must have been experienced by those He healed! The lame man leaps for joy. The leper who had to cry "unclean" as he lived in a graveyard outside the city, begging for bread, unable to go home and embrace his wife or children, is suddenly cleansed! Peter's mother-in-law feels her incapacitating, nagging fever leave her, and out of joyful gratitude rises to minister to those in the house! The blind man who never saw a sunrise nor his mother's face suddenly sees the splendors of nature and the faces of loved ones! The palsied fellow who had to be car-

ried from place to place suddenly feels strength in his body
enabling him to rise and walk! The bent woman who for
eighteen years couldn't lift herself up straightens up at the
command of Jesus and glorifies God for joy! The man who was
deaf and suffering from a speech impediment suddenly has his
ears opened and the string of his tongue loosed! No wonder,
though ordered not to tell anyone, he cannot help publicizing
it everywhere out of sheer happiness. Unbounded joy made
many a cured person disobey Jesus' command to keep it quiet.

Many expressions of Christ command joy positively or nega-
tively. "Be of good cheer," He said to a man He was about to
both heal and forgive. He also spoke, "Be of good cheer," to the
troubled disciples when they saw Him walking on the water,
mistaking Him for a ghost.

Joy-killing fear He ordered banished. How often He said,
"Fear not." He dispelled His disciples' fear when He quelled
the raging storm on the Sea of Galilee (Matthew 8:26). He
warned against anxious worry over material needs in the sermon
on the mount (Matthew 6:25-34). He calmed Jairus' parents,
"Fear not: believe only, and she shall be made whole" (Luke
8:50). To His followers He said, "Fear not, little flock; for it is
your Father's good pleasure to give you the kingdom" (Luke
12:32).

"Peace to you" or its equivalent was another utterance that
promoted joy. To the trembling woman who furtively touched
the hem of His garment to be cured of a longstanding illness
and who was forced to reveal her identity, He said, "Go in peace,
and be whole of thy plague" (Mark 5:34). Someone has said,
"Peace is joy resting, whereas joy is peace dancing." Jesus bequeathed peace to His own (John 14:27), that in the midst of
tribulation they might have peace (John 16:33). The terrified
disciples in the upper room on the day of resurrection He
greeted with "Peace be unto you" (Luke 24:36).

To the discouraged disciples the Lord twice gave miraculous
catches of fish. Downhearted at His impending death they heard
Him say, "Let not your heart be troubled" (John 14:1). He
promised them a Comforter like unto Himself (John 14:16).
To weeping Mary He brought joy.

The sinful found the joy of forgiveness through His love.
The Samaritan woman was so overjoyed that she forgot her

waterpot. Zaccheus joyfully received Christ as his ugly cheating past was forgiven.

Those who keep His word will be happy. The beatitudes begin with "Blessed," promising a joyful spirit to those who practice Christlike virtues. Our Lord spread cheer wherever He went, for His desire is that the sunshine of His joy may be found in our lives as well.

HE WAS SERENE, SELF-POSSESSED, EVEN SINGING IN THE FACE OF PERSONAL DIFFICULTY AND DISASTER

He Was Content

Covetousness disrupts contentment. Thoughtful assessment of blessings dispels grumbling and results in thankful praise. A satisfied soul makes a joyful person. Not a single gripe has been recorded among our Lord's words.

The Lord offered thanks many times. He was grateful for daily bread. Before feeding the 5,000 and the 4,000, He lifted up His heart in recognition of His Father's favor in the form of food. Reminder of the Lord's bounties should produce joyful worship.

Christ also thanked His Father for revealing deep spiritual truth to the simple disciples while hiding it from the so-called wise people. He was grateful that one doesn't have to have his B.A. or Ph.D. degree to understand the abc's of spiritual truth.

He also thanked God for answered prayer, "I thank thee that thou hast heard me. And I knew that thou hearest me always" (John 11:41, 42).

In addition, the night before He died, the Lord thanked His Father for the bread and wine which pictured His crucified body and shed blood (Matthew 26:26, 27).

Our Lord urged contentment in regard to food, clothing and drink. He practiced what He preached. His joy filled Him with gratitude.

He Was Poised

Thoroughly put to rout by Jesus' words and deeds, the frantic Pharisees, letting rage overthrow reason, held a council to destroy Him. Though they were filled with madness, Jesus was undisturbed. Not indifferent to self-preservation He withdrew but did not flee in panic. His retirement was graced with majestic calm.

He had a wholesome outlook on life. When the Pharisees narrowly objected to healing on the sabbath, His broader, healthier view realized that they in inconsistency would without hesitation rescue a sheep that had fallen into the pit on the sabbath. Hence He proceeded to heal on the sabbath despite their hypocrisy and anger. He knew He was in the right.

Not the worrying kind, He rested in the Father's care which enabled Him to live above adverse circumstances. An aura of serenity surrounded Him in all situations.

Doctors tell us that when a thick layer of troubles hangs oppressively over a person preventing him from rising above it into a realm of occasional joy, that person is a candidate for a psychosomatic illness. To avoid such illness we are advised to make our attitude and outlook as cheerful and pleasant as possible. Possession of the joy of Christ has undoubtedly kept many people from psychosomatic breakdown.

Humor involves the recognition of contradiction without loss of inner peace. The Lord not only spotted but spotlighted the inconsistencies of the religious leaders of His day. Hypocrites who made long prayers after swindling widows out of property, or who tithed fragments of plants while neglecting to be merciful, were the objects of His humor. He described the Pharisees as those who went around microscopically examining the eyes of others to discover a speck therein while at the same time their own Pharisaical eyes which did the searching had a piece of lumber protruding from them. He also described the Pharisees as those who with fringe of their shawl strained out an insect from their drink but who then proceed to swallow the grotesque hulk of a camel, long neck, one hump, two humps, lumpy knees, hoofs and all. Thus our Lord used humor. Godly humor springs from divine joy within and buttresses man in his struggles with the frustrations, tensions and depressions of life.

He Sang in the Face of Personal Disaster

The Lord's wish for His followers to have His same joy is all the more remarkable when the circumstances under which they were uttered are recalled. It was on His way to Gethsemane that He said, "Let not your heart be troubled," and "I will not leave you comfortless," and "My peace I leave with you," and "These things have I spoken unto you, that my joy might remain in you, and that your joy might be full." In fact, it was in the garden where He prayed "that they might have my joy fulfilled in themselves" (John 17:13). In a few hours He would be arrested, scourged, mocked, crucified, dead. Yet He was filled with joy.

The night before His death, after instituting the Lord's Supper, He sang a hymn, probably part of Psalms 113 - 118. John the Baptist had been beheaded; His relatives thought Him out of His mind; His crowds had dwindled; His disciples would soon forsake Him and flee; Judas was about to betray Him; cruel nails would soon snuff out His life. What was His attitude? Did He complain, find fault, grumble at the way fate had treated Him? No, He sang! So joyful was He in the face of disaster that He sang a psalm in full knowledge that in twenty-four hours He would be dead after suffering the pangs of the cross. In fact, it was the joy of the Lord which gave Him strength to face the ridicule and pain. His triumphal self-composure on the cross sprang from joy within.

This is why two decades later Paul and Silas, after false accusations, beating and imprisonment in the inner jail, could sing praises to God at midnight (Acts 16:25). This is why Christians can rejoice when persecuted and treated despitefully. Sorrow and joy are not incompatible. Beneath sorrow can be a substratum of joy which gives strength in the hour of grief. This explains why Paul said he was sorrowful, yet rejoicing. The Christian can be joyful in the midst of miseries, while the non-Christian is often miserable in the midst of his so-called joys.

Where there is the joy of the Lord, singing will be an integral part of life, whether in public worship or private spontaneity. A newspaper writer in a large Canadian city recently asked why congregational singing is so bad in many churches. If you visit some poor little gospel hall or tabernacle where so many of the economically and socially underprivileged worship out of paperbacked songbooks, they really sing. But if you go to the large stone cathedrals or big brick temples of the larger denominations at the city corner where there are towers, spires, stained glass windows and Cadillacs at the curb, striped trousers and mink, you may hear a gentle humming if you listen hard. His explanation was that people don't practice during the week enough, nor do they possess zeal for the Lord. Perhaps the reason they sing so little between Sundays is they have so little devotion to the Lord.

Someone has said, "If you can't sing your theology, there's something wrong with it." We have something to sing about: an omnipotent, loving God above, a Saviour who came to earth to die for us on the cross, the Holy Spirit who lives within, the record of God's message in the Bible, the forgiveness of sins, and a hope of life immortal in a land where our joys shall be forever perfect and our love forever full. A Communistic, atheistic magazine recently naively plugged Christianity, when it reported the diary entries from a member of the Communist youth organization who infiltrated a group of Soviet Christian youth in 1960. After describing a Baptist meeting, it remarked how the service featured hymn-singing of which the writer commented, "That is their game, you see. They make use of the opportunity to sing as a bait to draw people to religion." The real reason the Christian youth sang was that they had something to sing about, for they were possessed by the joy of Christ.

The Man of Sorrows bequeathed to us a legacy of joy. He came to give the more abundant life, as He proclaimed the glad tidings of the kingdom. One bishop remarked that people will be surprised at last in the presence of Christ in the world to come to find the Lord so genial. In the parable of the pounds the servant who foolishly hid his talent had a mistaken opinion of his master, calling him "an austere man." But those who used their talents wisely were told to enter into the joy of the Lord.

Finding Christ is like finding buried treasure with which nothing else can compare and for which one sells all else to joyfully possess it. Jesus said, "Rejoice because your names are written in heaven." The Gospel is good news: Christ died and rose. No wonder the women and disciples had great joy when the truth gripped them. Failure to have the joy of the Lord is sin for God's children.

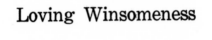

Loving Winsomeness

11

Loving Winsomeness

THE SUPREME TRAIT OF CHRIST which we are bidden to emulate has not received specific treatment in the previous chapters. This quality Christ Himself enjoined, "A new commandment I give unto you, that ye love one another; as I have loved you, that ye also love one another" (John 13:34). Paul expressed it this way, "Walk in love, as Christ also hath loved us" (Ephesians 5:2).

Christlikeness Can Be Summed Up in Love

The reason that love has not been given separate discussion is because every one of the qualities handled in preceding chapters is an aspect of love. In other words, love is actually the topic of consideration in every one of the chapters whether it is expressed in non-retaliation, service, self-denial, friendliness, forgiveness, humility, gentleness, longsuffering or joy. Love is compounded of these elements. Love is the whole of which these are the parts, the hub from which these various spokes proceed.

Christlikeness Relates to Inner Life

Christlikeness is not orthodoxy in the realm of doctrine, as mandatory as sound theology may be for the man of God. Christlikeness is love in the area of the disposition.

> May the mind of Christ, my Savior,
> Rule in me from day to day,
> By His love and power controlling
> All I do and say.

May we not lose the sense of importance of this inward life by placing more emphasis on the sins of the outer life? Immorality and drunkenness we may condemn strongly, all the while regarding selfishness, envy and criticism as insignificant. In reality, sins of the flesh are less satanic than sins of the spirit. Because he has no physical body the devil can not be

123

guilty of gross physical sins like immorality or alcoholism. But the devil is guilty of the sins which ushered the fall into the universe and ultimately into the world: pride, envy, lying. The sins that nailed Christ to the tree were not sins of the flesh like adultery or drunkenness, but sins of the spirit, envy, covetousness, lying. How easy to rebuke others for practices for which we have no Scriptural grounds for condemnation, and how easy to rebuke them with an unlovely, critical spirit which is clearly forbidden in the New Testament and which runs directly counter to the disposition of Christlikeness which is specifically demanded of us. One lady who didn't believe in reddening her face with make-up had no hesitation about blackening another woman's character.

Christlikeness Revolves Around the Cross

Significantly, most of the qualities of Christ's example we are bidden to follow center in the cross.

We are not to retaliate because when reviled during the proceedings immediately before and during the cross He reviled not back.

Appeal to self-denial mentions taking up the cross. Because He forgave we are also to forgive. The place which made forgiveness possible was the cross. The command to humility is enforced by Christ's condescension, not only to manhood and servanthood, but to the shameful death of the cross.

Patient endurance in persecution is encouraged by the example of Christ who for the joy set before Him endured the cross. The love of Christ is to dominate us because "Christ also hath loved us, and hath given himself for us an offering and a sacrifice to God" (Ephesians 5:2). Later in the same chapter husbands are told to love their wives, "even as Christ also loved the church, and gave himself for it" (Ephesians 5:25).

The night before the cross the Lord stooped to the menial service of washing the disciples' feet.

Primarily the cross made possible reconciliation to God. Secondarily, it illustrates many qualities of Christ which God wants us to cultivate. Thirdly, it provides the dynamic for Christlikeness, for apart from the life of Christ within there can never be the likeness of Christ without.

The Lord's Supper can provide a powerful incentive to Christlikeness. Not only does this ordinance provide a memorial of Christ's crucified body and shed blood for our forgiveness, but it should remind us of His exemplary conduct during passion hours, as illustrated in His love, non-retaliation, forgiving spirit, patient endurance, humility, service and self-denial. Thus, participation in the Lord's Supper can make us thankful not only for pardon, but can provoke us to copying Christ.

A boy lost in Chicago was taken to the nearby police precinct where an officer knew the major landmarks. He asked the lad if there was any train station, pier, airport or bus terminal near his home. The boy knew of none. When the boy was asked if he knew of any building, he lit up, "There's a big church with a cross lit day and night. And if you take me to the foot of that cross, I'll know my way home." The cross of Christ not only starts us on the heavenly way and provides a dynamic for the trip, but also gives a vivid picture of the Christlike behavior expected during the heavenward journey.

> By looking to Jesus,
> Like Him thou shalt be;
> Thy friends in thy conduct
> His likeness shall see.

Christlikeness Has Winsome Power

A century ago gold seekers in Montana struck gold in a lonely spot. Because they needed additional supplies and equipment they went to the nearest town after swearing each other to absolute secrecy. Though the vow was faithfully kept, when they started their return to the gold, no less than 300 other gold seekers tagged along. Who had given them away? No one. They had given themselves away, for their beaming faces had betrayed the secret.

Christlikeness is a potent apologetic for the Christian faith. People would rather see a sermon than hear one. If we belong to Christ, we ought to live like Him. "He that saith he abideth in him ought himself also so to walk, even as he walked" (I John 2:6). Wearing a button announcing our Christian faith, or carrying a Bible to advertise our belief, or verbally declaring our allegiance to Christ are legitimate ways of witness. But the indispensable method without which all others are useless and sometimes even harmful is living Christ so people can readily see Him in us. So often what we are speaks so loudly people cannot hear what we say. We must live Him as well as talk Him.

A group of Chinese pastors in the interior of China were once asked what it was about Christ that impressed them most. None mentioned any miracle. One elderly pastor replied, "His washing His disciples' feet." General consensus showed that this moral quality made the biggest impact on them. That a dignified teacher should overstep the lines of class to assume the slave's place was an impressive moral wonder.

How would your life measure up if someone were hired to shadow you for several days to see if you lived in a Christlike way? Some years ago a hospital official watched the lives of professing Christians with whom he came in contact in a large denominational hospital in Atlanta, Ga. "They just don't live what they preach," he concluded, "and if they can't, I can't either."

Someone mentioned the godly life of the pastor of the Baptist Temple, Dr. Will H. Houghton. The hospital official decided to see if this man's life was true to his profession. So he hired a plain-clothes detective to follow Dr. Houghton everywhere he went for several days. At the end of the period the detective declared, "He lives it; there's no flaw there."

These words were inescapable evidence. They rang in the man's ears in an hour of great despair when he was about to take his life. With the prayers of his godly wife, these words helped him accept the Saviour. He spent his spare time laboring for the Master in many ways, including the holding of street meetings. His daughter attended Moody Bible Institute, where this story was reported in the student newspaper. The article ends with the daughter's question, "Suppose Dr. Houghton had not lived a sincere, true Christian life — one that would bear watching — where would my dad be today?"

A minister's little boy, after his father had moved to a different parish, rushed in after the first morning of play, "Mother, I've found such a good little girl to play with here. I hope we never move again."

"I'm so happy," said the mother. "What is the little girl's name?"

"Oh," replied the child with sudden seriousness, "I think her name is Jesus."

"What do you mean?" exclaimed the startled mother.

"Well," replied the boy, "she is so lovely and kind that I did not know what other name she could be called but Jesus!"

Too often our dispositions are so cross, irritable and mean that exactly the opposite would have to be said about us. Would that we should live so like Christ that people would wonder if our name was Jesus.

> Let the beauty of Jesus be seen in me,
> All His wonderful passion and purity;
> O Thou Spirit divine, all my nature refine,
> Till the beauty of Jesus be seen in me.

Joseph Smith's

FIRST VISION

CONFIRMING EVIDENCES AND CONTEMPORARY ACCOUNTS

MILTON V. BACKMAN, JR.

Second Edition
Revised and Enlarged

BOOKCRAFT
SALT LAKE CITY, UTAH

Library of Congress Catalog Card Number: 80-65981
ISBN 0-88494-399-2

Second Edition
First Printing, 1980

Lithographed in the United States of America
PUBLISHERS PRESS
Salt Lake City, Utah

Joseph Smith's

FIRST VISION

CONFIRMING EVIDENCES AND CONTEMPORARY ACCOUNTS

MILTON V. BACKMAN, JR.

Second Edition
Revised and Enlarged

BOOKCRAFT
SALT LAKE CITY, UTAH

Library of Congress Catalog Card Number: 80-65981
ISBN 0-88494-399-2

Second Edition
First Printing, 1980

Lithographed in the United States of America
PUBLISHERS PRESS
Salt Lake City, Utah

Joseph Smith's
FIRST VISION

Contents

Illustrations

Preface to Second Edition

For several years *Joseph Smith's First Vision* has been out of print. Two major factors suggest a rising demand for the book: The increased interest which members of the LDS Church are showing in their historical heritage, and the desire which many have in particular to read all of Joseph Smith's accounts of the beginnings of the Restoration. It was therefore decided to make this book available again.

Even before the publication of the first edition, critics were at work attacking the writings of the Prophet Joseph Smith relating to the First Vision and to his testimony regarding that sacred religious experience. These attacks have continued. It was therefore decided to strengthen the evidence still further by the inclusion of 1820 accounts of revivals which appeared in the *Palmyra Register* and by offering a succinct reply to the critics. This has been done in the present edition by the addition of appendixes P and Q.

It is believed that this additional material will be of genuine interest to all who are seeking a better understanding of the beginnings of the restoration of the gospel.

Preface to First Edition

As Paul journeyed along the road to Damascus, he was suddenly surrounded by a brilliant light. After falling to the ground, he heard a voice saying, "Saul, Saul, why persecutest thou me?" Paul replied, "Who art thou, Lord?" And the Lord said, "I am Jesus whom thou persecutest." (Acts 9:3-5.) This vision is recognized by Christians as the major turning point in the life of one of the world's most devout saints and energetic missionaries. Other revelations ensued in which truths were unfolded to this resolute leader. When Paul addressed the Galatians, he reminded these converts that the gospel which he preached was "not after man," for he neither received it of man nor was taught it by mortals, but learned the things of God through revelation from Jesus Christ. (Galatians 1:11-12.)

Sacred history clearly testifies that God has periodically directed his children through prophets. The Lord instructed Adam, Noah, Abraham, Isaiah, Jeremiah, Peter, John, Paul, and many other influential spokesmen. Amos astutely observed: "Surely the Lord God will do nothing, but he revealeth his secret unto his servants the prophets." (Amos 3:7.)

Although we know of many instances in which God has appeared to man, there are only a few accounts preserved in our scriptures in which the Father and Son have manifest themselves simultaneously. When Jesus was baptized, witnesses heard the voice of his Father affirm, "This is my beloved Son, in whom I am well pleased;" and the "Spirit of God" descended "like a dove" and landed upon the Savior. (Matt. 3:16-17.) When Peter, James, and John returned from a "high mountain" on which Jesus had been transfigured, they too heard a voice declare, "This is my beloved Son: hear him." (Luke 9:28-36.) And in the midst of being stoned, Stephen was filled with the Holy Ghost "and saw the glory of God, and Jesus standing on the right hand of God." (Acts 7:55.)

While manifestations of both the Father and Son together have occurred in only a few known instances, and theophanies (appearances of God to man) have been limited to special occasions in the history of mankind, these dramatic events have taken place; and undoubtedly, many communications between God and man have not been recorded nor preserved. Ecclesiastical history, however, informs us of a series of apostasies and restorations. Men have continually perverted the truth, and God has perennially intervened to restore the gospel for the benefit of mankind.

In the latter days, one of the most important manifestations in the history of mankind occurred in the beautiful Genesee country of western New York. The dispensation of the fulness of times was inaugurated by both the Father and the Son appearing and speaking to a young man who was kneeling in prayer. Since Joseph Smith's First Vision was one of the most significant events in the history of mankind, it is fitting that the precursors to the Restoration and the immediate historical setting of this vision be examined. In a work entitled *American Religions and the Rise of Mormonism,* I described the preliminaries to the Restoration, outlining developments occurring from the time of the disruption of the Primitive Church through the Reformation to the colonization of the New World and the birth of the early Republic. After describing the national historical setting of Mormonism in that publication, I decided to focus my attention on conditions existing in western New York at the time of the First Vision. A description of the immediate historical setting of Mormonism is followed in the present work by a discussion of the recitals of the First Vision and an analysis of the concepts unfolded to the Prophet in 1820.

After learning of Joseph's remarkable experience in the sacred grove, some ask, What evidence exists that Joseph Smith was a prophet and received a visitation from the Father and Son? Since this question arises, this book concludes with a brief summary of several distinct evidences of the divine calling of Joseph Smith.

Acknowledgments

This publication could not have been completed without the generous support of Dr. Truman G. Madsen, director of the Institute of Mormon Studies, and Dr. Lane Compton, director of the Research Division, of Brigham Young University. As a result of two grants, I was able to devote part of two summers in Palmyra and vicinity and along the East coast gathering information.

I am also indebted to many gracious and competent librarians, especially individuals working in the Brigham Young University Library; the LDS Church Historian's Office; the Palmyra Public Library; the American Baptist Historical Society; the Presbyterian Historical Society; the New York Public Library; the Library of Congress; the Rochester Public Library; the Ontario, Geneva, Rochester, and Pennsylvania historical societies; and the Wyoming Seminary located in Kingston, Pennsylvania. I further extend appreciation to Elder Howard W. Hunter, LDS Church Historian, and Earl Olson, Assistant Church Historian, for permission to include in this book Appendixes A-I, which are selections from some of the valuable manuscripts located in the Church Historian's Office; and to Don Perry of Shortsville, New York, for permission to reproduce from the files of the Shortsville Enterprise Press valuable information on the early history of the town of Manchester.

In the preparation of this book, I have been helped immeasurably by the counsel of a number of scholars. I am grateful to my father, Milton V. Backman, and to Dr. Richard L. Anderson for reading the manuscript and offering many perceptive suggestions throughout the writing of this work. I wish to thank Dr. Leonard J. Arrington and Dr. Charles D. Tate for their constructive criticisms of the portion of Chapter 3 which appeared in the Spring, 1969, issue of *BYU Studies*.

I further extend my gratitude to Dr. Paul R. Cheesman for locating many of the recitals of the First Vision which he included in his Master's thesis and for supplying me with many of the pictures included in this work. Other pictures were provided through the assistance of the LDS Church Information Services. Maps included in this work were prepared by Dr. Robert L. Layton.

A number of students enrolled at Brigham Young University helped in the research and typing, and to these individuals I extend my appreciation, especially to John and Susan Matthews, Mark Grover, Katherine A. Taylor, and Nora Sue Andersen.

To my wife, Kathleen, I owe a special debt of gratitude for sustaining me during a most busy period in life and, while raising three children, reading and re-reading the manuscript and offering many pertinent recommendations concerning content and style.

CHAPTER 1

The Yankee Expansion

Early in the decade of the 1840's a unique community rapidly emerged in the American wilderness adjacent to the graceful banks of the Mississippi. This city, known as Nauvoo the beautiful, was a peaceful but temporary refuge for members of the most bitterly persecuted religious society in American history.

The leader of the denomination, which had been organized in 1830, was a tall, robust farm boy, named Joseph Smith. He was a man of remarkable ability, a religious leader, a city planner, mayor of the largest city in Illinois in the early 1840's, a commander of migrations, the highest ranking officer of the local militia, a presidential candidate, and a competent author and historian. One of the visitors to Nauvoo — Josiah Quincy, the mayor of Boston — recognized that Joseph Smith was directing a movement that would grow and expand and would continue to influence profoundly the lives of innumerable people. "It is by no means improbable," Quincy astutely observed,

> that some future text-book, for the use of generations yet unborn, will contain a question something like this: What historical American of the nineteenth century has exerted the most powerful influence upon the destinies of his countrymen? And it is by no means impossible that the answer to the interrogatory may be thus written: Joseph Smith, the Mormon Prophet.[1]

Today, Latter-day Saints living throughout the world solemnly testify that Joseph Smith was one of the greatest

---

[1]Josiah Quincy, *Figures of the Past* (Boston, 1883), 376-400.

leaders of the ages and one of the most influential prophets to be guided by the hand of God

The event that initially directed Joseph Smith along a path leading to the rise of a powerful religious movement occurred in a beautiful, peaceful grove located in western New York.

Born in 1805, amidst the rugged mountains of Sharon, Windsor County, Vermont, Joseph Smith had grown up in Vermont and New Hampshire; and when he was about ten migrated with his family to Palmyra, New York. When the family arrived in this village, the region had already evolved from a primitive wilderness to a settled community. In fact, the rapidity of the settlement of western New York was one of the remarkable episodes in the history of America.

When the first battles of the American Revolution erupted, a priceless history, later published as the Book of Mormon, lay hidden in a virtually unknown wilderness. During the colonial era, Americans had pushed their frontiers to western Massachusetts and Connecticut; they had moved into western Pennsylvania and had expanded their civilization into the fertile Shenandoah Valley and the western sections of what is today the Carolinas. One area, however, which the colonists had not penetrated with success, was western New York. The only serious white penetrations into this region were the small settlements located near the banks of the Mohawk from Schnectady to a few miles east of the area called German Flats.[2]

Western New York, Home of the Iroquois

One of the facts which hindered an expansion of the new American culture into the primitive New York wilderness, was the powerful confederation of Indians known as the Iroquois. About 1500 A.D. five tribes of the same linguistic stock united for the purpose of waging war and defending themselves from other Indians. Under the probable leadership

---

[2]W. Pierrepont White, "Indian Possessions and Settled Areas in New York State from 1771 to 1820," *The Rochester Historical Society Publication Fund Series,* VII (1928), 225, 227.

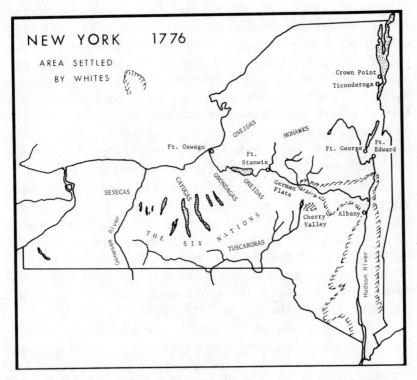

FIG. 1. NEW YORK, 1776, INDICATING INDIAN POSSESSIONS AND
AREAS SETTLED BY WHITES

of a Mohawk named Hiawatha, the Mohawks, the Oneidas,
the Onondagas, the Cayugas, and the Senecas agreed to resolve
their internal problems through arbitration; and when all
were in harmony with a declaration of war, the warriors from
all these tribes vowed to fight together against their enemy.
The Mohawks, located between Utica and Albany, protected
the eastern door of the confederation; and the Senecas, located
west of Seneca Lake, were the guardians of the west; while
the other three tribes protected the center of the Indian
nation. About 1715, the Tuscaroras migrated from the Carolinas and joined the confederation, expanding the five nations
to a confederation of six nations.[3]

---

[3]*Ibid.*, 226-27; Clark Wissler, *Indians of the United States* (Garden City,
New York: Doubleday, 1948), 110-12.

The Iroquois were among the most formidable Indian foes the European immigrants encountered. They not only established an effective organization, but they enjoyed a much higher standard of living than most North American Indians. The people lived in long bark-covered houses. The women cultivated the fields, raising maize, beans and squash; and they produced maple sugar. Meanwhile, the men were active as hunters, spending much time hunting deer. Although most of their clothes were made of deerskin, they produced some cloth and were skilled in the production of black pottery.[4]

For several centuries, the Iroquois succeeded in protecting their lands from encroachment by other Indians and by the white settlers from the east. But during these years, their strength was gradually dissipated because of constant fighting with other Indians. Although the six nations succeeded in winning the wars against those of their race, they were unable to combat the devastating attack launched by the whites during the patriots' struggle for independence.

After the American Revolution erupted, the six nations could not agree concerning which power they should support. The confederation therefore remained neutral but, except for the Oneidas and some Tuscaroras who supported the Americans, most of the Iroquois united with the British. Since these warriors were a constant threat to the inhabitants of border settlements and occasionally terrorized and massacred frontiersmen, General George Washington ordered American troops to drive this enemy from their beloved lands.[5]

Sullivan's Campaign Against the Indians

The devastating maneuver which opened the door for expansion by a maturing civilization occurred in 1779. Under the effective command of General John Sullivan, Continental troops plunged into the heart of the Seneca territory, destroying fields, orchards, shelters, and harvested corn. Burning about forty villages, this army drove most of the Senecas

---

[4]Wissler, *op. cit.*, 118, 125.

[5]Diedrich Willers, Jr., *The Centennial Celebration of General Sullivan's Campaign against the Iroquois in 1779* (Waterloo, 1880), 97-99.

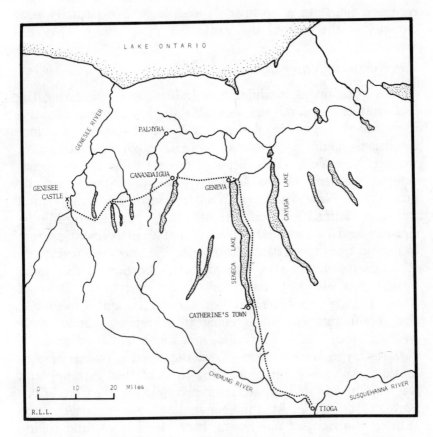

FIG. 2. GENERAL JOHN SULLIVAN'S ROUTE INTO WESTERN NEW YORK

to the Niagara country, and transformed an Indian paradise into a desolate wilderness.[6]

Sullivan's men not only crushed the power of the Indian confederation, but the troops advertised their adventures with spirited enthusiasm. They informed Americans that western New York was a beckoning paradise, containing an abundance of fertile land, scenic lakes, running streams, extensive forests, and wild fruits and game. After learning that choice inexpensive land was available to industrious pioneers, many veterans

[6]*Ibid.,* 157-58. See also Charles P. Whittemore, *A General of the Revolution, John Sullivan of New Hampshire* (New York: Columbia University Press, 1961), ch. 9.

returned home to a postwar depression and eventually suc-
cumbed to the lure of the west.

The Hartford Convention, 1786

In addition to subduing the Indians and publicizing the
fact that choice land was available in the Genesee country,
it was necessary to resolve the problem of ownership before
conditions could be favorable for the rapid colonization of
western New York. This disputed territory was not only considered the land of the Iroquois but was regarded as the
property of New York and Massachusetts, and one section
was also claimed by Connecticut. Early charters of Massachusetts and Connecticut provided that their boundaries were
to extend from the Atlantic to the Pacific and were to include
all lands uninhabited by Christians. A portion of this same
country had also been conveyed by the king to the Duke of
York. During the American Revolution, the states examined
their conflicting claims, agreeing to surrender title to their
western lands. After the initial secessions had been made, a
vast region in western New York remained a source of contention. An agreement concerning most of this disputed land
was finally adopted at an assembly held in Hartford, Connecticut, in 1786. At this convention, Massachusetts was
granted the right of purchasing from the Indians and selling
6,000,000 acres lying east of the preemption line, a line running north and south from the Pennsylvania border to Lake
Ontario and located immediately east of Geneva, New York.
Massachusetts also secured the right of preemption to 230,000
acres located along the Susquehanna River in Broome and
Tioga counties. In return, New York was granted all rights
of sovereignty and jurisdiction over this territory, including
the power of government. Eventually, Connecticut relinquished
her title to southwestern New York, but secured the right
to sell land in northeastern Ohio, known as Connecticut's
Western Reserve.[7]

---

[7]Alexander C. Flick, ed., *History of the State of New York* (New York
City: Columbia University Press, 1935), V, 115-17, 145.

Phelps and Gorham's Purchase

Fearful that the compromise adopted at Hartford might not be enduring and might be plagued with heavy debts, politicians in Massachusetts decided not to complicate matters in New York by holding her western lands for speculative purposes and agreed to dispose immediately of this property. The most enticing offer of purchase was submitted by Oliver Phelps and Nathaniel Gorham, two wealthy speculators who had combined forces. Born in Windsor, Connecticut, Phelps had settled in Massachusetts shortly before the Revolution and had accumulated a fortune through trading and merchandising. While serving in the army during the Revolution, he had become acquainted with several officers who participated

FIG. 3. NEW YORK, 1786, SHOWING THE PHELPS AND GORHAM'S PURCHASE

in Sullivan's campaign and had been favorably impressed with
their descriptions of the beautiful Genesee country. Gorham
had also acquired wealth by his own initiative and had been
a participant in framing the Constitution of the United States.
These bold entrepreneurs secured from Massachusetts, in 1788,
the vast section of western New York for what amounted to
less than three cents an acre.

The purchase price of the land west of the preemption
line was low, but Phelps and Gorham were to pay the money
to the state during a three-year period. Seeking about fifty
associates to assist them, the speculators sold large sections
of land to other financiers. They also had to persuade the
Indians to sell or relinquish all claims to lands stretching
from the preemption line to the Genesee River. With the help
of others, Phelps accomplished the mission with the Indians
at a council held at Buffalo Creek in the summer of 1788.
The approximate 2,600,000 acres ceded by the Indians became
known as Phelps and Gorham's Purchase. The two businessmen were unable, however, to meet their original financial
obligations to Massachusetts; and although the period for
payment was extended, Phelps and Gorham retained only one-
third of their original purchase. Robert Morris, the financier
of the Revolution, expanded his business interests, secured
the region west of the Genesee River, and promoted the colonization of that country.[8]

Jemima Wilkinson, the Public Universal Friend

While Phelps and Gorham were securing title to choice
land in the Genesee country, the first group of pioneers established their homes in the region which had belonged to the
Senecas. These settlers were devout disciples of Jemima Wilkinson, the first native-born American to organize a religious
society in the New World. After asserting that during a
serious illness she died and that her body was repossessed
by another spirit, this former Quaker commenced her ministry

---

[8] Flick, op. cit., 152-58; O[rsamus] Turner, History of the Pioneer Settlement of Phelps and Gorham's Purchase, and Morris' Reserve (Rochester,
1852), 140-42, 162.

in Rhode Island in 1776. She was no longer Jemima Wilkinson, she declared, but the Public Universal Friend. She had been commissiond by God to preach repentance to "a lost and guilty, perishing, dying World, to flee from the wrath which is to come; and to give an Invitation to the lost Sheep of the house of Israel to come home." After announcing to others that she had been transformed during a miraculous vision, the Universal Friend was condemned and maligned by innumerable critics. In the midst of growing opposition and oppression, this controversial woman decided to seek an asylum from the unregenerate world and establish a new Jerusalem in the wilderness of New York.

In the spring of 1788, an advance party of Universal Friends, primarily New Englanders, located a site for the religious community about a mile west of Seneca Lake (southwest of Fayette). Two years later, the Universal Friend assumed direction of the Jerusalem community. There she remained until her death on July 1, 1819; whereupon the small society, which had already begun to wither, slowly disintegrated.[9]

Migration into the Hill Cumorah Country

In order to stimulate colonization of western New York, Phelps sent an expedition into the region in 1788, and a base of operations was established near the north shore of Lake Canandaigua. Surveyors hastened into this region, dividing the land into townships (six-mile squares) according to the pattern employed by the federal government in its division of the Northwest Territory. During the summer and fall of 1788, Phelps also hired workmen to construct a crude road from Geneva to Canandaigua, the first to be blazed in that region. Immediately after this road was completed, an extension was built northward from Canandaigua into the wilder-

[9]Herbert A. Wisbey, Jr., *Pioneer Prophetess: Jemima Wilkinson, the Publick Universal Friend* (Ithaca: Cornell University Press, 1964), 105-112, 163, 168.

ness where the town of Manchester is now located.[10] Consequently, the path had been opened for the Yankee invasion
of the Genesee country.

Ontario County, a Mother of Counties

Shortly after the convention at Hartford, the New York
legislature anticipated the imminent settlement of western
New York and in January, 1789, created a new county from
Montgomery which was named Ontario after the great lake
which originally formed its northern boundary. This county
embraced not only the territory within its current boundaries,
but also included the land located in Steuben (a county formed
in 1796), Genesee (created in 1802), parts of Monroe and
Livingston (formed in 1821), Yates and part of Wayne (the
last two counties being formed in 1823). Eventually, Ontario
County was divided into towns. In 1790, there were four towns
in this extensive area; and in 1800, nineteen. One of the towns
created between 1790 and 1800 was named Palmyra and was
originally an area twelve miles by six miles. In the year that
Wayne County was formed, the town of Palmyra was divided
into two townships, the western half being named Macedon
and the eastern section (an area six miles square) retaining
the name of Palmyra.

Located immediately south of the town of Palmyra was
another geographical unit created in the 1790's named Farmington Town, which originally consisted of two townships.
In 1821, Farmington was divided. The west portion retained
the name Farmington; the eastern section was named Burt,
but was renamed Manchester Town (and is also called the
township of Manchester) in 1822. At the time of the First
Vision, the Smith family was living in the town of Farmington, but the area where they lived was first renamed Burt
and then Manchester.

After clusters of homes and businesses emerged within
the towns, villages were named and later incorporated, and

---

[10]Turner, op. cit., 163.

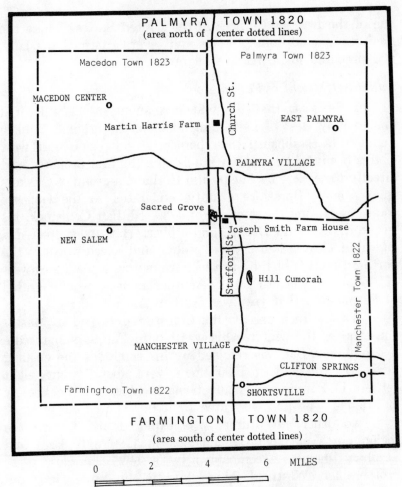

FIG. 4. TOWNS OF PALMYRA AND FARMINGTON, 1820

many of these communities adopted the name of the town or township in which the settlements were located.[11]

Probably no one spent the winter of 1788-1789 in Canandaigua, but early in 1789 permanent settlers migrated west to Canandaigua village where Phelps and Gorham established

[11]White, op. cit., 229; Hamilton Child, Gazetteer and Business Directory of Ontario County, New York for 1867-8 (Syracuse, 1867), 45-46, 49-52; Horatio Gates Spafford, A Gazetteer of the State of New York (Albany, 1824), 400-401.

one of the first land offices in the United States. There the pioneers erected homes, stores and taverns, farmed the land, and prepared for a massive migration.[12]

Initial Settlement of Farmington

In the year that the first permanent colonists located immediately west of Lake Canandaigua, the original Yankee immigrants established their homes in the region northwest of this beautiful lake. After purchasing the first property sold directly to settlers by Phelps and Gorham, a group of Quakers from Adams, Berkshire County, emigrated to the Genesee country. During the summer of 1789, Nathan Comstock, his two sons Otis and Darius, and Robert Hathaway erected a log cabin, cleared four acres of ground and sowed wheat in the northern section of the town of Farmington, a few miles west of the Joseph Smith farm. Another pioneer who migrated to Farmington that year was Nathan Aldrich.

All these men except Otis Comstock returned to Massachusetts for the winter. Otis was left in Farmington to care for the stock, but was rejoined by his comrades the ensuing year. By the end of 1790 there were about twenty-eight settlers in Farmington, many being members of the Society of Friends, who had emigrated from Berkshire County.[13]

Two other adventurers who explored and farmed the region north of Lake Canandaigua in 1789 were Ezra and Stephen Phelps. Accompanied by a few comrades, these brothers left Westfield, Massachusetts, in June, 1789, and settled near one of the highest drumlins located in the Erie-Ontario lowland, later known as "Hill Cumorah" or the "Mormon Hill." After burning brush and clearing land, these industrious men planted corn and ascertained that the area was fertile and productive. A few years after returning to Massa-

---

[12]The first known white pioneer to settle Canandaigua (and first known settler west of Seneca Lake) was named Joseph Smith. He erected a block house on Main Street where he opened a tavern. A few years later, he moved to Farmington and there erected the first frame building and with the assistance of Jacob Smith built the first sawmill in that town in 1795. Turner, *op. cit.*, 163, 222.

[13]*Ibid.*, 217-19; "Old Newspapers," *The Palmyra Courier*, August 4, 1871, 3.

FIG. 5. THE HILL CUMORAH

The earliest known artist's sketch of the Hill Cumorah, published in J. W. Barber and Henry Howe's *Historical Collections of the State of New York* (1841).

chusetts, they again traveled west and settled permanently in the Finger Lake country.[14]

Meanwhile, "Bob" Robinson located his home in the land which had been cultivated by the Phelps brothers, and in 1790 purchased as part of his farm the property which included the Hill Cumorah.[15]

Colonization of Palmyra

While Farmington was being settled, other pioneers commenced clearing the heavily wooded region north of this town. Township No. 12, range 2, containing 21,120 acres, was purchased by John Swift and Colonel John Jenkins for £ 1,320, or about one shilling an acre. During the summer of 1789, these land speculators worked long hours surveying their property; and the subsequent year, John Swift moved into the region with his family, building the first log home located within the present limits of Palmyra village. In the year that Swift located his home in Palmyra, Webb Harwood and his wife (other pioneers from Adams, Berkshire, Massachusetts) and three of their friends — Noah Porter, Jonathan Warner, and Bennet Bates — settled in this same town. Two other settlers who arrived in Palmyra in 1790 were David White and Lemuel Spear, Spear being a veteran from Massachusetts who arrived with his family of eleven children. Originally, the pioneer settlement founded by John Swift was called "Swift's Landing" or "Swift Town," but soon was changed to "Toland," and in 1796 was renamed "Palmyra."[16]

Another early settler of Palmyra was Nathan Harris, who was accompanied by his wife Rhoda Lapham Harris. Nathan migrated from Rhode Island in 1793 and in February, 1794, purchased six hundred acres of land from John Swift for $300 in New York currency. After securing this land,

---

[14]"Old Newspapers," *The Palmyra Courier,* January 26, 1872, 3; February 2, 1872, 3.

[15]*Ibid.,* January 19, 1872; 3.

[16]Book of Deeds, I, 223, Ontario County Clerk's Office, Canandaigua, New York, hereafter cited as Deeds. Turner, *op. cit.,* 378-80; "Old Newspapers," *The Palmyra Courier,* August 4, 1871, 3; [W. H. McIntosh, ed.], *History of Wayne County, New York* (Philadelphia, 1877), 134.

he built a log home on the north end of Wintergreen Hill, one
of the few hills in that area which at the time was barren
of timber. Occasionally neglecting his farm, Nathan spent
much of his time fishing and hunting deer and wild ducks.
This rugged outdoorsman gained the reputation of being one
of the most skilled hunters and fishermen of the area. "Uncle
Nathan" was not only called "Trout Harris" but was often
referred to as the Nimrod of the settlement; and according
to Palmyra folklore, Nathan shot the last wolf killed in that
vicinity.

Part of the land which Nathan purchased was deeded to
his son, Martin, who mortgaged his farm on August 5, 1829,
for $3,000 to E. B. Grandin to pay for the printing of the
Book of Mormon. This money was to be paid to Grandin,
the printer of the sacred record, within eighteen months. In
case of default, Grandin was authorized to sell, at public
auction, sufficient land to pay the accrued debt. Partly due
to the boycott of the translated record by the people of Palmyra, Joseph Smith was unable to raise sufficient funds to
pay Grandin within the eighteen-month period specified by
the contract. Martin Harris, therefore, again aided the Prophet
by selling 151 acres of his farm to Thomas Lakey, at a private
sale on April 1, 1831. This land was sold for approximately
$3,000, which was undoubtedly paid to Grandin.[17]

The extreme eastern section of the town of Palmyra was
originally colonized by settlers from Southampton, Long Island.
In 1788, eleven bold adventurers agreed to relocate their homes
somewhere in the American west. After three years of searching, two explorers from this group wandered into a heavily
forested valley containing rich soil and a meandering stream.
That same year these men convinced their partners of the
advantages of this site, and part of the group — consisting of
Elias Reeves, William Hopkins, Joel Foster, Abraham Foster,

---

[17]Deeds, VI, 45; "Old Newspapers," *The Palmyra Courier,* May 3,
1872, 3; Wayne Cutler Gunnell, "Martin Harris — Witness and Benefactor" (Master's thesis, Brigham Young University, 1955), 37-38. Copies of
the contracts between Martin Harris and E. B. Grandin and Thomas Lakey
are located in the appendix of his thesis.

and Luther Sanford — purchased the land from John Swift.
The following year these Long Island settlers migrated to
East Palmyra with their families and commenced building a
society where that village stands today.[18]

While frontiersmen were erecting log homes in East Palmyra, the west portion of Palmyra Town (the area that became
the township of Macedon in January, 1823) was settled primarily by immigrants from Massachusetts, Connecticut, and
Rhode Island. A number of these pioneers were Quakers who
worshipped for many years with the members of the Society
of Friends living in the northern part of Farmington. Eventually church buildings and small businesses emerged near the
heart of this town, and the community was named Macedon
Center.[19]

Settlement of Manchester

Early in the decade of the 1790's, frontiersmen also began
clearing the forests where the communities of Manchester
and Shortsville are now located. After purchasing land from
Phelps and Gorham, Lot 19 Township 12, Joab Gillet, accompanied by his wife, three sons, and six daughters, erected the
first log home in Manchester village in 1793. Settlements
southwest of this village commenced three years earlier when
Sharon Booth located his home in a hamlet named Shortsville.
After initiating the colonization of that area, Booth moved
to Manchester in 1794, and there became one of the influential
leaders in organizing the Methodists living south of the Hill
Cumorah. Stephen Phelps also was one of the earlier settlers
of Manchester, but after living there for a few years moved
to Palmyra where he opened a tavern.[20]

---

[18]*History of Wayne County,* 136; Turner, *op. cit.,* 388; Deeds, I, 230-31.
[19]*History of Wayne County,* 117-19.
[20]Charles Brown, "Manchester in the Early Days," Files of the Shortsville Enterprise Press, October 18, 1902; October 25, 1902, copy located in
the Brigham Young University Library. This collection contains selections
of articles which appeared in the *Shortsville Enterprise* and typewritten
copies were placed on file in the publisher's office. See also "Old Time
School Matters," Files, June 7, 1889.

The eastern section of Manchester commenced in 1800, when John Shekell left his home in Maryland and settled east of Shortsville in a village that was named Sulphur Springs and then renamed Clifton Springs. Although Shekell was a southerner who transported the first slaves into the area, the three blacks were eventually freed. Earlier the New York legislature had passed a law providing for the gradual emancipation of slaves, and since a strong sentiment existed in that state against slavery, and the Finger Lake country was settled primarily by immigrants from the North, few slaves and few Negroes lived in the area where the Smiths settled in the early nineteenth century.[21]

Methods of Travel by Yankee Invaders

Many of the earliest immigrants to the Genesee country journeyed into the wilderness by boat. Ezra Phelps and his companions traveled from Massachusetts to Manchester by sailing along the Mohawk River, transported their boat to Wood Creek, and followed that stream to the largest lake located within the borders of New York, Lake Oneida. After traversing this body of water, the men proceeded down the outlet to the Seneca River and sailed down this river to Geneva. Then they walked to Canandaigua and continued northward to the Hill Cumorah.[22]

The Long Island settlers of East Palmyra also employed the network of the river highways to transport themselves and their belongings to their new home in the west. During the winter of 1791-1792, these craftsmen built a two-and-a-half-ton sailboat and on April 1, 1792, proceeded down an inlet to the Atlantic. After sailing up the Hudson, the party of six men and two women entered the Mohawk River and continued to Albany. After arriving at Albany, they transported their vessel sixteen miles overland to Schenectady. Then they continued along the Mohawk to Fort Stanwix,

---

[21]Brown, *op. cit.*, February 27, 1903.
[22]"Old Newspapers," *The Palmyra Courier*, January 26, 1872, 3; February 2, 1872, 3.

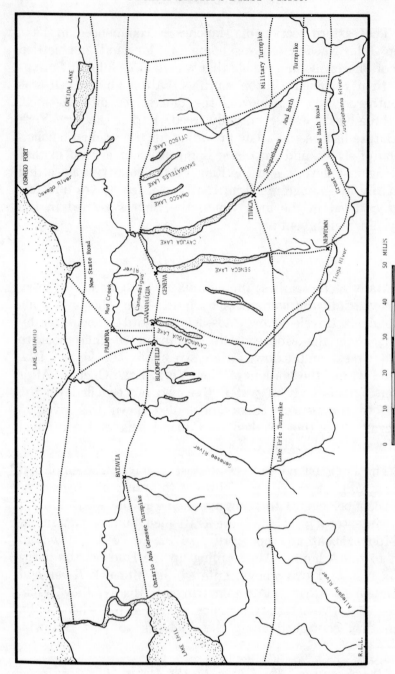

FIG. 6. MAIN ROADS AND RIVER HIGHWAYS LEADING INTO WESTERN NEW YORK ABOUT 1800

now Rome. For the second time the Long Island settlers were forced to hoist their vessel from the water. After being placed on rollers made of logs, their boat was pushed almost a mile to Wood Creek. Upon their arrival at this stream, the immigrants met five other groups migrating west, three traveling to Geneva, one to Palmyra, and the other to Cayuga. Accompanied by a parade of boats, the adventurers continued by sailing down the creek to Lake Oneida. In two-and-a-half hours they sailed across the twenty-one-mile lake. They traveled down the Oneida Outlet, followed the Clyde River to Mud Creek, and continued along this stream. After traveling for weeks in an open boat, being exposed to heavy rains and chilling winds, they arrived at East Palmyra where they had selected home sites the preceding year. Since they were welcomed by a turbulent, pelting storm, they overturned their boat and used this vessel as a temporary shelter until they succeeded in building log homes.[23]

While some immigrants were traveling west by boat, others packed corn, wheat, beans, cooking utensils, clothes, and additional supplies in covered wagons, and had their goods pulled across the primitive roads by oxen, or sometimes by horses. Some of the early settlers also drove cattle and horses across the rolling hills, and took geese, ducks, and chickens west by fastening them to their wagons.[24]

Other pioneers of this era penetrated the frontier without the aid of boats or wagons and walked two hundred miles or more carrying on their backs or in their arms the possessions which they considered most vital for the inauguration of a new life. When the Comstocks and Robert Hathaway traveled to Farmington in 1789, some proceeded part way by boat, one rode a horse, and the others walked, driving cattle before them. Since a calf was born during the journey, Otis Comstock carried the young, struggling animal miles across the Genesee plains. The following year, some of these same

[23]"Old Newspapers," *The Palmyra Courier,* March 1, 1872, 3.
[24]"Obituary of Sunderland P. Gardner," Files of the Shortsville Enterprise Press, February 18, 1893; "Old Newspapers," *The Palmyra Courier,* March 15, 1872, 3.

Quakers, accompanied by their families, traveled for more than a month in drenching rains as they carved their own paths into the New York woodlands.[25]

During the winter, when a mantle of snow covered the ground, many immigrants traveled by sleigh, but as the snow thawed and the land became bogs of mud, the pioneers sometimes exchanged their sleighs for wagons and plodded the remainder of the way west through ridges of spongy soil.

Migration of Smith Family from Vermont to New York

During the first two decades of the nineteenth century, methods of transportation did not change appreciably as far as most immigrants were concerned; and the Smith family, who in 1816 or thereabouts followed the early wave of immigrants, experienced the same kind of trials and inconveniences that many other pioneers endured. Joseph Smith, Sr., had preceded the other members of the family west, had located a new residence in Palmyra, and had hired Caleb Howard to assist his wife and children in the move from Norwich, Vermont.[26] Howard, however, did not prove to be a trustworthy hand. He squandered the family's funds by drinking and gambling and then rode in the Smith wagon, forcing Joseph and others to walk. Under normal conditions the trek would not have been so difficult for Joseph, but the young boy, who was about ten, had not fully recovered from an operation which had been performed a few years earlier while the Smiths were living in Lebanon, New Hampshire. Portions of the bone had been removed from Joseph's left leg, and the boy was still hobbling on crutches when he started for New York. On occasions, during the biting winter weather, they would journey twenty, thirty and almost forty miles along snow-covered trails. Fortunately, while the Smiths owned a wagon, they were accompanied by another family, named

---

[25]Old Newspapers," *The Palmyra Courier*, August 4, 1871, 3; Turner, *op. cit.*, 218.

[26]Joseph Smith, History, Note A, LDS Church Historian's Office, Salt Lake City, Utah, hereafter referred to as LDS Church Historian's Office.

Gates, who owned several sleighs; and occasionally the Smiths were invited to ride with that family.[27]

The Prophet's grandmother, Lydia Mack, also started west with the family, but after traveling only a few miles this elderly woman was injured by the upsetting of one of the vehicles. Deciding to tarry with relatives living in Royalton, Vermont, Lydia failed to fully recover and died a few years later before rejoining the others.[28]

As the Smith family traveled through Utica, New York, Caleb Howard attempted to steal the wagon belonging to this group of pioneers. Lucy immediately summoned help, convincing others that she was being robbed; and the men who were present intercepted Howard, preventing him from accomplishing his malicious plan. The remainder of the journey was completed without the interference of Howard, but the family was so poor, especially after their meager funds had been squandered, that Lucy paid several managers of roadside inns with cloth and clothing, the last payment being made with a pair of Sophronia's earrings. During the final portion of the journey, Joseph was invited to ride in one of the sleighs belonging to the Gates family, one that followed the other vehicles. For some unknown reason, shortly before the family arrived at their destination, Joseph was beaten and "knocked down" by one of the Gates boys, the driver of the last sleigh. He was left on the trail while others, undoubtedly not knowing of his plight, rode into Palmyra. A stranger discovered the injured youth, picked him up, and carried the boy to the village where his father had decided to settle. Commenting on this journey, Lucy Smith exclaimed: "We . . . arrived at Palmyra, with a small portion of our effects, and barely two cents in cash."[29]

---

[27]*Ibid.*

[28]Lucy Mack Smith, *History of Joseph Smith,* ed. Preston Nibley (Salt Lake City: Bookcraft, 1958), 61. Although this later edition has been cited, the references cited in this work have been compared with the first edition and the quotations harmonize with the original publication.

[29]Joseph Smith, History, Note A; Lucy Mack Smith, *op. cit.,* 62-63.

CHAPTER 2

From Wilderness to Civilization

For several years after the initial colonization of the Genesee country there were no stores, no mills, no physicians, no ordained ministers and few implements of labor in the towns of Palmyra and Farmington. Nevertheless, through ingenuity and vigorous work, the early settlers secured the food, clothing, and shelter which they needed. The people were prepared to sacrifice, and their immediate success encouraged others to join them in transforming the virgin forest into productive communities.

Securing the Land

Since land was plentiful and labor was scarce, it was not difficult for the original white inhabitants to purchase large farms for themselves and their sons. Some of the first settlers of that region purchased land for twenty-five cents an acre and earned a dollar a day for their labors. Although money was scarce, a few frontiersmen earned sufficient in one day to procure four acres of land; and in the early years of the nineteenth century, annual sales from wheat produced sufficient revenue for a few industrious laborers to purchase yearly a new farm for one of their sons.[1]

Much of the land purchased by John Swift was surveyed into one-hundred- and two-hundred-acre lots; the smaller lots being situated adjacent to Mud Creek, and the two-hundred-acre plots being located in the northern part of the town. Many purchased this land from Swift for less than one dollar an acre. One immigrant, for example, bought a hundred-acre

[1]Files of the Shortsville Enterprise Press, March 13, 1903.

lot for what amounted to seventy-five cents an acre; and another pioneer secured from Swift two hundred acres for sixty-two cents an acre.[2]

Between 1790 and 1800, land in the area currently known as Manchester had increased from about twenty-five cents to approximately four dollars an acre. Some of the most valuable property in that country was located on either side of the Canandaigua Outlet where the falls provided valuable sites for mills. Five hundred acres of this more expensive land was sold in 1804 for five dollars an acre to Theophilus Short, the entrepreneur known as the founder of the small industrial complex which became Shortsville.[3]

Some of the early pioneers of the Finger Lake country exchanged farms in New England for unsold land in New York. Nathan Herendeen was offered one thousand acres in Farmington for his farm in Berkshire County, Massachusetts; and one frontiersman of Manchester exchanged his farm in Windham County, Connecticut, which was valued at twenty dollars an acre, for land selling for four dollars an acre in western New York.[4]

Even though land on the basis of prices in the east was inexpensive during the initial phase of colonization, some of the pioneers could not afford to buy property and squatted in the area near Hill Cumorah. Eventually the land which the squatters had improved was sold and those uprooted were forced to more further west, where all too frequently a repetition of their unfortunate experiences occurred.[5]

Life on the New York Frontier

Although the earliest settlers of the Genesee country began farming immediately after their arrival in that wilderness, the wild fruits growing on the land, the game in the

---

[2]"Old Newspapers," *The Palmyra Courier*, October 13, 1871, 3; December 1, 1871, 3; February 16, 1872, 3.

[3]Files of the Shortsville Enterprise Press, January 9, 1903; February 27, 1903; File No. XXIV.

[4]*Ibid.*, September 6, 1890; March 21, 1903.

[5]*Ibid.*, January 16, 1903.

forests, and the fish in the streams provided these frontiersmen with a valuable source of food. In addition to wild plums,
a variety of berries were growing in the Finger Lake country,
such as blackberries, strawberries, raspberries, and cranberries.
During the initial years of colonization, venison provided the
settlers with much of their winter supply of meat; and the
outlet which flowed from Manchester to Lake Canandaigua
was well stocked with trout, white fish, black bass, and other
fish. Mud Creek also contained a variety of fish, including
some salmon. For a number of years, fishing was principally
done with nets; and occasionally a few men supplied an entire
community with the fish which the settlers desired.[6]

Not all the animals of that area were considered beneficial, for wolves and bears often preyed upon the sheep and
swine. On occasions, entire flocks of sheep would be slaugh-
tered in a night by the wolves, and bears frequently attacked
the hogs which ran wild in the commons.[7]

During the 1790's, small bands of Indians roamed the
Genesee country, trapping, hunting, and trading; exchanging
beaver pelts for baskets, flour, tobacco, and gunpowder. But
the number of Indians seen in that region declined rapidly,
just as the supply of venison and fish diminished as the area
was transformed.[8]

One of the major tasks facing the frontiersmen of western
New York was that of penetrating the heavily wooded land.
Originally, most of the land was cleared by "slashing." Trunks
would be chopped so that they would fall into a huge pile,
after which they would be burned. Some trees were growing
in areas where they could not be cut so as to form a pile.
These isolated plants were chopped into logs and then dragged
to the areas where the timber was burned. In order to expe-
dite this project, many pioneers sponsored work parties, invit-

_____

[6]O[rsamus] Turner, *History of the Pioneer Settlement of Phelps and
Gorham's Purchase, and Morris' Reserve* (Rochester, 1852), 168, 211.
[7]*Ibid.,* 191.
[8]"The Old and the New," *The Palmyra Courier,* April 12, 1872, 3.

ing their neighbors and other friends to assist them not only in levelling the trees but also in raising part of their homes.[9]

After the land had been cleared the farmers tilled the soil with crude wooden plows, usually drawn by oxen, and with a hoe made the final preparation for planting. They sowed seeds and harvested large crops of wheat and corn. They planted fruit trees and nurtured their apple and peach orchards. They cared for their cows, horses, sheep, hogs, chickens, and oxen. They gathered the winter supply of wood and from the local trees secured the wood used for making furniture and household items, such as eating utensils, mixing bowls, and chopping boards. Self-sufficiency was the rule of that age; and people worked from sunrise to sunset, six and sometimes seven days a week, in order to procure the goods they desired.

While raising large families the women, with the aid of their daughters, performed innumerable household chores, employing techniques that had been adopted by their pioneer ancestors. They ground corn on stumps hollowed out for that purpose. They spun and wove woolen and linen cloth from which they made the family clothes. They also made clothes from animal skins, and many Genesee farmers wore buckskin breeches throughout the cold winter months.[10] The women also helped outside. They aided their husbands and sons in maintaining the kitchen garden, successfully growing white potatoes, turnips, cabbages, squash, and other vegetables. They milked the cows, fed the animals, and sometimes helped the boys in herding the sheep and cows. Through mutual cooperation, families worked ceaselessly in creating a new environment.

The original homes of the settlers were crude in comparison to the mansions then located along the east coast and the homes constructed in the area in the early decades of the nineteenth century. Most of the log cabins built in the early 1790's were made without wooden doors or glass windows,

---

[9] Files of the Shortsville Enterprise Press, May 8, 1903.
[10] *Ibid.*, February 14, 1903.

these openings occasionally being covered with blankets. Much
of the furniture was homemade and the dirt floors were sometimes covered with split logs. When the logs became too soiled,
the inhabitants cleaned them by chipping, thereby creating
a fresh layer of wood.[11]

Journeys of the Genesee Settlers

While there was much work which constantly needed to
be accomplished at home, the Genesee farmers traveled long
distances in order to secure the goods and services which they
desired and in order to find markets for their grain. During
the summer of 1789, Darius Comstock walked almost twenty
miles weekly to Geneva in order to secure provisions, and
then returned to his cabin in the Farmington wilderness.[12]
In 1790 Ebenezer Spear was requested by one of his friends,
Webb Harwood, to procure wine for Harwood's wife who was
in a "delicate state of health." Spear walked from Palmyra to
Canandaigua but, failing to locate the wine there, headed east,
continuing to Utica and thence to Schenectady. At Schenectady he finally located the beverage, purchased six quarts
for medicinal purposes, and then returned to Palmyra. During
this fourteen-day journey in which Spear walked approximately
thirty miles a day, he slept on the ground in a knapsack on all
except four of the nights.[13]

Until mills appeared in 1794 and 1795 on Mud Creek and
the Canandaigua Outlet, the closest mill to the settlers of
Palmyra and Farmington was located near Seneca Lake at
the Jerusalem community. Occasionally farmers living in these
towns loaded their wagons with wheat and rode in ox-drawn
carts for four or five days along the winding trails leading to
the Jerusalem mill, returning home after a ten-day trip.[14]

Early pioneers of the Genesee country also rode or sailed
to Syracuse, a distance of about 70 miles from Palmyra, where

---

[11]*Ibid.,* December 26, 1902; January 2, 1903.
[12]Turner, *op. cit.,* 218.
[13]*Ibid.,* 381.
[14]*Ibid.;* "Old Newspapers, No. 18," *The Palmyra Courier,* March 15,
1872, 3.

they exchanged wheat for salt; and others journeyed along the roads leading to Utica, a distance of 120 miles from Palmyra, to sell their grain or to exchange agricultural products for nails, glass, and other finished products.[15]

Western Highways

Men walked and rode great distances during that era, but they also converted the rivers into major highways. Before the completion of the Erie Canal, not only was grain shipped east in large wagons but wheat and other goods were loaded on boats at and near Palmyra and shipped to many eastern markets.[16]

One of the frequently traveled paths of western New York, especially by those living in Palmyra and Farmington, was the Canandaigua road. It proceeded south from Palmyra village, ran less than a mile east of the Joseph Smith farm, passed the Hill Cumorah, bisected Manchester Village and entered Canandaigua, a distance of fifteen miles from Palmyra. In the early nineteenth century there were two main roads stretching west across western New York. One crossed the state in the area where the Erie Canal was constructed, passing through the main sector of Palmyra Village. Another artery west was located immediately north of the Finger Lakes. These two main routes were connected by the Canandaigua road.

For the convenience of the settlers of that region, a stage coach made daily runs along the Canandaigua road. According to the schedule of 1824, a coach left the Eagle Hotel in Palmyra Village daily at 7:00 A.M. and arrived at Canadaigua before 10:00 A.M. Leaving Canandaigua at 2:00 P.M. the stage returned along the same road and arrived each evening in Palmyra. The advertised one-way fare for such a trip was seventy-five cents.[17]

---

[15]Turner, op. cit., 212; Files of the Shortsville Enterprise Press, January 2, 1903; March 6, 1903; April 23, 1887.
[16]Turner, op. cit., 383; "The Old and the New," The Palmyra Courier, April 12, 1872, 3.
[17]The Wayne Sentinel (Palmyra), September 28, 1824.

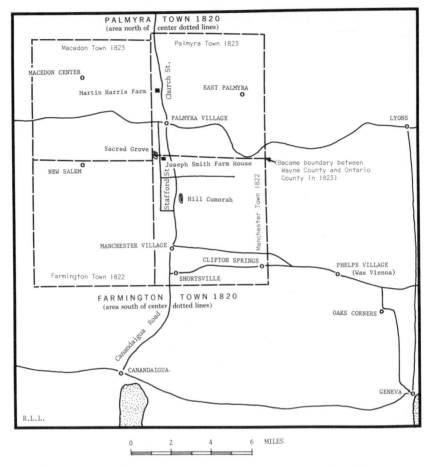

Fig. 7. Towns and Villages Located Near the Joseph Smith Farm

Many settlers living in Farmington regularly trekked along the Canandaigua road to Manchester village in order to conduct their business. Before Farmington was divided into two towns the residents of what became the town of Manchester participated in the Farmington town meetings. Many of the men elected to serve as local officials resided in Manchester and sessions were often held in the area which was formerly the eastern part of Farmington. During the period when the Smith family lived in western New York, local political matters were often discussed in buildings located in Manchester village, such as Nathan Barlow's store, Ebenezer Pratt's tavern, the local hotel, and the woolen factory.[18]

The justice of the peace court also drew many settlers in the 1820's to Manchester village. On January 19, 1830, for example, Joseph Smith, Sr., and Abraham Fish appeared before Nathan Pierce, justice of the peace, and confessed owing Lemuel Durfee "damages" amounting to $37.92. Although the records do not reveal the nature of the damages, the judge recorded that the accused admitted their guilt and on September 13, 1830, paid not only Durfee, but also the interest and the courts costs. And on June 28 of the same year, Joseph Smith, Sr., the father of the defendant Hyrum Smith, appeared before the justice of the peace in Manchester, admitted that his son owed $20.07 for "shoeing horses," and directed the justice to enter judgment against the defendant.[19]

Many settlers of Palmyra and Farmington also walked or rode through Manchester village on their way to Canandaigua. Canandaigua was not only a transportation center but was also the seat of government for the settlers of Ontario County and was an important business community for the farmers of that region of New York.[20]

While many settlers of the Genesee country journeyed to Canandaigua, others traveled to Geneva, located twenty-two miles from Palmyra, following various routes to their destination. Although the settlers of Palmyra and vicinity could have followed the road to Canandaigua and then proceeded east to Geneva, there were more direct routes to that community which passed through the village of Vienna, later renamed Phelps. The Vienna road, for instance, was situated north of Palmyra village and ran south towards Phelps and Geneva. Other well-trodden paths were blazed south of the Hill Cumorah, connecting Manchester center and Phelps.

[18]Files of the Shortsville Enterprise Press, November 28, 1902; February 20, 1903; December 4, 1903.

[19]Justice Records, 1827-1830, Town Clerk's Office, Clifton Springs, New York, microfilm copy located in Brigham Young University Library.

[20]While the Smith family resided in Palmyra, this village was located in Ontario County. After moving to Farmington, the family continued to reside in that county.

Since Geneva became an important merchandising and banking center, there were many factors which served as magnets drawing travelers to the village located near the shore of Seneca Lake. Palmyra merchants secured a major portion of their supplies from Geneva; and many residing in that section of western New York took advantage of the banking services available there.[21] While Martin Harris was attempting to raise money to pay for the publication of the Book of Mormon, this farmer hastened to Geneva to secure a loan from one of the bankers living in that village. Recalling this visit, an inquisitive businessman wrote:[22]

> Among the applicants for money who came to me at Geneva, as I now recollect, was one Martin Harris, of Palmyra, Wayne County. He brought a letter of introduction to me from a highly respectable citizen of that town, a Mr. Jessup, who was a leading man and an elder in the Presbyterian Church and on whose judgment I depended in respect to the character of the borrower and the value of the property in all cases of applications for loans from that quarter. From the letter of Mr. Jessup the bearer was introduced to me as a very worthy and substantial farmer, possessing a very excellent farm which would furnish a very ample security for the amount of money which he wished to obtain, viz. $1,300.00, and he commended Mr. Harris to me as a desirable borrower. As usual, my first inquiry of Mr. Harris was for what purpose he wanted the money. In reply to this, with some hesitation, he stated that he wanted it to pay for publishing a book. This excited my curiosity to know what sort of book it was that a farmer desired to mortgage his farm to publish. His answer to this was, that it was the Mormon Bible. This was the first that I had ever heard of the Mormon Bible and my curiosity was further excited in regard to it. I interrogated him as to its character and what it was. He then informed me that

---

[21]Files of the Shortsville Enterprise Press, April 23, 1887; January 2, 1903; March 21, 1903.

[22]A portion of a typewritten copy of a letter presumably written by Charles Butler is located in the Charles Butler Collection, Library of Congress.

the plates for it had been discovered by one Joseph Smith, a young man then living at Palmyra, whom he knew well and who had been guided in his discoveries by divine inspiration.

Although the banker was impressed with Harris' credentials, Martin Harris did not at this time secure the loan which he was seeking.

Barter and Exchange

Since money was scarce, the early farmers of the Genesee country were required to secure the necessary goods and services primarily through barter and exchange. Many merchants received wheat and cattle from the pioneers and sold to the people in return spices, cooking utensils, paper, shoes, and other commodities which the farmers desired but found difficult to produce. Because of the shortage of money, many were also unable to pay their taxes, and much property was constantly being placed on public sale because of the failure of farmers to pay their assessments.[23]

The Frontier Becomes a Community

While farmers and merchants continued to travel slowly along the well-trodden dirt trails leading to the political and economic centers of the Genesee country, the frontier posts rapidly evolved into bustling communities. Before 1800, log cabins began to be replaced by larger and more comfortable frame homes in what became Manchester township; and at the turn of the century a shop to repair agricultural implements and a blacksmith shop appeared in the area of Manchester village.[24] Early in the nineteenth century, other manufacturers emerged along the Canandaigua Outlet. This river flowed across the entire length of the township and was navigable up to Manchester village, where the flow was inter-

---

[23]Turner, *op. cit.*, 383. The Palmyra newspapers of the early nineteenth century contain numerous advertisements of land sales resulting from the failure of settlers to pay their debts.

[24]Files of the Shortsville Enterprise Press, November 28, 1902; April 17, 1903.

rupted by a fall which provided a valuable source of power. Another waterfall of about twenty-two feet was located about a mile southeast of this village at Shortsville; and many speculators living in that town believed that important industrial complexes would emerge near these two sites. Since the early promoters of Manchester village anticipated the rise of many factories in that area, they named their community after Manchester, New Hampshire, and a town in England of the same name.[25] In 1811 an enterprising group of citizens organized the "Ontario Manufacturing Company," and immediately thereafter constructed a woolen factory adjacent to the Canandaigua Outlet. This factory included a spinning jenny with seventy-five spindles, a jack with forty spindles, six looms, a fulling mill, and a coloring and dyeing shop. At that time there were only two other similar manufacturing establishments in New York state.[26]

Many other structures were erected in Manchester village during the first two decades of the nineteenth century. About 1809, Nathan Barlow built the first store in the village, and during the War of 1812 his merchandising establishment became a popular gathering place for individuals who desired to discuss the war and related topics. Meanwhile, one of the first settlers of the community, Ebenezer Pratt, erected a tavern which served for years as a rest stop for immigrants. In 1814 a hotel was built there.[27] Three years later, on January 14, 1817, the inhabitants of Manchester organized a library which contained histories, biographies, geographies, religious treatises, and other popular works of that age.[28]

Another manufacturing center began to emerge in the early nineteenth century at Shortsville. In 1804, Theophilus Short erected a flour mill and a saw mill in this hamlet, and

---

[25]*Ibid.*, April 3, 1903.
[26]*Ibid.*, April 17, 1903.
[27]"Reminiscences of Russell M. Rush," Files of the Shortsville Enterprise Press, March 6, 1903.
[28]Miscellaneous Records, Book C, 178, Ontario County Court House, Canandaigua, New York. Many of the books which were originally located in the Manchester library are now in the possession of the Ontario Historical Society, Canandaigua, New York.

eighteen years later constructed another flour mill north of his original business. Encouraged by Short's initial success, another industrious pioneer, William Grimes, erected a woolen mill on the south bank of the Outlet in 1816. During the early years that this business was in operation Grimes hired eight men to work in the factory, and in 1818 the mill was sold to Stephen Brewster who doubled its capacity. One year before Brewster purchased the woolen mill, E. K. Case, Jet Abbey, and Alvin West erected a paper mill in the community and began producing paper from cloth pulp, providing printers and farmers throughout the area with this commodity. According to the reminiscences of one old settler, while Stephen Brewster was one of the proprietors of the Shortsville paper mill the paper produced was that sold to E. B. Grandin and used for the printing of the first edition of the Book of Mormon. Prior to 1820 a blast furnace was also constructed along the Outlet which contributed to the continued growth of this small manufacturing center.[29]

Although the growth of Manchester was rapid during the first two decades of the nineteenth century, the population increased slowly. In 1800, for example, there were only 633 settlers in Farmington (which included the town of Manchester). During the ensuing ten years the population of that town tripled (being 2215 in 1810) and then doubled during the period from 1810 to 1820 (there being 4,214 settlers in Farmington in 1820). In 1830, after Farmington had been divided, there were 1773 inhabitants in the township of Farmington and 2811 in Manchester, or a total in the two towns of 4,575, representing a growth of only 570 during the decade when the Smith family lived there. Since the Erie Canal was constructed a few miles north of the farms and factories of Manchester, the ambitious plans of the industrialists of Man-

---

[29]Files of the Shortsville Enterprise Press, April 17, 1903.

chester were not fully realized. The inhabitants of this town failed to reap the harvest created by this transportation artery.

The Transformation of Palmyra

While the first generation of white settlers were constructing mills and shops near the Canandaigua Outlet, others were conquering the wilderness adjacent to Mud Creek. Before the Smith family arrived in western New York, farms, homes, and clusters of shops had been established throughout the town of Palmyra; and the village of Palmyra had evolved from a primitive frontier outpost to a civilized community.

Within a few years after pioneers erected log cabins near Mud Creek, Yankee invaders began forming a village about one block south of this stream. As early as 1792 the main street of Palmyra was laid out near its present location. Trees were cut, stumps and logs were removed, and grass was levelled, thereby creating a path for the oxdrawn carts. Although the trail was not graded, wagons could pass through the area without encountering innumerable obstacles. In the spring of 1793 a number of uprooted Americans purchased land along this trail, and in that same year a log school house was constructed in the emerging community on land donated by John Swift.[30] Before 1800, frame homes began replacing the rough log cabins and a tavern appeared along Mud Creek. Shortly after the turn of the century a copper shop, a tannery, a merchandising store, and the first two-story home were also constructed in Palmyra village.[31]

The energetic leader who more than any other individual promoted the transformation of Palmyra was the same speculator who was partly responsible for the settlement of that

---

[30]"Old Newspapers," *The Palymyra Courier*, February 23, 1872, 3.

[31]"Old Newspapers," *The Palmyra Courier*, September 1, 1871, 3; February 28, 1872; *History of Wayne County, New York* (Philadelphia, 1877), 137.

community. John Swift was a man of tremendous energy, diverse activities, and humanitarian spirit. He built Palmyra's first wool-carding machine and grist mill. He served as the first moderator of the Palmyra town meeting and was chosen supervisor and pound-tender. He became captain of the local militia, and not only donated land for the first school erected in the village but also gave to the community land for a grave-yard and church. After serving in many capacities he died in poverty in 1814; and later his remains were exhumed and placed in the cemetery which he had donated to the citizens of Palmyra.[32]

In 1812, a few years before the Smith family arrived in Palmyra, the main street of the village was crossed by one major road. Running south from Main, this road was called Canandaigua; and continuing north towards the Martin Harris farm, the same road was called Church Street. Today, four Protestant meetinghouses are located on the four corners made by the intersection, but the only meetinghouse in Palmyra village from 1811 to 1822 was located on Church Street, a short distance from the village's one intersection and immediately next to the cemetery. Across from the old Western Presbyterian church on the east side of Church Street were two homes. Only one home was located near the intersection along the Canandaigua road.[33]

While only a few buildings had been erected on Canandaigua and Church Streets, there were structures in 1812 on

[32]"Old Newspapers," *The Palmyra Courier,* September 1, 1871, 3; February 23, 1872, 3; *History of Wayne County,* 140-41.

[33]*History of Wayne County,* 142. It was not until about 1870 that four churches were located on the famous Four Corners. In 1832 a Presbyterian meeting house was erected on the site where the present Western Presbyterian church stands. A Baptist stone meeting house was built on the Four Corners in 1841 and then rebuilt in 1871. In 1867, the Methodists erected a church on this corner; and in 1873 the Episcopalians completed their church which replaced the wooden structure which had been used for about forty-five years. See *Wayne County Journal* (Palmyra), June 6, 1872; Thomas Cook, *Palmyra and Vicinity* (Palmyra, 1930), 249-54.

*Approximate Location of the Homes and Business Establishments
Along the Main Street of Palmyra About 1812
[unless otherwise indicated]*

1 Shirtliff homestead

2 Solomon Tice's property

3 Silas Hart's home

4 Azel Ensworth's tavern and stables

5 James and Orin White's two-story brick store [c. 1817]

6 Clothiery of Andrew G. Howe

7 Franklin House (stage tavern and saddler and harness shop of Solomon Hathaway)

8 Residence, law office and store of William Howe Cuyler

9 Joseph Colt's home

10 Ira Selby and Stephen Phelps' long, wooden two-story store

11 Steven Phelps' tavern (two-story frame building)

12 House belonging to Dr. Robinson

13 Johnson, the tailor

14 Samuel Jennings' store

15 William T. Hussy's home

16 "Democratic" school house

17 Stephen Skellinger's home

18 William Cook's cooper shop

19 Henry Jessup's property (tannery and home)

20 Dr. Gain Robinson's home and drug store [Located further west, near present town line]

21 Zebulon Williams' property

22 William Jackway's home and blacksmith shop

23 John Hurlbut's home and distillery

24 Benjamin Cole's two-story home

25 Zachariah Blackman's blacksmith shop and shelter for teams

26 Asa Lilly's tavern (Lilly's Coffee House)

27 Timothy C. Strong's book store [c. 1817]

28 Washington Hall

29 Western Presbyterian Church

30 Old Cemetery

31 James Benson's home

32 Abner Cole's law office

33 Ezra Shepardson's home

34 Store of Nathaniel H. and George Beckwith

35 A. H. Reed's tailor shop

36 Abraham Shattock's saddlery

37 A. McIntyre's drug store

38 John B. Robson's home

39 Nathan Thayer's store

40 Levi Thayer's home

41 Joseph Colt's store

42 Samuel Wagstaff's store

43 Patrick O'Rourke's store

44 Peleg Holmes' home

45 John Swift's home

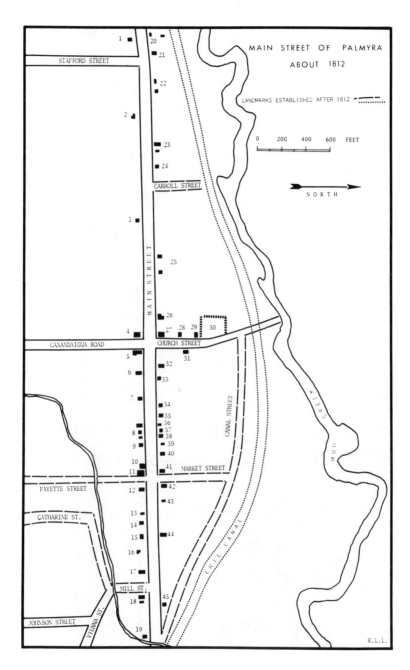

FIG. 8. MAIN STREET OF PALMYRA ABOUT 1812

Fig. 9. Main Street of Palmyra About 1840

As the street appeared looking west from the area near the Eagle Hotel and as published in J. W. Barber and H. Howe's *Historical Collections of the State of New York* (1841).

nearly every lot on either side of Main between the inter-section and Durfee's mill. The mill had been constructed adjacent to the creek on the east edge of the village. Located along this main thoroughfare were about eighteen homes, a number of offices, several saddler and harness shops (one at either end of the village), two tailor shops, a blacksmith shop, a tannery, a distillery, a shelter for animals, and a schoolhouse. All the frame homes, which had replaced the log cabins, were interspersed among the shops, offices, and store; and many proprietors were living in dwellings located at the rear of their place of business. Most of the homes were surrounded with picket fences, and large poplars shaded the residential prop-erty.[34]

The rapid transformation of Palmyra continued while the Smith family lived in the Genesee country. According to the census of 1820, 748 persons were engaged in agriculture, 190 in manufacturing, and 18 in commerce in the town of Palmyra (which included Macedon). This enumeration further speci-fied that forty-six free blacks and no slaves resided in the town.[35] In the early 1820's, there were also within the present limits of Palmyra town three grist mills, eight saw mills, one fulling mill, one iron works, five distilleries, and two asheries. One of the grist mills was located along Mud Creek near the eastern edge of Palmyra village, and another was situ-ated about a mile west of the village. At that time, within the village there were thirteen dry good stores, three drug stores, three inns, two tanneries (one of which employed forty hands), and a number of other businesses.[36]

Economic Pursuits of the Smith Family

According to tradition, after the Smith family arrived in Palmyra they "rented a small frame building on the eastern outskirts of the village near where Johnson Street takes off

[34]*History of Wayne County,* 142. See Appendix L.
[35]Population schedules of the Fourth Census of the United States, 1820 (Washington: National Archives, 1959), Microfilm Roll 62, New York, Vol. 1.
[36]Horation Gates Spafford, *A Gazetteer of the State of New York* (Albany, 1824), 400-01.

Vienna."[37] The mother of the Prophet, Lucy Mack Smith, recalled that although the family possessed few material goods, "not from indolence, but on account of many reverses of fortune," she "was quite happy," for the family had been reunited and she was again partaking of her husband's affection. Lucy also said that, in order to earn sufficient money to begin payments on a farm, she established a business in the village, painting oil cloth coverings for tables. By her exertions this industrious mother succeeded in paying for the furniture which was placed in the Smith home.[38] Meanwhile, Joseph Smith, Sr., and the oldest sons Alvin and Hyrum, also undoubtedly secured employment in and near the village, where, according to one contemporary (Pomeroy Tucker, whose memory was not always reliable), they engaged in gardening, harvesting, well-digging and merchandising. Tucker also specified that they sold in their shop "gingerbread, pies, boiled eggs, root-beer, and other like notions of traffic," and mentioned that sometimes they sold goods on the village streets from a mobile cart.[39] Within a few years, they had saved sufficient funds to begin payments on a farm.

Smiths Move to Farmington (Now Manchester)

After living in Palmyra village for about two years, the family moved in 1818 to a heavily wooded region known as "the North Woods." Having initiated payments on a hundred-acre farm, according to Lucy they cleared about thirty acres of land during the first year. They also erected a "snug log-house" which was "neatly furnished" and provided, in Lucy's opinion, comfortable living. This home has also been described as "a small, one-story, smoky log house," which was divided into two rooms on the ground floor, and had a low garret, where there were two rooms. "A bedroom wing,

---

[37]Willard W. Bean, A.B.C. History of Palmyra and the Beginning of Mormonism (Palmyra, 1938), 12.

[38]Lucy Mack Smith, History of Joseph Smith, ed. Preston Nibley (Salt Lake City: Bookcraft), 63-64.

[39]Pomeroy Tucker, Origin, Rise and Progress of Mormonism (New York, 1867), 12.

built of sawed slabs, was added afterward."[40] Conditions must have been crowded in this home, for as the year 1820 unfolded there were nine in the family. Alvin, the oldest boy was about twenty-one; Hyrum was nineteen; Sophronia was sixteen; Joseph, Jr., had just turned fourteen; Samuel was eleven; William was eight; and Don Carlos was three. One-and-a-half years later, on July 18, 1821, Lucy, the last of the Smith children, was born. Shortly after the birth of Lucy, the family initiated the construction of a much larger frame home. This project was under the direction of Alvin, who undoubtedly was an excellent carpenter; and before Alvin's death in November, 1823, the frame of the new home had been raised. According to Lucy, the material was procured for the "speedy completion" of this residence shortly after Joseph learned that a priceless, sacred record was located in a hill three miles southeast of the Smith farm.[41]

The property which the Smiths improved was situated about a half-mile west and two miles south of the intersection of Main and Canandaigua in Palmyra village and was located on the south side of the line which, in 1818, divided the towns of Palmyra and Farmington. Between 1821 and 1823, the northern edge of this farm became the boundary separating the town of Palmyra (which was included in the new county of Wayne in 1823) and Manchester, a new town in Ontario County created from Farmington.

Originally, Township No. 11, Lot 1, the land on which the Smith family located, had been given by Phelps and Gorham to their wives, Rebecca Gorham and Mary Phelps, and from these women had been conveyed in 1790 to Israel Chapman. Four years after Chapman secured the land, he sold about 5700 acres to William Bacon for £616, or two shillings an acre. In the same year that Bacon obtained the property, he sold this lot and 7,600 additional acres for eleven shillings an acre to Thomas Morris and James Wadsworth. These men in turn sold this 300-acre lot and nine other lots of similar size to

---

[40]Files of the Shortsville Enterprise Press, April 3, 1903; Lucy Mack Smith, op. cit., 64; Tucker, op. cit., 13.
[41]Lucy Mack Smith, op. cit., 85, 331-46.

Fig. 10. The Joseph Smith Farmhouse As It Appears Today

Nicholas Evertson of New York City in 1795 for £2,400, or
sixteen shillings per acre. It was during the thirty years in
which the Evertson family retained the land that the Smiths
initiated payments on the farm.[42]

According to Lucy Mack Smith, the final payment on
their farm was not due until December 25, 1825, but through
deception and intrigue others sought to prevent the family
from securing the deed. Although the enemies of the Smiths
succeeded in preventing these people from securing title to
the land, the family received assistance from their friends;
and on December 20, 1825, Lemuel Durfee purchased from
the heirs of the deceased Nicholas Evertson the one-hundred-
acre Smith farm, including their home and barn, for $1,135,
or $11.35 an acre. After purchasing the land at the request
of the Smiths, Durfee allowed the family to continue living
on the farm for a number of years.[43]

Activities of the Smith Family

Even though the Smith family lived in Manchester for
more than a decade, during their residence in that town they
undoubtedly traveled to Palmyra village more frequently
than to the other villages in that area. Palmyra village was
only two-and-a-half miles distant, while New Salem was four
miles west, Manchester five miles south, Canandaigua about
nine miles south, and Vienna (now Phelps) about thirteen
miles southeast of the Smith farm.

Members of the Smith family regularly traveled to Palmyra village to purchase needed supplies and attend church.
According to one contemporary, Orsamus Turner, Joseph
Smith, Jr., frequently visited the village to secure a copy of
the local paper, *The Palmyra Register,* and to "find an odd
job" in the "store of Seymour Scovill." Turner further recalled that the young man also attended sessions of the "juve-

[42]Deeds, I, 187-88; II, 267-68; III, 118; XX, 39; XXXXIV, 232-34.
[43]*Ibid.,* XXXXIV, 232-34; Lucy Mack Smith, *op. cit.,* 93-99.

nile debating club," a society that moved from the village to "the old red school house on Durfee street."[44]

The economic pursuits of the Smith family were not limited to developing the land in northern Manchester and working in Palmyra village. Since the family was poor and was striving to improve living conditions, including making annual payments on their farm, young Joseph and his older brothers engaged in various activities including farming, digging wells, manufacturing, and selling goods produced at home — such as black-ash baskets, birch brooms, cakes, sugar, and molasses.[45] In the earliest known recorded recital of the First Vision, Joseph Smith emphasized that after settling in western New York his family was in "indigent circumstances," and that therefore all the children who "were able to render any assistance . . . were obliged to labor hard for the support of" the family.[46] The fact that Joseph Smith, Jr., was not enumerated in the census of 1820 indicates that the fourteen-year-old boy was perhaps not living at home when this census was taken, possibly being employed by others.[47] Contemporaries have reported that Joseph worked for William Stafford, who lived about one mile from the Smith farm.[48] There is also a reference (which might not be valid) concerning Joseph's working for Jacob Chamberlain and "occasionally for others" in the vicinity of Waterloo;[49] and there are various reports of Joseph's engaging in unusual economic activities, some of which seem fantastic and are undoubtedly rumors designed to discredit

---

[44]Lucy, Samuel and Hyrum were active members of the Western Presbyterian Church until 1828. Records of the Session of the Presbyterian Church in Palmyra, II, located in the Western Presbyterian Church, Palmyra, New York, 11-13, microfilm copy located in the Brigham Young University Library. Turner, op. cit., 213-14.

[45]Tucker, op. cit., 14.

[46]Kirtland Letter Book, 1829-1835, 1-2, located in the LDS Church Historian's Office. Although the account appears in Appendix A with the punctuation and spelling as it appears in the original, in the main body of this work the spelling in the quotations has been corrected.

[47]Census of 1820, Farmington, No. 524.

[48]E. D. Howe, *Mormonism Unvailed* (Painesville, 1834), 237-40.

[49]Scrapbook of articles from old newspapers located in the Waterloo Historical Society, 46.

the Prophet.[50] Nevertheless, contemporaries have asserted that Joseph Smith worked in various towns located in the Genesee country.

Remarkable Growth of Palmyra

Although the number of inhabitants in Manchester town increased slowly while the Smith family lived there, the population of Palmyra continued to increase. At a time when the population of the United States was almost doubling every twenty years, the number within the town of Palmyra doubled during the first decade of the nineteenth century, increasing from 1,137 to 2,614. Then during the subsequent twenty years from 1810 to 1830, census reports indicate that the population had reached 3,724, and in 1830, after the town had been divided, there were 3,427 residents in Palmyra and 1,989 in Macedon, or a total of 5,416 in the region which was originally the town of Palmyra. At the time of the First Vision, there were almost 100 families and about 700 inhabitants living in Palmyra village; in 1822 the population was estimated at 800 and three years later there were close to 1,000 settlers there, repesenting approximately 37 percent of the entire town's population.[51] By 1830, the population of the village had increased to almost 2,000, which represented about 60 percent of the citizens living in that town.[52]

Palmyra a Canal Town

While describing the remarkable alteration of Palmyra village during the 1820's, one reporter enthusiastically proclaimed, "The whole village has undergone a visible change." The most noticeable transformation he observed occurred in 1822 when a section of the Erie Canal was constructed between Mud Creek and Main Street. In fact, he said with a passionate bias, "There is no village on the line of our famed canal, that has felt the benefits which flow from the internal channel of commerce, more sensible than Palmyra."[53] Although he

---

[50]Tucker, op. cit., 232, 248-49.
[51]Spafford, op. cit., 400-01; Palmyra Herald, Canal Advertiser, June 19, 1822, 2.
[52]Wayne Sentinel, September 26, 1828.
[53]Ibid.

incorrectly speculated that Palmyra would become one of the major business centers of the state, that community did become one of the important canal towns of western New York.

It is almost impossible to exaggerate the impact of this waterway on the economic lives of the settlers, not only in Palmyra and other sections of New York but in many other states. As early as 1817, under the direction of Governor DeWitt Clinton, New York undertook this mammoth project, regarded as the greatest engineering feat in American history up to that time. A fifteen-mile stretch of the canal was completed in 1819, connecting Rome and Utica. In November of that year, while one group of engineers were working within four miles of Palmyra village surveying the area, another body of men who were supervising the construction of this mammoth project were considering three possible routes, one of which passed through the village of Palmyra. In December it was announced that the big ditch would be built parallel to the Main Street of the village, and contracts were soon released. In 1822, a 250-mile stretch of the canal was completed connecting Rochester and Utica, and the following year boats could travel from Rochester to the Hudson. The marriage of the waters of the Erie and of the Atlantic was finally consummated in 1825.

The 363-mile canal was an immediate financial success. Although the canal cost about seven or eight million dollars to construct, the traffic was so extensive that tolls collected during the first nine years more than paid for that original cost. Most important, this canal reduced the time required to ship goods from Buffalo to New York City from 20 to 6 days and the cost of such shipments from $100 to $8 a ton.[54]

As the canal was being constructed one block north of the Main Street of Palmyra, shipping docks, warehouses, and other buildings needed for the canal trade appeared in the heart of the village. Then after the big ditch had been dug

---

[54]Harry J. Carman and Harold C. Syrett, *History of the American People* (New York: Alfred A. Knopf, 1959), I, 473-75: *Palmyra Register,* November 10, 1819, November 17, 1819, December 8, 1819; *Palmyra Herald,* October 9, 1823, November 13, 1823.

across the town of Palmyra, innumerable long, shallow boats, drawn by mules, constantly traversed the village, moving parallel to Main and passing over an aqueduct constructed on the outskirts of the village. Countless immigrants heading west, innumerable tourists, and many businessmen seeking wheat to ship to eastern markets arrived in the community. To accommodate the increased number of travelers, the Phelps tavern was rebuilt, enlarged to a three-story building in December 1824 under new proprietors, and renamed the Eagle Hotel. It is apparent that Clinton's big ditch precipitated the establishment of new businesses and the construction of many buildings in the community which reminded some observers of a quaint village in the Netherlands.[55]

Palmyra Newspapers

Shortly before the transportation revolution began in western New York, the first newspaper constituted in what is now Wayne County appeared in Palmyra village. On November 26, 1817, Timothy C. Strong began publishing a weekly entitled the *Palmyra Register*, and he continued editing this newspaper until the fall of 1823 — with occasional changes in title, such as *Western Farmer* and *Palmyra Herald, Canal Advertiser*. In October of 1823 the newspaper was sold to Pomeroy Tucker and E. B. Grandin, the latter of whom subsequently became the publisher of the Book of Mormon. The new editors changed the name of this newspaper to *The Wayne Sentinel*.

Two other newspapers, both having short lives, appeared in Palmyra during the 1820's, *The Palmyra Freeman* and *The Reflector*. *The Reflector*, initiated in September, 1829, was published by Abner Cole, ex-justice of the peace who published under the pseudonym Obadiah Dogberry, Jr. This newspaper published on "Winter Green Hill" was devoted to "science, amusement, and ironical castigation."[56] While the Book of Mormon was being printed, Cole secured a copy of portions of

[55]*History of Wayne County*, 141.
[56]*Ibid.*, 145.

the manuscript and commenced issuing that work in serial form in January, 1830, in violation of the copyright. After learning of this activity, Joseph traveled from his home in Harmony, Pennsylvania, to Palmyra and threatened to sue Cole. Immediately the publication of this serial discontinued. Meanwhile, the inhabitants of Palmyra had gained their first glimpse of the new witness for Christ.[57]

Libraries in Palmyra and Vicinity

The early Genesee settlers' zeal for knowledge is not only reflected by the appearance of a growth of newspapers but also by their establishment of libraries and bookstores throughout western New York. A library was organized in the village of Palmyra during the winter of 1822-1823. In January, 1817, also, settlers of Manchester village established a public library. For many years the Manchester library was located in the home of the librarian, John Pratt. Eventually, the collection was given to the Ontario Historical Society where it is currently being preserved.[58]

Bookstores in the Genesee Country

While the Smith family resided in Palmyra, many works were available in the T. C. Strong bookstore. During the month of October, 1818, for example, approximately three hundred volumes were advertised in *The Palmyra Register*, which included fiction works such as *Arabian Nights* and *Charlotte Temple*; Alexander Pope's *An Essay on Man*; biographies of Benjamin Franklin, George Washington, and Thomas Jefferson; Alexander Humbolt's history of New Spain and many other historical works; and approximately thirty religious treatises, including the works of Jonathan Edwards, John Wesley's *Sermons*, Benjamin Bell's *Strictures, upon the Doctrine and Discipline, of the Methodist Episcopal Church*, Ezra

[57]*The Palmyra Reflector,* January 2, 1830; January 13, 1830; January 22, 1830. Cole published selections from the First Book of Nephi and from the Book of Alma.

[58]*Wayne Sentinel,* December 3, 1823; Miscellaneous Records, Book C, 178, located in the Ontario County Court House, Canandaigua, New York; Files of the Shortsville Enterprise Press, July 26, 1890.

Ely's *Contrast Between Calvinism and Hopkinsianism,* Richard Baxter's *A Call to the Unconverted,* Hugh Blair's *Sermons,* Daniel Whitbey's *Six Discourses,* Alden Bradford's *Evangelical History, or a Narrative of the Life, Doctrines, and Miracles of Jesus Christ,* and Elhanan Winchester's *Lectures on the Prophecies.* In addition to the works which were identified, Strong sold classical, medical and law books; Bibles; "together with a general supply of School Books, and Stationary."[59]

While many works were available in Palmyra village, countless other books and pamphlets were being sold in Canandaigua, Geneva, West Bloomfield, and other surrounding communities. As early as 1815, a proprietor in West Bloomfield advertised that he had for sale more than one thousand volumes.[60] Therefore, while the Smith family resided in western New York, many of the publications of that age were being circulated in the area, and the ideas of many eastern intellectuals and theologians were being disseminated among the settlers of the Finger Lake country.

Early Publishers in the Genesee Country

Books were also published in increased numbers by the inhabitants of western New York while the Smith family was living there. Writings of the Genesee farmers were printed in Canandaigua, Geneva, Auburn, Ithaca and other New York villages. In 1820, Benjamin Bell published a work in Palmyra reflecting some of the contention which existed during that age. Bell unfolded the nature of the work in his title, *The Mystery of Iniquity Unveiled; or, a True History of the Rise and Progress of the Difficulties Between Rev. Wm. Clark, and some of the People in the Town of Wolcott, Seneca County. Together with the Trials of Benjamin Bell.*

Education in Western New York

As the population increased, new schools were established throughout the towns of Palmyra and Farmington. The earli-

---

[59]*Palmyra Register,* October 6, 1818; October 13, 1818; October 20, 1818.
[60]*Ontario Messenger,* April 25, 1815.

est public school records of Manchester which have been preserved, reveal that in 1828, classes were being held in fourteen districts. This record further states that schools were in session on an average of about eight months a year, and children from five to sixteen were attending the one-room schools. The students studied the three R's and geography, using as texts, Lindley Murray's *English Grammar;* Noah Webster's *The American Spelling Book;* Lyman Cobb's *A Just Standard for Pronouncing Dictionary;* Jedediah Morse's *The American Universal Geography* and *Geography Made Easy;* William Channing Woodbridge's *A System of Universal Geography;* and Jacob Abbot Cumming's *First Lessons in Geography and Astronomy, An Introduction to Ancient and Modern Geography,* and *The Pronouncing Spelling Book.*[61]

The school system of Palmyra was similar to that of Manchester and other sections of New York; and inhabitants, such as the Smiths, who lived on the border of two towns were served by a common school. One summary of educational developments within New York state and Ontario County was published in 1820. According to this report, nine-tenths of all children living in that state who were five to sixteen years of age were receiving some education. Within the thirty-four towns of Ontario County there were at that time 434 schools with 23,439 children being taught. After presenting this analysis, the editor of the *Ontario Repository* asserted, "This certainly presents a flattering picture for all who feel an interest in the moral character of the rising generation."[62]

The school teachers of that age were poorly paid, receiving in Manchester in 1828 less than $45 annually. Many of the teachers boarded with the parents of the children; and families who provided room and board for the teachers were

---

[61]Public Schools, 1828-1915, located in the Town Clerk's Office, Clifton Springs, New York, microfilm copy located in the Brigham Young University Library. See also, *Palmyra Herald,* March 12, 1823, p. 4.

[62]*Ontario Repository,* March 21, 1820. A few early nineteenth-century records of the Palmyra schools have been preserved and are located in the Public Library in Palmyra. A microfilm copy of these records has been placed in the Brigham Young University Library.

not required to pay as much as others for the schooling of their children. Consequently teachers, such as Oliver Cowdery — who taught on Stafford Street — were welcomed to reside temporarily with families such as the Smiths.[63]

In the summer of 1820 an academy was opened in Palmyra village where students studied Latin and Greek. Four years later an independent school was also established there and pupils gathered in the upper room of the academy where they were taught geography, mathematics, astronomy, surveying, grammar, reading, and writing.[64]

Education of a Latter-day Prophet

The formal education of Joseph Smith was apparently neglected while he was living in the Genesee country. Joseph said that because he was obliged to assist in supporting his family, he was "deprived of the benefit of an education." The Prophet admitted, however, that he received instructions in reading, writing, and arithmetic, "which constituted his entire literal acquirements."[65] Since Joseph was not able to attend the local elementary school as often as he desired, the young man undoubtedly was not enrolled in the grammar school nor the private school established in Palmyra village.

While commenting on the character and intellectual traits of her son, Lucy Mack Smith observed that Joseph was a "remarkably quiet, well-disposed child," adding that ''he seemed much less inclined to the perusal of books than any of the rest of our children, but far more given to meditation and deep study."[66]

Even though young Joseph was probably not an avid reader and received a meager formal education, he was a humble, inquisitive youth who sought knowledge concerning the world in which he lived and God's plan of salvation.

---

[63]Public Schools, 1828-1915; Files of the Shortsville Enterprise Press, File No. XXXIII.

[64]Palmyra Register, May 10, 1820; December 15, 1824; June 21, 1825.

[65]Kirtland Letter Book, LDS Church Historian's Office.

[66]Lucy Mack Smith, op. cit., 67, 82.

His interest in religion led to innumerable questions, the questions resulted in conflicting replies, and the inconsistent answers precipitated additional inquiries. "How can I know the truth?" Joseph asked. His seeking and searching were not in vain, for the quest of the fourteen-year-old boy eventually guided him along a path leading from a primitive log cabin to a peaceful grove. On a glorious spring day in 1820, while the young man was kneeling in prayer, the genuine education of a prophet commenced.

CHAPTER 3

Awakenings in the Burned-Over District

The Yankee invasion of western New York not only precipitated tremendous economic, political, and educational
advancements in that section of the nation, but also led to
ecclesiastical transformation of the Genesee country. While
the industrious pioneers were clearing forests, harvesting crops,
erecting mills, creating villages, establishing schools, and forming town governments, they were also organizing congregations
and building houses of worship. This conquest of the Genesee
wilderness paralleled the initial phase of the Second Great
Awakening, for at the same time that Protestantism was being
transplanted from New England, Pennsylvania, and eastern
New York to the former home of the Iroquois, a spiritual
quickening occurred in the early Republic. Eventually, western
New York became the ecclesiastical storm center of this enlivenment. As countless unchurched Americans engaged in
a quest for religious truth, religious enthusiasm increased, piety
seemed more evident, and church membership increased at a
steady, rapid pace.[1]

Neglect of Formalized Religion

When the immigrants of the 1790's initiated the colonization of the Finger Lake country, organized religion was probably at its lowest ebb in the history of America. As the
eighteenth century drew to a close, there were fewer churches

---

[1]For additional information on the preliminaries to the restoration and
the religious climate in America during the colonial period and the early
Republic see Milton V. Backman, Jr., *American Religions and the Rise of
Mormonism* (Salt Lake City: Deseret Book Co., 1970).

and less ministers per population than during any other era, whether it be the colonial period or the decades of the twentieth century; and church membership at that time was probably lower in this land than in any other Christian nation. In 1800, only about 7 percent of the American population was classified as active church members.[2]

There are many factors which explain the reason for the neglect of organized religion in late eighteenth and early nineteenth century America. Most inhabitants of the new nation lived on isolated farmsteads and, not being in a position to attend church regularly, became indifferent toward formalized religion. Many children matured without reading the Bible, attending church, or receiving even occasional edification from spiritual leaders. In most homes, not only were Bible study and church attendance neglected, but family prayers and observance of the Sabbath were not adhered to as taught by the Puritans.

Since many Protestant churches attempted to limit membership to the recognized believers or the acknowledged elect, strict requirements for membership were maintained in most congregations. Excommunications were frequent. Individuals convicted of immorality, using profane language, neglecting to attend church, or failing to observe the Sabbath were sometimes disfellowshipped or excluded from the privilege of being enumerated among the visible saints. Also, members of the Society of Friends were occasionally excommunicated for marrying without authorization outside the denomination. The fact that few blacks had been converted to Christianity and that young children were not enumerated on most membership reports provides further insight into the reasons church membership was at such a low level in early America. Negroes comprised about 20 percent of the population and young children about double that proportion at the turn of the century. Consequently, most membership records of the eighteenth century reflected only the names of white adults

---

[2]*Ibid.*, 283; Edwin Scott Gaustad, *Historical Atlas of Religion in America* (New York: Harper and Row, 1962), 162.

who had expressed a converting experience, endorsed one of the popular creeds of Christendom, and faithfully complied with the laws of the church to which they belonged.

While the percentage of active church members probably declined very gradually during most of the eighteenth century, the American Revolution played a role in precipitating the continued decline of religious activity in America. During this irrepressible conflict, the Church of England, which had been one of the dominant religions of colonial America, was nearly destroyed. This faith having been branded as the Tory church, its members witnessed the destruction of some of their meetinghouses and the exodus of many of their rectors. Before the war, there were about three hundred Anglican clergy in the thirteen colonies. When the church was reorganized after peace had been restored there were only approximately one hundred recognized ministers to serve the needs of the members of the Protestant Episcopal Church. Following the most critical period in the history of this denomination, membership in 1800 was reported at but twelve thousand.[3]

The Dutch Reformed Church also suffered as a result of the war. Many of their meetinghouses were located in the Hudson River valley, one of the areas where invading armies continually maneuvered; and some of the Dutch ministers fled the land, leaving their members without spiritual guidance.

Since members of the Society of Friends were conscientious objectors, Quakers sometimes experienced the pains of oppression; and when members of this faith united under the leadership of George Washington, the fighting Quakers were excommunicated.

During the war for independence, a militant form of deism was transplanted from France to America, resulting in the post-war publication of the initial anti-Christian books to be circulated in America. The first widely read work in this

---

[3]James Thayer Addison, *The Episcopal Church in the United States* (New York: Charles Scribner's Sons, 1951), 74; Walter H. Stowe, "The Clergy of the Episcopal Church in 1785," *The Protestant Episcopal Church Historical Magazine,* XX (September, 1951), 253.

country which critically attacked the Bible and the Christian religion was Thomas Paine's *The Age of Reason*, published in 1795. Converts to this movement tended not to join deistic societies, but concentrated on condemning organized religion, thereby contributing to the decline of religious activity in the new nation.

As pioneers pushed the boundaries of settlement further and further west, the problems created by the frontier environment increased. Following the Revolution there were not sufficient ministers in most faiths to fill the vacant pulpits located along the eastern seaboard, and the deficiency in the east could not be compared with the lack of trained clergy in the west. As a new century approached, the problem of providing rural Americans with formalized religion seemed almost insurmountable to many inhabitants of the early Republic.

Recognizing that vast numbers of Americans were without a formal religion and that many pioneers were seeking God, spiritual leaders of several Protestant faiths launched effective missionary programs. The societies which overcame the handicaps created by the American frontier and established programs designed to carry their version of the gospel to rural America increased rapidly in membership and became, numerically speaking, the dominant faiths of the pre-Civil War era.

Baptist Farm Preachers

The first major convert faith, the first religion to grow primarily by converting unchurched Americans rather than by immigration, was the Baptist denomination. These Protestants solved the problem of a shortage of ministers by not requiring their elders to be college graduates, but ordained many men who claimed an inward call to preach. For most Baptist elders of the early Republic, preaching was an avocation rather than a profession. They did not rely on parish contributions for their support, earning much of their livelihood from farming and other economic pursuits. Their farms became bases of operation. In addition to providing spiritual edification for members of their parishes, these farm preachers periodically traveled to other neighborhoods where they spread their innermost convictions. Although there were few Baptist congregations in this land prior to 1750, by 1800 this denomination had become the nation's largest religious community.[4]

Methodist Circuit Riders

Even though the Baptist faith was America's first convert religion, the fastest growing church in the early Republic was the Methodist society. By 1820 this faith had approximately the same numerical strength as the Baptists, but it surpassed that religion in membership during the decade of the 1820's, becoming the largest body of Protestants in America during the remaining years of the nineteenth century.[5] The Methodists divided America into conferences and districts and then subdivided the districts into circuits and stations. Although resident ministers were generally assigned to communities where there was a Methodist meetinghouse, most groups were served by traveling ministers. After preaching locations were determined within the circuits, itinerants were appointed to preach regularly in the designated places of worship. The circuits were called two-week, three-week, or four-week circuits, depending on the period required to contact the members at each station. Ministers were usually appointed to a circuit for only one or, at the most, two years, and the presiding elders of each district were assigned to a region for no longer than four years. By this ingenious system, vast numbers of Americans living in rural communities received regular spiritual edification.[6]

Congregationalism in the New Nation

Since most of the original settlers of western New York emigrated from New England, the Congregational church was in the best position to benefit from the Yankee invasion of

---

[4]Gaustad, op. cit., 52, 167.

[5]Ibid., 43, 52-53.

[6]William Thacher, "A Sketch of the History and Present State of Methodism in Connecticut," The Methodist Magazine, V (January, 1822), 33-36.

the Genesee country. These Protestants, however, failed to develop an effective missionary program and continued to maintain an educated clergy. There were not only few Congregational clergy to send west, but the well-trained college graduates sometimes were not the most effective preachers among the woodsmen of rural America. In an attempt to promote missionary work, the Connecticut General Association decided to cooperate with the General Assembly of the Presbyterian church. A Plan of Union was adopted in 1801 specifying that the inhabitants of the west could decide whether they were to function under a Presbyterian or a Congregational system of church government. By this maneuver, competition between Presbyterians and Congregationalists was minimized and members of these societies (whose Calvinistic theology was similar) united their efforts in organizing congregations in the west. The plan, however, proved to be most advantageous to the Presbyterians, for most congregations who united hired a Presbyterian minister and adopted a representative system of church government rather than a Congregational polity that maintained the autonomy of each congregation. The majority of settlers probably believed that the system of government which stimulated increased cooperation of societies was most advantageous. Presbyterianism, therefore, triumphed at the expense of Congregationalism in many areas, including the region where the Smith family lived. By 1822, the Association of Ontario had been dissolved and most Congregational societies had joined the Presbytery of Geneva.[7]

Expansion of Presbyterianism

Multiple forces placed the Presbyterian church in a favorable position to expand into western New York. In addition to benefiting from the alliance with the Congregationalists, Presbyterian theology was similar to New England Calvinism, the historic faith of many of the early immigrants. Furthermore, many uprooted Pennsylvanians pushed across the border

---

[7]David E. Ellis, and others, *A Short History of New York State* (Ithaca: Cornell University Press, 1967), ch. 16.

into the Genesee country. Some of these settlers had once lived in New England or had descended from Puritans who had colonized Massachusetts or Connecticut. Other emigrants from the Keystone state had descended from pioneers who had been reared in northern Ireland or Scotland where Presbyterianism was the dominant faith.

Although Presbyterianism became one of the leading faiths of the Genesee country, there were factors which impeded the thrust of Presbyterianism into western New York. Leaders of this denomination, with few exceptions, refused to ordain men who had not been trained in a recognized theological school; and there were insufficient educated clergy to supply the Genesee farmers with adequate spiritual guidance. Since some congregations were not favored with a full-time minister, members residing in certain communities, such as Manchester, did not receive regular spiritual direction; and instead of prospering, some groups dissolved. Even though Presbyterianism became the third largest Protestant society in the new nation, this denomination did not maintain the remarkable pace of growth set by the Methodists and Baptists.[8]

Roman Catholicism in Early America

Partly because of oppressive legislation and religious bigotry, the Roman Catholic church did not prosper in the thirteen colonies; and few members of this faith participated in the Yankee invasion of the Genesee country. Early in the nineteenth century, Roman Catholicism had been branded as an illegal form of worship in New York. Members of this communion were not permitted to proselyte, erect cathedrals, nor celebrate public Mass in that province. Although the English Toleration Act of 1689 was extended to America, granting Trinitarian Christians the right to organize congregations, this privilege was not extended to the Roman Catholics.[9] Moreover, before the end of the first decade of the

---

[8]Backman, op. cit., 291-2.

[9]John Webb Pratt, Religion, Politics, and Diversity: The Church-State Theme in New York History (Ithaca: Cornell University Press, 1967), 37-39. Trinitarian Christians in colonial America were defined as individuals who held that God was three persons of one essence.

eighteenth century, the Church of England had become the tax-supported state religion in the four lower counties of New York and in all the South. In New York and portions of the South, however, this legislation was ineffective. Nevertheless, Trinity church, an Anglican society in New York City, received some financial support from the state.

Birth of Religious Liberty

During the American Revolution, a new religious era was inaugurated. While Americans were struggling to advance democracy and preserve their inalienable rights, the patriots effectively expanded the religious rights of mankind. At that time, America became a laboratory for the framing of constitutions which included, in many instances, a state bill of rights. The right of freedom of conscience became a legal reality in many of the new states, and accompanying this extension of freedom was the dissolving of the Anglican establishments. During the debates in New York a few critics sought to retain curtailments on the rights of Catholics and non-Trinitarian Protestants. When restrictions were proposed, outspoken legislators raised the same question which Roger Williams had asked a century earlier, "Who is the authority capable of judging which faith is correct?"[10] Suggestions for limitations on the religious rights of men were buried under the new spirit of the enlightenment and the practical politics created by the religious pluralism which engulfed the new nation. Amidst the growing spirit of toleration, which was fanned by the Revolution, delegates of New York framed the state constitution of 1777. One of the priceless milestones along the path leading to religious liberty was Article 38 which declared:

> Whereas we are required by the benevolent principles of rational liberty, not only to expel civil tyranny, but also to guard against the spiritual oppression and intolerance, wherewith the bigotry and ambition of weak and wicked priests and princes, have scourged mankind:

---

[10]*Ibid.,* 85.

This Convention doth further, in the name and by the authority of the good people of this State, ORDAIN, DETERMINE AND DECLAIR that the free exercise and enjoyment of religious profession and worship, without discrimination or preference, shall forever hereafter be allowed within this State to all mankind. Provided that the liberty of conscience hereby granted shall not be so construed, as to excuse acts of licentiousness, or justify practices inconsistent with the peace or safety of this State.[11]

By this and other such maneuvers, a new religious climate was created in the young Republic and ministers of all denominations — Christians and non-Christians, Protestants and Catholics, Trinitarians and Arians — were granted the legal right to preach and to organize societies not only in western New York but in many other sections of America.

THE EMERGENCE OF PROTESTANTISM IN THE HILL CUMORAH COUNTRY

The Society of Friends

Shortly after arriving in Farmington and Palmyra, the immigrants of western New York commenced holding religious services in their log homes. Probably the first Protestant meetings conducted in these towns were held about 1790 in the cabins of the Quakers of Farmington; and possibly these services were the first held by Protestants on a regular basis in the area west of the Jerusalem Community.[12] Since members of the Society of Friends did not believe in a paid ministry, lay members were appointed to supervise the ecclesiastical activities of these Christians. After gathering in their small homes, the men sitting on one side of the main room and the women on the other, the Friends sat and meditated until one of their number arose, bore his or her testimony and then sat down. There were no opening nor closing hymns,

---

[11]*The Constitution of the State of New York* (Fishkill, 1777), 31.
[12]A. B. Katkamier, ed., *The History of the Township of Farmington, New York,* (n. p., 1897), 22.

FIG. 11. QUAKER MEETINGHOUSE

Erected in 1816 and located about four miles west of the Joseph Smith farm, this meetinghouse is the only building standing today that was a religious edifice in the area at the time of the First Vision. The structure has been moved a short distance from its original site and is currently being used as a storage shed.

no formal prayers, and no ministerial sermons in the meetings, only silent worship interrupted periodically with solemn expressions of faith. The "unprepared" messages delivered by the Quakers were based on what Friends believed were the promptings of the Spirit.

About six years after these Christians began worshipping in their cabins, they erected the first Quaker meetinghouse located west of Utica. One section of this double-log building was used for religious services, the other served as a school for the children. This early meetinghouse was used from 1796 to December, 1803, when it was destroyed by fire. During the ensuing winter, Quakers living in that section of the Genesee country worshipped in Palmyra and then, during the summer of 1804, constructed a frame building, 44 feet by 32 feet, on the site of their log meetinghouse. At that time the society was composed of about seventy-five families, approximately forty-five of whom lived in the town of Palmyra, mainly in the area known today as Macedon.[13] Membership increased so rapidly that by 1816 their meetinghouse was considered too small. Instead of enlarging their church, the Friends constructed a larger building across the road, about four miles due west of the Joseph Smith farm and immediately east of New Salem village, sometimes referred to today as "Pumpkin Hook." Since a schism occurred in this society in 1828, the edifice was used by the Hicksites until 1926, when it was sold and moved a short distance down the hill to the point where it stands today as a storage shed. This structure is the only building standing today near the Smith farm which served as a house of worship at the time of the First Vision. After the division of the congregation the Orthodox Quakers returned to the old frame building, where they resumed their testimony meetings. These Friends continued to meet there until 1876 when the edifice was replaced by the attractive white church which stands today.[14]

---

[13]Records of Farmington Monthly Meetings, 1803-1816, 15-16, 19, microfilm copy located in the Genealogical Society of The Church of Jesus Christ of Latter-day Saints; [W. H. McIntosh, ed], *History of Ontario County, New York* (Philadelphia, 1876), 194.

[14]*History of Ontario County*, 194.

Since it was more convenient to hold Sabbath services in homes or schools situated near clusters of Quakers rather than to travel four, five or sometimes ten or more miles to the meetinghouse located near New Salem village, Friends were authorized to hold regular services in the southern section of Farmington and in the town of Palmyra. The Friends living near Macedon Center were granted permission to hold meetings in the home of Asa Aldrich in 1808. These energetic Protestants also constructed a meetinghouse in 1816 which was about 30 feet by 40 feet.[15] In the same year that the houses of worship were erected in Farmington and Macedon, Quakers living in the southern section of Farmington and in Canandaigua were authorized to hold services in a school; and members residing near Palmyra village were authorized to meet in the home of Anna Durfee. Three years later the Palmyra services were held alternately in the homes of Pardon Durfee and Peter Harris.[16] Both of these societies constructed meetinghouses in 1823. The Palmyra church was a one-story building, 24 feet by 40 feet. It was located on Walker Road near the farms of Lemuel Durfee and Peter Harris,[17] being situated less than one mile northeast of the Martin Harris farm and about two miles from Palmyra village.

The Baptist Denomination

The Baptists who settled in the vicinity of the Smith home were also among the first to create a religious society in western New York. The initial steps to establish a Calvinist Baptist congregation were taken in 1796 when a few believers in the area known today as Manchester, organized. While meeting in the homes of members, the society continued to increase in membership. By 1804, eighty-two had been baptized into fellowship; and six years later these Bap-

---

[15]Prior to 1823, the society which met in Macedon was referred to as the Palmyra Friends and the society in Palmyra was named the East Palmyra Friends. Farmington Monthly Meetings, 1803-1816, 195; Farmington Monthly Meetings, 1816-1831 (Pt. 17), 17, 285.

[16]Farmington Monthly Meetings, 1816-1831 (Pt. 17), 11, 42, 46, 57, 87, 93, 119.

[17]*Ibid.*, 269.

tists built a log church. This wooden building served the needs of these Protestants for only a few years. In 1815 the Baptists constructed a larger stone edifice which was the only meetinghouse in Manchester village at the time of the First Vision.[18]

Four years after the Baptists of Manchester united, nineteen believers living in and near Palmyra village began holding services in the home of Lemuel Spear. A number of these Calvinist Baptists had belonged to the congregation in Manchester but withdrew to form their own society. These Protestants were the first to hold religious services in Palmyra village, and in 1802, membership had grown to nearly seventy. In the summer of 1808 a productive awakening erupted in that community and about one hundred joined this Christian communion. During that year of religious quickening, these Protestants constructed a meetinghouse (approximately 40 feet by 50 feet) about two miles west of Palmyra village.[19]

Between 1816 and 1820 the Baptist society located in what is today the towns of Palmyra and Macedon continued to prosper, adding about one hundred to their faith during this period. After a number of members had been dismissed from the mother church to join other Baptist communions, membership in 1820 was enumerated at 151.[20]

Records dating back to the nineteenth century reveal many other incidents in the historic life of the Calvinist Baptist congregation of Palmyra. In December, 1821, Elder Eliphalet Spencer replaced Reverend Jeremiah Irons, the original

---

[18]Minutes of the First Baptist Church of Farmington are located in the American Baptist Historical Society, Rochester, New York. See also *Minutes of the Fifty-Eighth Anniversary of the Ontario Baptist Association* (Canandaigua, 1871), 13; Files of the Shortsville Enterprise Press, August 4, 1883.

[19]*Minutes of the Twenty-Sixth Anniversary of the Wayne Baptist Association* (Lyons, 1860), 11-15; *The Massachusetts Baptist Missionary Magazine*, II (March, 1810), 280-81; Fred G. Reynolds, *One Hundred Years' History of the First Baptist Church of Macedon, N.Y.* (Macedon, n.d.), 3-5. The earliest records of the First Baptist Church of Macedon (then called Palmyra) are located in the American Baptist Historical Society.

[20]*Minutes of the Twenty-Sixth Anniversary of the Wayne Baptist Association*, 12.

preacher who had served the church during the years of its initial development and growth. After Elder Spencer resigned in November, 1822, James C. Barrett commenced serving as preacher in March, 1823; but since Barrett had not been ordained, ministers from neighboring communities performed the ordinances of baptism and the Lord's Supper. A significant awakening began shortly after Barrett commenced ministering to the Baptists of Palmyra and Macedon, and 96 were baptized in less than two years.[21] In the mid-1830's the Baptists of Palmyra separated from the Macedon congregation, occupying the old Presbyterian church located adjacent to burial hill until November 1838, when this historic church burned. Three years later the Baptists of Palmyra dedicated a new church in the village. The present brick edifice, located on the Four Corners, was dedicated in 1871, replacing the stone church which had been torn down.[22]

The Presbyterian Church

In the same decade that the Quakers and Baptists of Farmington organized, devout Calvinists united in worship in East Palmyra. Shortly after these emigrants from Long Island settled on the land which they purchased from John Swift, they gathered to pray, thanking their Creator for a safe journey into the American wilderness. In the latter part of 1793, Reverend Ira Condit, who was laboring as a missionary in Canandaigua, assisted eleven pioneers in organizing a Congregational society in the home of David H. Foster, which was one of the first groups of this faith to be constituted in western New York. By the end of 1806 the society had grown to about fifty members; and since the annex of one of their homes was too small to accommodate the congregation, members built a church in 1806 which was 54 by 64 feet. The following year they adopted a Presbyterian form of church government and united with the Geneva Presbytery, thereby

---

[21]*Ibid.,* 12-13; Reynolds, *op. cit.,* 5-6.

[22]*Wayne County Journal* (Palmyra), June 6, 1872; *Wayne Sentinel* (Palmyra), November 17, 1838.

becoming one of the earliest Presbyterian societies of the Genesee country.[23]

During the summer of 1816 a powerful revival erupted in the town of Palmyra, and the spiritual enlivenment continued throughout the winter. During this productive spiritual quickening, membership in the Presbyterian church nearly doubled. Consequently the congregation was divided in 1817. Fifty-six members separated from the mother church and formed the Western Presbyterian Church of Palmyra with Jesse Townsend as the first installed pastor.[24]

Members of the Presbyterian communion who organized three years prior to the First Vision immediately began holding services in the only church building which stood at that time in the village of Palmyra. This meetinghouse had been constructed in 1811 on land donated by John Swift, and was located on Church Street north of the Four Corners, adjacent to the cemetery where John Swift and Alvin Smith are buried. Originally the parish was an interdenominational church, but since most of the members leaned toward Presbyterianism, the assembly was periodically supplied by the Calvinist minister who resided in East Palmyra. While the Smiths lived in Palmyra village, members of this family probably worshipped occasionally with these Christians. Joseph stated that his mother, Lucy, his brothers Hyrum and Samuel, and his sister Sophronia, joined the Presbyterian church about the time of his sacred experience in the grove. Although records of the Western Presbyterian Church have not been preserved prior to 1828, the earliest available session book reveals that members of the Smith family attended the serv-

[23]Harriett M. Wiles, comp., Church Records of the Presbyterian Church of East Palmyra, Wayne County, New York, 1933, copy located in the Church Genealogical Society; W. B. Dada, A History of the Presbyterian Church of East Palmyra, N.Y., 1876, 7, 11-12, located in the Presbyterian Historical Society, Philadelphia, Pennsylvania; [Sarah Lines], One Hundred and Twenty-Five Years of the Western Presbyterian Church (Palmyra; n.p., 1942), 1-2.

[24]Dada, op. cit., 31; [Lines], op. cit., 2; Palmyra Wayne County. New York (Rochester: Woman's Society of the Western Presbyterian Church, 1907), 40-41. Since the East Palmyra church retained about sixty members. membership in the two congregations remained about the same for several years.

PALMYRA TOWN 1820

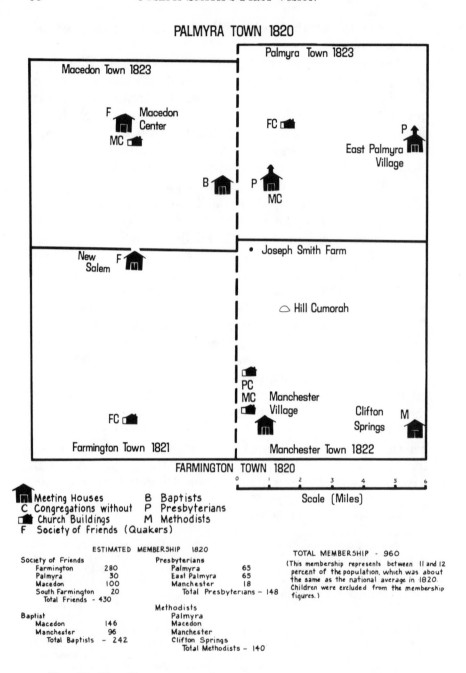

Meeting Houses
C Congregations without
Church Buildings
F Society of Friends (Quakers)

B Baptists
P Presbyterians
M Methodists

Scale (Miles)

ESTIMATED MEMBERSHIP 1820

Society of Friends
  Farmington   280
  Palmyra   30
  Macedon   100
  South Farmington   20
    Total Friends - 430

Baptist
  Macedon   146
  Manchester   96
    Total Baptists - 242

Presbyterians
  Palmyra   65
  East Palmyra   65
  Manchester   18
    Total Presbyterians – 148

Methodists
  Palmyra
  Macedon
  Manchester
  Clifton Springs
    Total Methodists – 140

TOTAL MEMBERSHIP - 960

(This membership represents between 11 and 12 percent of the population, which was about the same as the national average in 1820. Children were excluded from the membership figures.)

Fig. 12. The Churches of Palmyra and Farmington in 1820

ices of this society regularly until 1828; and then in March, 1830, Lucy, Hyrum, and Samuel were dismissed from the Lord's Supper, not because of any indictment concerning their moral or religious character, but because they had neglected to attend church for a year and a half and no longer desired to be affiliated with that body.[25]

Jesse Townsend continued to serve as minister of the Western Presbyterian Church from 1817 to the winter of 1819-1820, and then early in 1820 moved to Illinois, after which he served in Missouri. Returning to Palmyra in 1826, he became the minister in a neighboring town of Sodus from 1827 to 1831 and then continued to reside in Palmyra village, where he died in 1838 at the age of 72. Since a preacher had not been assigned to replace Townsend during the spring of 1820, undoubtedly Benjamin Baily, pastor of the church in East Palmyra, occasionally supplied the Presbyterians of Palmyra village with spiritual leadership. In January, 1822, Rev. Daniel C. Hopkins became the minister of that parish and continued to serve in that capacity for about two years. In February, 1824, Benjamin B. Stockton initiated his three-year period of leadership; and about the time of his arrival a major awakening erupted in that area which was one of the most powerful revivals that occurred in Palmyra.[26]

Another Presbyterian congregation was organized in the neighborhood where Joseph Smith lived in the year that the Western Presbyterian Church was constituted. This society

---

[25]*Palmyra, Wayne County,* 36; Records of the Session of the Presbyterian Church in Palmyra, II, 11-13, located in the Western Presbyterian Church, Palmyra, New York, microfilm copy in Brigham Young University Library. A selection from this record is reproduced in Appendix K. Sophronia might have withdrawn from this society earlier, being married in 1827.

[26]Franklin Bowditch Dexter, *Biographical Sketches of the Graduates of Yale College with Annals of the College History* (New York, 1907), IV, 695-96; *New York Observer,* September 1, 1838, 140; *Palmyra, Wayne County,* 47; Records of the Presbytery of Geneva, Book C, 253-54, located in the Presbyterian Historical Society, Philadelphia, Pennsylvania. A description of the revival that was occurring in Palmyra and vicinity in 1825 appeared in the *Wayne Sentinel,* March 2, 1825, which was a quotation from the *Religious Advocate* of Rochester, a Rochester newspaper that was first issued in the fall of 1824. See *The Rochester Telegraph.* September 7, 1824.

consisted of only eighteen members who met in homes in the town of Manchester. Since these Presbyterians were unable to support a settled minister, they were supplied irregularly by preachers appointed by the Geneva Presbytery. After about fifteen years of vicissitudes, they discontinued holding their meetings.[27]

The Methodist Society

The Methodists were also among the earliest Protestants to organize in the Genesee country. As early as 1798 members of this religious persuasion began holding prayer meetings in the home of Sharon Booth, one of the earliest pioneers of Manchester. Approximately four years before the Smith family arrived in the Empire state, not only had a Methodist class been constituted in Manchester village but small groups had commenced gathering on a regular basis in and near Palmyra village, Macedon Center, and Clifton Springs. At the time of the First Vision these classes, which usually consisted of less than thirty members, met in homes, barns, schools, and groves. Of these four groups, only the Methodists of Clifton Springs were holding services in a church building. The first Methodist meetinghouse constructed in Palmyra village was completed in 1822 and it was not until 1840 that the Methodists of Manchester, who numbered about forty at the time, erected a religious edifice in that community.[28]

Palmyra and Manchester were included in the Ontario circuit of the Genesee Conference in 1820.[29] This three-week circuit was divided into preaching stations so that every three weeks an itinerant minister would have contacted the people

[27]Charles H. Dayton and John Garth Coleman, *A Brief History of the Presbytery of Geneva and a Tribute to Some Early Ministers* (Shortsville, New York: Geneva-Lyons Presbytery, 1955), 5; Records of the Presbytery of Geneva, Book C, 92, 121; *History of Ontario County*, 195.

[28]Files of the Shortsville Enterprise Press, December 19, 1902; *Palmyra Wayne County*, 51; *History of Ontario County*, 181-82; Mary Louise Eldredge, comp., *Pioneers of Macedon and other Papers of the Macedon Center Historical Society* (Macedon Center, 1912), 132-33; [W. H. McIntosh, ed.], *History of Wayne County, New York* (Philadelphia, 1877), 148.

[29]Miscellaneous Records, Book C, 154, Ontario County Court House, Canandaigua, New York; *History of Wayne County*, 148.

living in Palmyra, Manchester and other stations, thereby providing the settlers with constant spiritual edification and guidance. Between the summer of 1819 and 1820, Andrew Peck and William Snow were assigned to this circuit.[30] Consequently, one of these itinerants would have preached regularly in Palmyra and Manchester and probably would have traveled frequently along the Canandaigua Road located within a mile of the Smith farm. The circuit-rider preachers not only delivered sermons to members of the Methodist classes who gathered at the designated preaching stations, but these conscientious crusaders periodically expounded Methodist tenets at district conferences, annual conferences, and other such gatherings.

Camp Meetings

One of the most effective missionary programs adopted by the Methodists to promulgate their faith was the camp meeting. Although Baptists, Presbyterians, and members of other religious societies also sponsored such meetings, and while Christians of various faiths participated in these services, the Methodists in western New York conducted more camp meetings in the early nineteenth century than did members of any other denomination. These meetings were usually held on the edge of a grove of trees or in a small clearing in the midst of a forest. After traveling many miles along dusty or water-logged roads, the settlers would locate their wagons and pitch their tents on the outskirts of the

---

[30]*Methodist Minutes* (New York, 1819), 51. From July, 1820, to July, 1821, the Ontario Circuit was supplied by Thomas Wright and Elihu Nash. *Methodist Minutes* (New York, 1820), 44. Some LDS historians have identified Rev. George Lane as possibly one of the ministers who participated in the religious excitement of 1819-1820. Rev. George Lane was appointed presiding elder of the Susquehanna District in northern Pennsylvania at a canference held in Vienna (now Phelps) during the summer of 1819. The following summer, Elder Lane attended the annual conference held in Niagara. Therefore, before and after the First Vision, this minister could have been in the area where Joseph lived. However, the Prophet did not identify the Methodist preacher who initiated the religious excitement in the place where he lived nor the individual he contacted following this memorable experience. For additional information on this preacher and his possible connections with Mormonism, see Larry C. Porter, "Reverend George Lane," *BYU Studies*, IX (Spring, 1969), 321-340.

FIG. 13. CAMP MEETING IN THE WEST, 1830-1835

A drawing by A. Rider depicting an American expression of religious fervor. Courtesy Library of Congress.

encampment. Farmers' markets and grog or liquor shops often sprang up near the camp grounds, thereby providing some farmers with unusual economic opportunities. The meetings frequently continued for several days, and sometimes one session would last nearly all day and into the night. Ministers would rotate preaching assignments so that one minister would immediately be followed by another, and at times two or three ministers would preach simultaneously in different parts of the camp ground. Itinerants not only preached lengthy sermons but devoted much of their time to counseling and to directing prayer circles and group singing.[31]

The numbers who attended camp meetings in New York in the decade of the 1820's varied considerably. There were times when only a few hundred gathered, and on other occasions thousands witnessed the proceedings. In a camp meeting held in Palmyra in 1826, one reporter estimated that 10,000 people assembled on the grounds to behold the spiritual drama.[32]

In some sections of early America, camp meetings frequently erupted into exciting spectacles in which enthusiasts demonstrated their emotional aspirations with a variety of physical demonstrations. During these exuberant meetings people went into trances, jerked, rolled and crawled on the ground, barked like dogs, and fell to the ground as though they had been hit by a piercing cannon ball, remaining unconscious for minutes or even sometimes for hours. In western New York at the time of the First Vision, however, physical demonstrations were rarely manifest, except for the occasional practice of falling to the ground and crying out for mercy. Nevertheless, some settlers who were attending these

---

[31]Charles Giles, *Pioneer: A Narrative of the Nativity, Experiences, Travels, and Ministerial Labours of Rev. Charles Giles* (New York, 1844), 266-70; "Religious and Missionary Intelligence," *Methodist Magazine,* II (December, 1819), 474-76; Eben Smith, "Progress of the Work of God on Hudson-River District," *Methodist Magazine,* V (December, 1822), 474-75.

[32]Theophilus Armenius, "Account of the Rise and Progress of the Work of God in the Western Country," *Methodist Magazine,* II (July, 1819), 272; Thomas Madden, "Good Effects of Campmeetings," *Methodist Magazine,* I (1818), 152-53; "Genesee Conference," *Methodist Magazine,* IX (August, 1826), 313.

New York meetings for the first time were alarmed by the piercing, dissonant commotions that would occasionally erupt. Some viewed with mixed emotions the weeping, the crying, the mourning, and the sighing which created loud noises in the encampment.[33]

In the neighborhood where Joseph lived, camp meetings and other services conducted by Methodists were held periodically at the time of the First Vision. Notices of such gatherings seldom appeared in the local newspapers, except when an unusual event occurred in connection with a particular meeting.[34] In June, 1820, the *Palmyra Register* reported a Methodist camp meeting in the vicinity of Palmyra because an Irishman, James Couser, died the day after attending the gathering and after becoming intoxicated. "It is supposed," the editor commented, that Couser "obtained his liquor, which was no doubt the cause of his death, at the Camp-ground, where it is a notorious fact, the intemperate, the lewd and dissolute part of community too frequently resort for no better object, than to gratify their base propensities." A quasi-apologetic clarification of this report was printed in a later edition of the Palmyra paper in which the editor stated that when he wrote that Couser "obtained his liquor at the Camp-ground," he did not mean that the Irishman obtained it within the enclosure of their [Methodist] place of worship, or that he procured it of them, but at the grog-shops which were established at, or *near* if you please, their camp ground."[35]

The Protestant Episcopal Church

As early as 1806, Episcopalians of Palmyra organized in one of the homes of the settlers and selected two church-

[33]Giles, *op. cit.*, 268; R. Smith, *Recollections of Nettleton, and the Great Revival of 1820* (Albany, 1848), 31-33, 71, 74, 123; T. Spicer, "A Short Sketch of the Revival of Religion in the City of Troy, A.D. 1816," *Methodist Magazine*, I (1818), 152-53.

[34]M. P. Blakeslee, Notes for a History of Methodism in Phelps, 1886, 7, copy located in Brigham Young University Library. Blakeslee discusses in his manuscript history a camp meeting held near Palmyra in 1818, in which twenty were baptized and forty converted to the Methodist society, and which was not reported in the newspapers and religious journals of that age.

[35]*Palmyra Register*, June 28, 1820; July 5, 1820.

wardens and eight vestrymen, John Swift being chosen one of the wardens. For almost twenty years this small group met sporadically, as did the Episcopalians of Farmington who organized in the home of John Shekell in 1807.[36] There were few traveling Episcopalian preachers who penetrated western New York in the early nineteenth century, and these supervising bishops or missionaries did not preach according to a regular schedule. Consequently, for many years most Episcopalians living in the Genesee country were without spiritual leadership and many small congregations disbanded.

After meeting irregularly for several decades, under the direction of Rev. Rufus Murray, the Episcopalians of Palmyra organized on a permanent basis in June, 1823. Murray served as rector for three years, and during this period meetings were held in the academy located across the street from the old Western Presbyterian Church. In 1827, during the pastorate of Rev. John Clark, these Protestants erected a wooden chapel on Main Street and then in 1873 completed the Gothic structure which stands today at the Four Corners. Originally this society, which was the first permanent Episcopalian communion to be organized in Wayne County, was named Zion's Church, but eventually it was renamed Zion's Episcopal Church.[37]

Other Protestant Faiths

Beyond the town limits of Palmyra and Farmington, but within fifteen miles of the Smith farm, other Protestants had organized and were meeting on a regular basis at the time of the First Vision. Episcopalians and Congregationalists were worshipping in Canandaigua and were spreading from that community the basic tenets of these faiths. Freewill Baptists were holding services east of the Smith home in an area known as Junius; and southwest of the Smith farm in West

[36]Miscellaneous Records, Book B, 51-52, 60, Ontario County Court House.

[37]Rev. John S. Carrie, *Zion Episcopal Church, Palmyra, New York* (n.p., n.d.); *Palmyra Courier*, August 17, 1866, November 26, 1858; The Zion Episcopal Church Records of Palmyra, Wayne County, N.Y., Part I, 1-2, located in New York Public Library.

Bloomfield, a society known as the Christians, Eastern Christians, or Eastern Christian Connection had been constituted in 1818 under the leadership of Rev. David Millard. Moreover, a few Universalists were living in the town where Joseph resided. Although the Universalists had not organized a religious society in that immediate locality, the controversial beliefs of these Protestants were being fanned through the Genesee country.[38]

The Second Great Awakening

The religious societies of Palmyra and Farmington and neighboring towns were organized during an era of increasing spiritual vitality that was not only evident in western New York but in many other parts of the new nation. In fact, during the six decades preceding the Civil War, innumerable spiritual quickenings erupted throughout this country; and many Americans living in the rugged frontier communities, in the rapidly growing urban area, and in the villages and towns of northern and southern United States turned their attention to organized religion. (This is often referred to as the second great awakening, as distinguished from the first great awakening which occurred from about 1739 to 1745.) Subsequently, church membership and religious zeal soared. Although in 1800 approximately 7 percent of the population was churched, in 1820 about 11 percent of Americans were active members of religious societies; in 1850 the percentage had increased to about 17; and by 1860, membership had reached 23 percent of the rapidly expanding population.[39]

A Burned-Over District

Although the innumerable spontaneous revivals which occurred during this second great awakening did not proceed from one community to another in a definable manner, and the quickenings did not spread from one state to another like a path created by a raging fire, one region in this land which

---

[38]*History of Ontario County,* 111-12, 220-21; G. A. Burgess and J. T. Ward, *Free Baptist Cyclopaedia* (Chicago, 1889), 474.

[39]Backman, *op. cit.,* 308.

was in an almost constant state of revivalism during the early nineteenth century was western New York. During the decades preceding the Civil War, revivals were so habitual and powerful in the area west of the Catskill and Adirondack Mountains that historians have labeled this ecclesiastical storm center the "Burned-over District."[40]

As in Kentucky, the winter of 1799-1800 was the era of a "Great Revival" in western New York. Since an innumerable series of spiritual quickenings followed this first major wave of enthusiasm, this powerful awakening initiated a new religious epoch in that region of America. Although one can locate evidence of spiritual enlivenment in a number of New York communities every year of the early 1800's, peak periods occurred when revivals erupted in more than the customary number of towns and villages, and unprecedented numbers joined the popular churches of that age. One of these apexes of religious fervor followed the low ebb which occurred during the War of 1812. Between 1816 and 1821, revivals were reported in more towns and a greater number of settlers joined churches than in any previous period of New York history. After a brief calm in which awakenings continued in a less spectacular manner, the grand climax in the "series of crests in religious zeal" occurred between 1825 and 1837.[41]

A Fruitful Field All Ready to Harvest

For a variety of reasons, western New York was in a favorable position for rapid church growth in the early nineteenth century. New York was not only growing and developing more rapidly than any other part of the nation, but the Genesee country had been invaded by pioneers who had emigrated from the section of the land where religious activity was higher than in any other portion of the United States. In 1776, for example, about 12 percent of the inhabitants of New England were churched in comparison to about 10 per-

---

[40]Whitney R. Cross, *The Burned-over District* (Ithaca: Cornell University Press, 1950), 3-4.

[41]*Ibid.*, 13; See also Smith, *Recollections of Nettleton and the Great Revival of 1820.*

cent in the Mid-Atlantic states, and approximately 5 percent in the south.[42] Many of the unchurched New Englanders, however, were religious-minded people, like the Smiths, who were seeking God and were desirious of joining God's true church. The reason why some of these immigrants were not members of a Christian denomination was that there was no meetinghouse in the neighborhood where they lived. Even though the church was the center of religious activity in the compact agricultural villages, many New Englanders lived on isolated farms located more than three miles from a church building, and farmers who lived far from a meetinghouse found it most inconvenient to attend church with any degree of regularity. Other immigrants were unchurched because they could not accept Congregationalism, which was the dominant faith in that section, or rejected the Calvinism proclaimed by most itinerant Baptists who were preaching in America at that time. If one did not endorse the five points of Calvinism, including predestination, there was in most instances no religious society in New England to which he could conscientiously unite. Consequently, many of the pioneers living in western Massachusetts, western Connecticut, and Vermont belonged to a generation in which vast numbers were unchurched but whose grandparents or parents had been active members of a Christian society.

Recognizing that many, but probably not the majority, of early settlers of the Genesee country were seeking organized religion, innumerable preachers of various denominations followed the immigrants and commenced preaching and organizing societies in the Finger Lake country. At the time of the First Vision, only about 11 or 12 percent of the settlers residing in the towns of Farmington and Palmyra were members of a Christian faith (which was the national average at that time), but many of these pioneers were interested in joining one of the communions which had been or was on the verge of organizing. Confronted with a perpetual stream of revivalistic sermons and witnessing the creation of many different

---

[42]Backman, op. cit., 277.

religious societies which espoused a variety of doctrines, large numbers of settlers residing in western New York (and many other parts of America) asked the question, "Which church should I join?" In the early nineteenth century, religious liberty was becoming a reality. The beliefs of many were being brought into harmony with many of the doctrines of the Restored Church; and vast numbers of Americans were engaged in a quest for religious truth. The field was white all ready to harvest.

Unusual Religious Excitement

One who was spiritually quickened while living in the Burned-over District was Joseph Smith. Joseph became keenly interested in organized religion during one of the higher waves of revivalism which swept across western New York. Approximately eighteen years after witnessing this spiritual phenomenon, Joseph recalled his experience from a distant vantage point. The Prophet asserted that in the second year after his removal to Manchester (which in 1820 was Farmington town), an "unusual excitement on the subject of religion" occurred in "the place" where he lived. "It commenced," he said, "with the Methodists, but soon became general among all the sects in that region of country." Then probably placing this religious quickening in an enlarged historical setting, Joseph declared, "Indeed, the whole district of country seemed affected by it, and great multitudes united themselves to the different religious parties."[43]

It is difficult to determine precisely what Joseph Smith meant when he said that there was unusual religious excitement in the place where he lived, for the Prophet did not elaborate on this statement, nor did he define the terms which he employed. The religious excitement mentioned by the Mormon Prophet might or might not have precipitated an immediate, substantial increase in church membership in his neighborhood. Although *revivals, quickenings, awakenings,* and *religious excitement* were terms used interchangeably by

---

[43]Pearl of Great Price (Salt Lake City: The Church of Jesus Christ of Latter-day Saints, 1952), 46.

authors of the early nineteenth century, these words were
employed to describe an increased interest in religion, a conversion of settlers from darkness to light, a reconversion of
former members, an extension of the power of godliness, an
outpouring of the spirit, and a visible change in the patterns
of conduct of individuals.[44] Although significant increases in
church membership are often indicators of the reality of a revival in a region, the absence of substantial membership increases
is not evidence that a spiritual quickening did not occur in a
community. Countless individuals joined churches many years
after they had experienced a profound spiritual change. Baptist and Quaker records and reports appearing in newspapers
and religious journals do not indicate any special revival in
Palmyra village in 1819 or 1820, but not all awakenings were
reported and records of the early 1820's are not available for
the Western Presbyterian Church and the Palmyra Methodist
society. When Joseph stated that great multitudes united
themselves to the different religious parties, he was not referring to the neighborhood where he lived, but identified the
membership increase with the "whole district of country."

There are many plausible explanations of what Joseph
meant by a religious excitement initiated by the Methodists
in the place where he lived. He might have had a spiritual
experience while listening to a circuit rider enthusiastically
proclaim his interpretation of the word of God in a home,
school, field, or grove in or near Palmyra or Manchester village. He might have been awakened while attending a district
conference or a Methodist camp meeting held near Palmyra
village or along the Vienna road near Phelps. One of the
contemporaries of Joseph, Orsamus Turner, concluded that
the Mormon Prophet became excited about religion while he
was attending a camp meeting held "away down in the woods,
on the Vienna road," a road that ran east of Palmyra village
and led to the village of Phelps.[45] This report of Joseph's

---

[44]Wm. Neill, "Thoughts on Revivals of Religion," *The Christian Herald,* VII (April 7, 1821), 708-11.
[45]O. Turner, *History of the Pioneer Settlement of Phelps and Gorham's Purchase, and Morris' Reserve* (Rochester, 1852), 214.

catching a "spark of Methodist fire" while attending a camp meeting along the Vienna road has been interpreted by several town historians as a meeting held in or near Phelps or in Oaks Corners, a small farming community situated southeast of Phelps village.[46]

Another possible explanation of Joseph's description of the historical setting of the First Vision is that his religious interests might have been enhanced directly or indirectly as a result of the many memorable services which were held in the town of Phelps, meetings which precipitated a powerful spiritual awakening in that section of western New York.

The historic gatherings which led to a great revival and created such an impression on the settlers in the town of Phelps began in July, 1819, when the Methodists of the Genesee Conference held their annual meetings in Phelps village, which was then called Vienna. Approximately one hundred Methodist ministers gathered in this small village during that summer to deliberate, to develop programs, to resolve controversies, and to receive edification, instruction, and annual appointments. The sessions of this conference were held in a clapboard meeting house, a newly completed Methodist church which was painted with yellow ochre and crowned with a diminutive cupola. Although this building contained no classrooms, carpets, or cushions, fairly comfortable seats with backs were installed shortly before the conference began.[47]

In addition to the special services which were held in connection with this conference, camp meetings were conducted following the deliberations; and during the ensuing twelve months (from the summer of 1819 to the summer of 1820) a "flaming spiritual advance" occurred in that region.[48]

---

[46]Mabel E. Oaks, *History of Oaks Corners Church and Community* (Phelps, 1954), 11; Hamilton Child, *Gazetteer and Business Directory of Ontario County, New York, for 1867-8* (Syracuse, 1867), 52.

[47]Journal of the Genesee Conference, 1810 to 1828, 76-84, copy located in Brigham Young University Library; Blakeslee, *op. cit..* 6-7; Helen Post Ridley, *When Phelps Was Young* (Phelps, 1939), 55.

[48]Blakeslee, *op. cit.,* 7-8; Ridley, *op. cit.,* 55.

Since the boundaries of the Genesee Conference stretched from the Catskill Mountains in the east to Detroit in the west, a distance of about five hundred miles, and from Upper Canada in the north to central Pennsylvania in the south, a distance of about three hundred miles, many itinerant preachers — from western New York, northwestern Pennsylvania, portions of Canada, Ohio, and other western regions — traveled through or near Palmyra and Farmington in the summer of 1819. It was common for those ministers to preach and participate in camp meetings while they were traveling to and from their annual conferences. It is not unreasonable, therefore, to assume that Joseph Smith might have attended meetings convoked by ministers of this conference held immediately before, during or shortly after the deliberations which took place in Phelps. And, since Joseph employed the phrase "place where we lived" while preparing a history of the Church in Missouri and Illinois, and since many farmers of that age traveled ten or fifteen miles to attend Methodist conferences or camp meetings, the unusual excitement might have occurred in the town of Farmington or one of the neighboring towns such as Phelps or Palmyra.

Ecclesiastical records clearly reveal that unusual gains in church membership occurred in 1819 and 1820 in many communities located within a radius of twenty miles of the Smith farm. Evidence that Baptists in the neighborhood where Joseph lived prospered from the religious stirrings is found in the membership reports of the Baptist society of Manchester village located about six miles south of the Smith farm. Twenty-two converts were added to this congregation in 1819, which was a significant growth for a church consisting of only 87 members in 1818.[49] When representatives of the Presbyterian churches assembled in Phelps in February, 1820, members of the Presbytery of Geneva reported that "during the past year more have been received into the communion of the Churches than perhaps in any former year," and the word

---

[49]*Minutes of the Ontario Baptist Association* (Canandaigua, 1818), 3; *Minutes of the Ontario Baptist Association* (New York, 1819), 2.

"perhaps" has been crossed out by pencil in the manuscript.[50] Presbyterian records further reveal that revivals were occurring in 1819-1820 in Geneva, Phelps, Rochester, Penfield, West Bloomfield, and Lima, all communities located within twenty miles of the Smith farm, and prospects of revivals were reported in Canandaigua and Waterloo, which probably means that an unusual religious excitement had commenced in these communities.[51] Freewill Baptist records indicate an unusual growth in the area of Junius, and Episcopalians issued encouraging reports from missionaries laboring in Phelps and Waterloo.[52] Methodist reports specify that in 1820, membership in the Lyons circuit, a circuit located immediately east of the Smith farm, doubled, increasing from 374 to 654 members.[53]

Quaker records of the Farmington Monthly Meeting, which included congregations located in Riga, Rochester, Palmyra, Macedon, Farmington, South Farmington, and Deerfield (the last-named group being located about forty or fifty miles south of Palmyra), further reveal unusual increases in church membership in the months immediately preceding the First Vision.[54] From 1803 to 1814 about thirteen new members were added to this monthly meeting annually, with the largest increase occurring in 1808, when twenty-two were added to the societies. Between 1815 and 1820, however, more than thirty-three persons were added annually to the worship meetings that comprised this body of Quakers. The largest increases occurred in 1817 when more than fifty were added, but many of these new members were children who had matured and were finally admitted into the church. The second largest increase in the early history of this monthly

---

[50]Records of the Presbytery of Geneva, Book C, 37-38.

[51]*Idem.; Extracts from the Minutes of the General Assembly of the Presbyterian Church* (Philadelphia, 1821), 22.

[52]Marilla Marks, ed., *Memoirs of the Life of David Marks* (Dover, N.H., 1846, 26; Charles W. Hayes, *The Diocese of Western New York* (Rochester, 1904), 53.

[53]*Methodist Minutes* (New York, 1820), 7; *Methodist Minutes* (New York, 1821), 27.

[54]S. Ricketson, *An Account of the Times and Places of Holding the Meetings Constituting New York Yearly Meeting of Friends* (Poughkeepsie, 1821), 10.

meeting occurred in 1819 when thirty-seven were admitted, nearly all of whom were adults. A comparison of these converts with individuals enumerated on the census of 1820 and the Quaker membership summary of 1828 indicates that at least thirteen of these newly admitted Quakers resided in Farmington, the town where Joseph lived. Evidence that the religious excitement among the Quakers reached a crescendo in 1819 is apparent when one continues to examine the copious records kept by this Protestant group. In 1820 there was an addition of twenty-six; then from 1821 to 1828, when a schism interrupted the growth of this society, an average of only sixteen new members were admitted annually.[55] Quaker records therefore inform us that in Joseph's neighborhood there were greater increases in church membership in the years immediately preceding the First Vision than during any other period in the early history of this denomination; and the Quakers were the largest religious society, numerically speaking, in the area where Joseph lived at the time of his remarkable experience in the sacred grove.

Membership Increases in the "Whole District of Country"

Ecclesiastical records further reveal that there was a great awakening in many other sections of western and eastern New York in 1819 and 1820. Although not complete nor always reliable, records compiled by the General Assembly of the Presbyterian Church provide one indication of the numbers affected during the initial phase of this great awakening. The average annual increase of membership in this church in western New York between 1812 and 1816 was about five hundred. In 1816, however, Presbyterian membership in the region west of the Catskill Mountains increased by 1050; in 1817, the increase was 1989; in 1818, 1516; and in 1819, 1513. During the year preceding the First Vision, the national increase in Presbyterian Church membership was approximately 6500, and the increase in the state of New York alone was

---

[55]Records of the Farmington Monthly Meetings, Pt. 11, Pt. 17. A summary of Quaker membership in Palmyra, Macedon, and Farmington in 1828 is located in Pt. 11 (1821-1843), 58-77.

2250, representing 35 percent of the national total. But what is also most significant is the fact that more than 67 percent of the New York converts came from the area west of the Catskill mountains. That means that 23 percent of the national increase in Presbyterian Church membership occurred in the "Burned-over District." The General Assembly of this church also reported in 1820 that awakenings were occurring in 54 congregations in New York, and the enumeration did not include the congregations in the Albany region where 1400 were added to the churches.[56]

National Calvinist Baptist records, which are very incomplete, reveal that about 22 percent of the reported additions to their societies during the period immediately preceding the First Vision, occurred in congregations located in western New York.[57] The 1820 minutes of fourteen of the nineteen Baptist associations of New York are available in the American Baptist Historical Society, and these records reflect that 2,425 believers were baptized into the Baptist faith in 1819. Reports for that year from six of the nine associations located west of the Appalachian Mountains indicate that 1,410 additions occurred in the churches located in western New York. According to the national statistics published by the Baptists, the most significant increase in the United States in 1819 occurred in the Madison Association where more than 500 converts were baptized, the largest additions taking place at Homer, Truxton, Petersburg, and Nelson, New York.[58] In that year too, more than two hundred were admitted by baptism into the Saratoga, Cayuga, and Otsega associations. Except for Saratoga, all of the churches included in these alliances of Baptist societies were located in western New York. Baptist membership records further reveal that in 1820, 2,137 were baptized into the New York societies (based on reports from

[56]*Minutes of the General Assembly of the Presybterian Church in the United States of America from its Organization A.D. 1789 to A.D. 1820* (Philadelphia, n.d.), 516, 574-75, 634-35, 667, 696, 742.

[57]*Proceedings of the Baptist General Convention in the United States, at their Second Triennial Meeting* (Philadelphia, 1820), 308-309.

[58]*Idem., Minutes of the Madison Baptist Association* (Morrisville, 1820).

THE GREAT REVIVAL
OF 1819–1820
in Western, Central, and Upstate New York

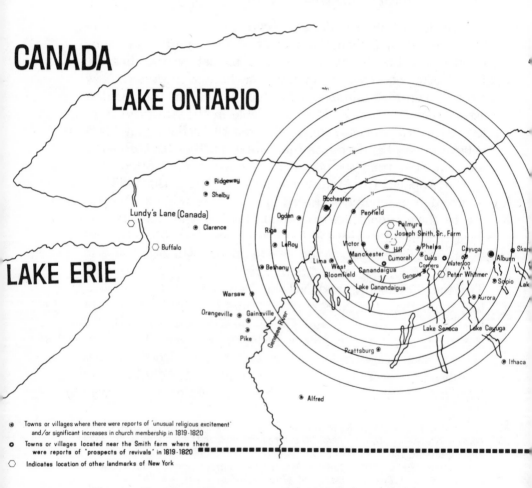

Towns or villages where there were reports of "unusual religious excitement"
and/or significant increases in church membership in 1819-1820

Towns or villages located near the Smith farm where there
were reports of "prospects of revivals" in 1819-1820

Indicates location of other landmarks of New York

Fig. 14. The Great Revival of 1819-1820 in Western New York

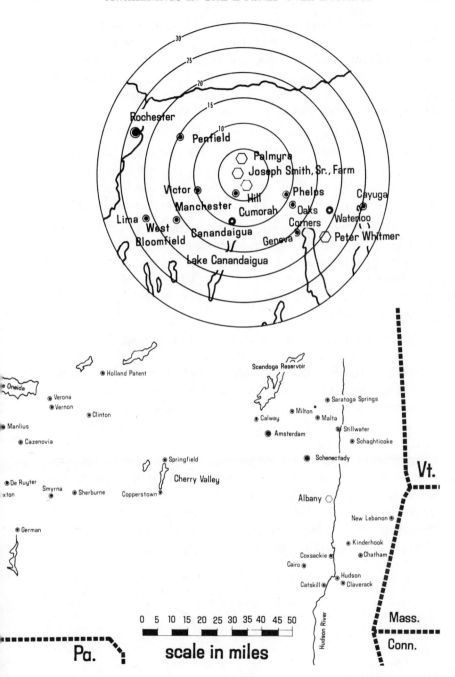

sixteen associations). The largest additions in that year occurred in the Cayuga Association, where 199 were baptized,
and which included the societies located in the vicinity where
Joseph lived. Also the congregations located in Phelps, Gorham, Sodus, and Williamson experienced unusual increases
in church membership at the time of the First Vision.[59]

Methodist membership figures further reveal substantial
increases in membership in the "Burned-over District" at
the time of the First Vision. In 1820 there was an increase
of 2,256 members in that region, which was the largest annual
increase reported by this group for that section of America.[60]

Not only were there substantial increases in church membership of the Methodist, Presbyterian, and Calvinist Baptist
societies in the region of country where Joseph Smith lived,
but there were also additions in the Christian denomination,
the Freewill and Seventh-day Baptist societies, and other
Protestant faiths.

While summarizing the spiritual quickenings that awakened America into a new reality of the divinity of Christ, one
editor declared in 1820 that there were currently more reports
of revivals in religious publications than in any previous era.[61]
Although an unusual spiritual phenomenon was occurring in
various sections of America, New York state, especially the
area stretching from Albany to Buffalo, was the ecclesiastical
storm center of the new nation at the time one of the most
remarkable visions was unfolded to mankind. Accounts of
the enlivenments which occurred in western and upstate New
York in 1819 and 1820 were advertised in Palmyra, and the
record number of baptisms occurring in the area east of Lake
Cayuga and in the region of Albany was enumerated in the

---

[59]*Minutes of the Ontario Baptist Association* (Canandaigua, 1820), 2-4.
[60]*Methodist Minutes* (1820), 27-28; *Methodist Minutes* (1821), 27.
Since the district of Ontario was created in 1819, there was a realignment
of the districts in the area where the Smith family lived prior to the First
Vision. It is therefore difficult to determine the precise increase in membership of the Methodists at that time. Nevertheless, the records indicate
a doubling of membership in 1820 in the area where the Smith family lived.
[61]"Revivals of Religion," *The Western New York Baptist Magazine,* III
(August, 1820), 91.

local newspaper, the *Palmyra Register*.[62] Joseph Smith therefore undoubtedly knew that unusual religious quickenings were occurring in New York in 1819 and 1820, that great numbers were joining churches, and that additions were being made in the various denominations located in the vicinity where he lived.

When Sarepta Marsh Baker, one of the converts of the Great Revival of 1819-1820, who lived in Phelps, recalled the quickenings which followed the annual Methodist conference held in her community in 1819, she employed an expression remarkably similar to Joseph's account. "The revival," she observed, "was a religious cyclone which swept over the whole region round about and the kingdom of darkness was terribly shaken."[63]

Although one cannot define precisely what Joseph meant by "the place where we lived" and the "whole district of country" by employing the tools of modern historical research, various primary sources clearly demonstrate that there were substantial increases in church membership in many sections of western New York at the time of the First Vision. There is not only evidence of religious excitement occurring in the area where Joseph Smith lived in 1820, but one can substantiate the Prophet's accounts of great multitudes joining churches in the whole region of country by defining district of country as an area within twenty, fifty, or one hundred miles of the Smith farm, or by adopting a definition of western or upstate New York. The most reliable sources, therefore, reveal that Joseph Smith's brief description of the historical setting of the First Vision is in harmony with other contemporary accounts of the great awakening which occurred in New York in 1819 and 1820. Indeed, the Mormon Prophet penned a brief but reliable description of the enlivenment which occurred in the "Burned-over District" at the time he launched his quest for religious truth.

---

[62]*Palmyra Register,* September 13, 1820; August 16, 1820.
[63]Blakeslee, *op. cit.,* 7-8.

CHAPTER 4

The "War of Words and Tumult of Opinions"

An Era of Ecumenism

One of the widely-publicized religious characteristics of modern America is the powerful movement of Christian unity. Today there is a constant, friendly dialogue between Protestants of various denominations and between Protestants and Catholics. This spirit of ecumenism is beginning to create new religious alignments. For example, after most Congregationalists united with a body called Christians, these two societies merged with former members of the Evangelical Church and the German Reformed Church, creating the United Church of Christ. At the time of writing (1970) plans are being discussed for the uniting of this society with eight other Protestant faiths which would produce an estimated membership of twenty-five million.

The modern spirit of unification and denominational cooperation is evident today in many sections of western New York. During the summer of 1958, the Presbyterian minister of Shortsville, a hamlet located about eight miles south of Palmyra, was hospitalized and members of this congregation united in weekly worship with the Methodists of Manchester village. A few miles south of Manchester, in Canandaigua, Baptists and Presbyterians have merged permanently, creating a Baptist-Presbyterian Church.

The modern ecumenical movement is partly the result of a new reformation which is de-emphasizing dogma. While one spectrum of Protestantism is clinging to the historic or traditional beliefs, another wing within most large Protestant societies has endorsed a new theology in the sense that they are reinterpreting classical Protestantism and are popularizing concepts that do not harmonize with the old-time religion. As a result of the increasing acceptance of a liberalized theology, striking diversity of opinion has evolved within many Protestant congregations and Catholic parishes. The views of some Baptists are more in harmony with the beliefs of many Methodists and Presbyterians than they are with the espoused convictions of many other Baptists. To avoid conflict, many ministers do not preach from the pulpit precise descriptions of belief. Many theologians are emphasizing the need for each generation to formulate its own creed and for each individual to determine his own patterns of faith. A few years ago, after a group of Protestant ministers gathered socially, one of the clergy suggested that his colleagues discuss a traditional Christian tenet, such as the fall, the atonement, or life beyond the grave. Because this preacher dared suggest that the spiritual leaders engage in such a doctrinal discussion, he was regarded by some as an intellectual curiosity.

An Age of Theological Discord

Although the spirit of ecumenism has engulfed many Protestant congregations of the twentieth century, one hundred and fifty years ago members of these same denominations were engaged in innumerable theological confrontations. Revivalists and lay members engaged in numerous and vigorous debates concerning doctrines. Authors wrote and circulated countless polemical theological treatises. Christians argued vehemently over doctrines that today are seldom discussed in most congregations of the Genesee country. In describing the historical setting of the First Vision, the Prophet Joseph Smith aptly declared:[1]

> My mind at times was greatly excited, the cry and tumult were so great and incessant. The Presbyterians were most decided against the Baptists and Method-

---

[1]Pearl of Great Price (Salt Lake City: The Church of Jesus Christ of Latter-day Saints, 1952), 47.

ists, and used all the powers of both reason and sophistry
to prove their errors, or, at least, to make the people
think they were in error. On the other hand, the Baptists
and Methodists in their turn were equally zealous in
endeavoring to establish their own tenets and disprove
all others.

In the midst of this war of words and tumult of
opinions, I often said to myself: What is to be done?
Who of all these parties are right; or, are they all wrong
together? If any one of them be right, which is it, and
how shall I know it?

What was the nature of the theological struggle dividing
Christians in the neighborhood where Joseph lived in 1820?
What were the doctrines that precipitated the "war of words
and tumult of opinions" which erupted in the Genesee country
in the early nineteenth century?

These questions can partially be answered by determining
the location of the churches that had been constituted prior
to 1820 in the area where Joseph Smith lived, by examining
the creeds adopted by these Protestants, and by investigating
the controversial religious tracts which were circulated in western New York at the time of the First Vision.

Congregations in Joseph Smith's Neighborhood

Within a radius of eight miles of the Smith farm, four
Protestant denominations had organized congregations and
were holding meetings regularly in 1820 — Quakers, Baptists,
Presbyterians, and Methodists. In addition to four congregations of Friends, within eight miles of the Smith farm there
were three Presbyterian societies and two Baptist congregations; and at the time of the First Vision four groups of Methodists were worshipping regularly in the towns of Palmyra and
Farmington.

Within fifteen miles of the Smith farm other Protestants
had organized and were holding weekly Sabbath services in
1820. Congregationalists and Episcopalians were meeting in
Canandaigua. Freewill Baptists were worshipping regularly in

Junius; Eastern Christians or members of the Eastern Christian Connection were assembling in West Bloomfield; and Episcopalians of Palmyra sporadically assembled to worship according to the rites of their church.

Although the views of the Universalists were also being fanned in the area by means of pamphlets written by their apologists and by a few enthusiastic spokesmen living within seven miles of the Smith farm,[2] there is no evidence that Roman Catholics had constituted a society in that section of New York, nor are there records informing us that Catholics were active participants in the war of words that rocked the Genesee country in the early nineteenth century.

When Joseph Smith identified the denominations engaged in a theological confrontation, he mentioned three faiths, the Presbyterians, Baptists, and Methodists. It is understandable why the Prophet referred to these societies, for they were three of the four faiths who had organized congregations within a few miles of his log home, and members of his family divided their interests primarily between the Presbyterians and Methodists. The only Protestant group not mentioned by the Prophet which had organized prior to 1820 in the neighborhood where he lived was the Society of Friends. Being opposed to a salaried clergy, Quakers did not support their religious leaders financially and few Quaker missionaries were preaching in the Genesee country at the time of the First Vision. Most Friends lived peaceably on their rural farms and seldom engaged in rigorous debates with other Christians. The literature published in the vicinity where Joseph lived does not include debates between Quakers and other Protestants, but does include controversial debates, sermons, or vehement discussions emphasizing distinct theological positions of the Presbyterians, Baptists, Methodists, Episcopalians, Eastern Christians, and Universalists. Consequently, even though

---

[2]One of the pamphlets advertised for sale in the Palmyra book store in 1818 was Elhanan Winchester's *Lectures on the Prophecies,* which contains an excellent description of the Universalist belief concerning life beyond the grave. See also Files of the Shortsville Enterprise Press, March 3, 1883.

young Joseph undoubtedly learned some of the peculiar tenets of the Quakers, he did not mention this religious body as a major participant in the war of words.[3] However, as the Prophet considered the tumult of opinions which created a theological barrier among Christians, he probably not only remembered disputes between Presbyterians, Baptists, and Methodists, but also contemplated some of the unusual beliefs held by the Friends and other Protestants.

Baptism a Source of Contention

One doctrine which precipitated innumerable theological debates and produced a noticeable "tumult of opinions" among the early settlers of western New York was the belief concerning baptism. What are the prerequisites for baptism? Are infants proper subjects for this sacrament? What is the proper mode of baptism? What is meant by baptismal regeneration? These were questions which were continually discussed by Genesee farmers, merchants, craftsmen, and ministers.

Methodists, Presbyterians, Congregationalists, and Episcopalians unitedly insisted that infants were proper subjects for baptism and that sprinkling and pouring were proper modes. Children, many argued, are baptized into future repentance and faith, for the efficacy of baptism is not confined to the occasion when it is administered. It is a sacrament, some added, that replaces circumcision, which was a token of God's covenant with Abraham. Baptism, therefore, is a sign or indication that God will tend to save the children of believers. And members of these denominations asserted that the quantity of water performed in this rite was not important.[4]

---

[3]Although Joseph did not mention the Quakers as one of the denominations participating in the war of words, it should be remembered that omission from a written text does not mean necessarily exclusion, for when men describe events they do not always include all details in their account.

[4]*Anabaptism Disproved* (New York, 1818) aptly summarizes the controversy concerning baptism which divided Protestants in Joseph's neighborhood at the time of the First Vision. See also John Wesley, *Sermons, on Several Occasions* (Hudson, 1810), 237-41; and Jacob Catlin, *The Gentiles Inheritance of the Blessing of Abraham Through Jesus Christ. A Sermon Respecting Infant Baptism* (Canandaigua, 1799), 25-26.

Replying to those arguments, the Baptists and Eastern Christians insisted that, according to the Bible, the essential prerequisites to baptism were faith and repentance, and that since infants could not believe nor repent, small children were not proper subjects for that ordinance. There is no scriptural warranty, they added, for the belief that circumcision was replaced with baptism, nor is there a New Testament reference of an infant being baptized. Although they admitted that there were references in the Bible to all within a household being baptized, these Protestants declared that there was no scriptural evidence that there were infants in these families. Moreover, members of these societies emphasized that immersion was the only proper mode of baptism. The Greek word "baptizo" from which the English word "baptism" is derived, they explained, means immersion; and in the New Testament this rite was compared to a death, burial, and resurrection. Sprinkling and pouring, they concluded, are not symbolic of a burial and are modes of baptism which are not in harmony with New Testament Christianity.[5]

In response to arguments employed by Baptists to support their conviction concerning baptism, some ministers charged that Baptists incorrectly cited the baptism of Jesus as an example of the recommended form of this sacrament. John the Baptist, some contended, was baptizing Jesus as part of a Jewish rite, not as a Christian ordinance. John's baptism was one of repentance and preparation for the kingdom which was to come, and was not the same as the rite administered by the apostles.[6] Moreover, theologians of the early nineteenth century reasoned that there is only one instance of early Christians baptizing possibly by immersion, and that was the case of Philip and the eunuch in which the rite was performed "accidentally" by plunging the candidate in the water. Even in this instance, some specified, there is

---

[5]John Gill, *Infant-Baptism, A Part and Pillar of Popery* (4th ed., Boston, 1805), is one of many Baptist publications which was republished in western New York and contains a description of the position of this society concerning baptism.

[6]*Anabaptism Disproved*, 13-14.

no way of determining the depth of the water; and since baptisms were performed, they explained, in prisons and homes and in places such as Jerusalem where there was a lack of sufficient water to immerse candidates, it is inconceivable that all early Christians were baptized by total immersion. "Surely," one apologist declared, "those who can believe that the jailor and his household were immersed under" a variety of "forbidding circumstances, can believe anything they wish." When Paul referred to being buried in baptism, men further reasoned, he meant in a pure symbolic sense, for we are not really baptized into the death of Christ.[7] Furthermore, men asserted that the word *baptizo* has more than one meaning and includes the concept of wetting or washing with water.[8]

Most Protestants of western New York also replied to the Baptists by insisting that we should not deny our infant children baptism. "If you say," one man declared, "that infants must not be baptized, because they cannot believe, do you not also say in effect that they must not be saved because they cannot believe?" Faith, some insisted, is only a requirement of adults, not children. Since "it is clear that baptism succeeds circumcision, as a seal of the same covenant, . . . of course it ought to be administered to our infant offspring."[9]

Baptists and Eastern Christians were not silenced by the arguments advanced by their Protestant opponents, for such reasoning merely added fuel to the fire of contention. Most Protestants, they retorted, "are ever restless and uneasy, endeavoring to maintain and support, if possible, their unscriptural practice of infant baptism," which should more properly be labeled "infant sprinkling."[10] Christ's baptism, they insisted, is an example which all should emulate. Following the precepts taught by the Savior, the apostles baptized only those who had faith and only performed the ordinance by immersion. "The apostolic churches," they added, "consisted only of baptized believers, or of such who were baptized upon pro-

---

[7]*Ibid.*, 15-18.
[8]*Ibid.*, 24.
[9]*Ibid.*, 26, 29.
[10]Gill, *op. cit.*, 3-4.

fession of their faith." Our critics, Baptists concluded, have failed to provide any scriptural warranty for infant baptism or of a baptism performed by sprinkling.[11]

One of the most perplexing concepts that divided Protestants in the area where Joseph lived was the doctrine of baptismal regeneration. In 1818, William Bacon delivered a sermon in the Presbyterian church of Waterloo which incited many settlers of the Finger Lake country. Individuals who profess that baptism is regeneration, he charged, maintain incorrect opinions. "Baptism is not regeneration," he asserted. "Everyone who knows from experience, what it is to be born again, knows it is not baptism."[12]

In an attempt to clarify the Episcopalian position concerning baptismal regeneration and expose the "misrepresentations" appearing in Bacon's work, Rev. Henry U. Onderdonk published two tracts in Canandaigua in 1818. Regeneration, he explained, means a change of state or character and is a change from being out of to being within the visible church. This change, he continued, "is effected in baptism, and by the Spirit or Holy Ghost; the minister being His agent. . . . Hence Christian baptism consists of two parts; viz: washing done by the minister; and regeneration effected by the Holy Ghost."[13]

Onderdonk made no attempt to define precisely the term "baptismal regeneration," but recited various conflicting theories concerning the meaning of these words. He emphasized that regeneration, when coupled with baptism, might be interpreted in either a figurative or a literal sense. What is important, Onderdonk suggested, is that the term is scriptural. After citing Titus 3:5, the rector insisted that the term "washing of regeneration" was another method of saying baptismal regeneration. Concluding his defense, Onderdonk

---

[11]*Ibid.*, 31-32.

[12]William Bacon, *Regeneration, the New Birth. A Sermon delivered May 10th, 1818, at Waterloo* (Waterloo, 1818), 10-11.

[13]Henry U. Onderdonk, *An Appeal to the Religious Public, in Behalf of the Protestant Episcopal Church, against the Slanders and Sophistry Printed under the name of Rev. W. Bacon* (Canandaigua, 1818), 31.

stated ambiguously that the precise meaning of the phrase was a "mystery; revealed in scripture, but not to be explained by men."[14]

Although immediately prior to the First Vision a heated debate concerning baptismal regeneration was going on in the area where Joseph lived, the war of words did not center on the subject of the necessity of baptism. While Episcopalians were accused of holding to the essential nature of the ordinance, Onderdonk, one of the leading spokesmen of that faith in the area where Joseph lived, refused to be precise in his interpretation of this doctrine. Meanwhile, Calvinist Baptists and Presbyterians living in the Genesee country definitely contended that baptism was not essential, but was a sign of one's regeneration.[15] Also, the Methodists emphasized that baptism was a symbol of the new birth. Even though John Wesley commented that the church supposes that "all who are baptized in their infancy, are at the same time born again" or regenerated, Methodists of the early republic did not teach that baptism was necessary for salvation. It is not to be assumed, Methodists exclaimed, that a person cannot be saved nor regenerated without baptism.[16] Quakers agreed with other Protestants in rejecting the essential nature of that ordinance. In fact, Friends rejected all sacraments, denying that one should be literally baptized by water.[17]

Since some members of the Smith family were "proselyted to the Presbyterian faith" and others, including the Prophet, "became somewhat partial to the Methodist sect," it would appear that immediately prior to the First Vision family discussions might not have concentrated as much on the subject of baptism as on the concept of predestination versus foreordination.[18] While Presbyterians and Methodists agreed that

---

[14]Henry U. Onderdonk, *Baptismal Regeneration: Briefly Defended and Explained* (Canandaigua, 1818), 1-5.

[15]Bacon, *op. cit.,* 9-10.

[16]Wesley, *op. cit.,* 237; Jonathan Crowther, *A True and Complete Portraiture of Methodism* (New York, 1813), 193-94.

[17]Henry Tuke, *The Principles of Religion, as Professed by the Society of Christians, Usually Called Quakers* (New York, 1837), 86.

[18]Pearl of Great Price, 47.

infants were proper subjects for baptism, that sprinkling was
a proper mode for this rite, and that baptism was not essential for salvation, they disagreed sharply concerning man's
role in the salvation experience.

Calvinism vs. Arminianism

Protestants living in the area where the Smith family
resided were divided into two major spectrums of thought,
some being Calvinists and other Arminians. Presbyterians,
Calvinist Baptists, and Congregationalists insisted that man
was totally depraved and that, before the creation of man,
God decreed that a select group, known as the elect, would
inhabit heaven and all non-regenerates would suffer everlasting punishment in hell. They further asserted that only the
elect benefited from the atonement, that a man could not
reject the call when offered by God, and that the elect could
not fall. Meanwhile Arminians, such as the Methodists, Quakers, Freewill Baptists, Eastern Christians, and Episcopalians,
proclaimed that although man inherited the original sin and
was depraved, man was not totally corrupt, for he was given
the free will to accept or reject the gift of salvation. In addition to emphasizing man's role in the salvation experience,
these Protestants averred that man could fall. Therefore, they
concluded that all believers who persevered to the end benefited from the atonement, and asserted that because of God's
foreknowledge he predicted, but did not decree, the final fate
of mankind.

The tone of this controversy was aptly unfolded in one
of the tracts published in western New York in the early
nineteenth century that described a debate which originated
in Palmyra between a Presbyterian minister, Benjamin Bell,
and a Methodist preacher. The vigorous argument centered
on the subject, "Did God from eternity, absolutely and uncon-
ditionally foreordain whatsoever came to pass?" The Presbyterian alleged that since "all things, visible and invisible,
matter and motion, were originally, constantly and entirely
dependent on God," our Father not only decreed the end but

determined "the means to attain the end." This means, the
Calvinist explained, that God offers faith to mankind according to a predetermined decree and thereby provides for the
salvation of all whom he elects.[19]

In response to the Presbyterian position, the Methodist
asserted that God created man as a free moral agent; and
the dogma, he added, that man is absolutely and entirely
dependent on God destroys man's free will.[20]

"God's free agency," Bell charged, "produces our free
agency; that God's working in us, both to will and to do, is
the cause of our working out our salvation with fear and
trembling." "To say that all men" are capable of choosing
salvation for themselves is "to deny man's total moral deprav-
ity" and man's "absolute dependence on God for all we have
and are." Did not Christ say, God's will, not man's will, be
done? (Matt. 26:39.) And did not the Savior also declare,
"No man can come to me, except the Father which hath sent
me draw [elects] him." (John 6:44.)[21]

It is absurd to believe, the Methodist retorted, that God
would "predestinate and bring into existence, all the vile
enormities involved in the conduct of guilty man." Predestination "palms iniquity on God, and excuses guilty man." The
doctrine of unconditional election cannot be reconciled with
the concept of man's free will, he reiterated. Although God
knows the fate of mankind, the Methodist concluded, God has
not determined the final fate of his children. God proffers
grace to all mankind, and men have the God-given gift of
accepting or rejecting this precious pearl.[22]

Innumerable quotations from the Bible were constantly
cited by Presbyterians and Methodists of the early Republic
to support their conflicting beliefs. As men listened to their
debates, some clearly perceived that the Old and New Testa-
ments were susceptible to a variety of interpretations.

---

[19][Benjamin Bell], *Strictures, upon the Doctrine and Discipline, of
the Methodist Episcopal Church* (Utica, 1812), iii-v, viii.
[20]*Ibid.,* 18.
[21]*Ibid.,* viii, 22.
[22]*Ibid.,* 30-31, 74.

The Bible and Modern Revelation

The vehement debates over baptism, predestination, and man's role in the salvation experience merely opened the gates of perennial controversy. While most Protestants of the early Republic insisted that the Bible was the sole norm of faith, the Quakers emphasized that latter-day revelation was the primary source of determining religious truth. Every man and woman, they said, had the capacity of being a prophet and of receiving revelation as did the prophets of antiquity. Writings of biblical prophets, they reasoned, were inferior to current revelation because during the transmission of their works, errors of additions, omissions, and mistranslations were made by incompetent and unreliable scribes.[23]

One of the major problems encountered by Quakers was that of determining who among their members and leaders received inspiration from God and who were deceived by Satan. Since Friends claimed that everyone had the capacity of being a prophet and since men and women received conflicting messages, the problem of determining religious truth was not resolved. Some insisted that the founder of this faith, George Fox, proclaimed the word of God and that Robert Barclay, an early convert, had incorporated these truths in his *Apology*. Therefore, Barclay's popular treatise was regarded by many Quakers as a correct expression of faith, and Friends living in the area where Joseph resided accepted the basic tenets located in Barclay's defense of Quakerism. But this work too, proved unsatisfactory in resolving the theological issues which erupted. In 1828, the Quakers were rocked with a debilitating schism. As in other parts of the new nation, members of the four congregations in the area where the Smiths lived divided into the Orthodox and Hicksites. This, and other such divisions, severely impeded the growth of Quakerism in the nineteenth century.[24]

---

[23]Robert Barclay, *An Apology for the True Christian Divinity* (London, 1736), 5, 26, 80-83. Many editions of this work were published in early America. See also Tuke, *op. cit.,* 22, 34.

[24]Farmington Monthly Meetings, 1831-1843, Vol. 48, 77.

Eternal Punishment vs. Universal Salvation

Men of that age also engaged in debates concerning life beyond the grave. While many preached the literalness of hell, others contended that hell was a condition and not a place; but most concluded that all unregenerated or non-converted souls would suffer some kind of everlasting punishment in hell. The Universalists, however, were the principal opponents of the traditional view of damnation, proclaiming that eventually or immediately after death all men would be saved and enter heaven. Through the power of God, they declared, every knee would bow and everyone confess that Jesus is the Christ. Therefore, they concluded, as in Adam all die, even so in Christ would all be made alive — meaning, in their opinion, that all would enter the kingdom of God.[25]

Trinitarianism vs. Arianism

Although most of the Protestants living near the Smith farm endorsed creeds which specified that God was three persons of one essence, during the years immediately preceding the First Vision the Nicean view was attacked by David Millard, the minister who organized an Eastern Christian church in West Bloomfield. After Millard initiated a crusade against the traditional Protestant and Catholic concept of God, a Presbyterian minister denounced Millard's conviction, declaring that the unorthodox preacher was denying the divinity of Christ. Consequently, in 1818, Millard published in Canandaigua an apology concerning his concept of Deity, entitled *The True Messiah Exalted.*[26] Launching his attack, Millard announced that there was no scripture which stated that God was three persons of one essence. There are, however, he said, innumerable references informing us of the separate nature of the Father and the Son. In defense of this position, he cited the fact that Christ prayed to his Father, came forth from

---

[25]Elhanan Winchester, *Lectures on the Prophecies* (Ballston Spa., New York, 1811), 10-11, 27-30, 76-78.

[26]David Millard, *The True Messiah Exalted, or Jesus Christ Really the Son of God, Vindicated; in Three Letters to a Presbyterian Minister* (Canandaigua, 1818), 5-6.

FIG. 15. DAVID MILLARD

Minister of the Eastern Christian Church of West Bloomfield at the
time of the First Vision.

the Father, and did not know the date of his Second Coming, as did the Father. "The whole tenor of scripture," he asserted, "concurs in the testimony, that Christ is verily the Son of God, as really so as Isaac is the son of Abram."[27]

Millard further declared that it was not only unscriptural to believe in the Nicean God concept but that it was unreasonable to hold to this view. "Three Gods are not one God, any more than three times one are one," he stated, "or two and one are one: which not only destroyes the rules of multiplication and addition, but is flat inconsistency."[28]

The controversial restorationist theologian further insisted that God is a spirit, meaning an immaterial being, and that the Holy Ghost is not a distinct person but an influence of God.[29]

Attitudes Concerning Authority

Another doctrine which precipitated controversy among Protestants of the Genesee country was the concept of authority. Most Protestants, including Presbyterians, Methodists, and Baptists, held that every Christian was a priest, directly encountered God, and received grace directly from God. In their opinion, the authority to teach and baptize was conveyed directly by Christ to the early Christians and had remained with God's true followers since that age. The ministerial office, they taught, was conferred upon incumbents through the congregations (or their representatives). By calling an individual, congregations delegated to the minister the right to exercise the duties of his office. The rite of ordination was considered a public acknowledgement of the call.

Two denominations, the Friends and Episcopalians, rejected the popular Protestant concept of a priesthood of believers. Since Quakers did not believe in any ordinances, they did not recognize any need for special authority; and Episcopalians insisted that only bishops possessed the power

27 *Ibid.*, 14-20, 26.
28 *Ibid.*, 8.
29 *Ibid.*, 10.

of ordination. This authority, they claimed, had descended in an unbroken line from the apostles and had been preserved by Anglican and Episcopalian bishops.[30]

Other Debatable Issues

In the early nineteenth century, preachers of the Genesee country not only proclaimed conflicting views concerning baptism, man's role in the salvation experience, sources of religious truth, life beyond the grave, the nature of God, and the source of authority, but also taught various beliefs concerning the Lord's Supper, church government, and other subjects. When Reverend William Bacon launched his widely heralded attack on the Episcopalians who had recently organized a congregation in Waterloo, he not only challenged their view concerning baptismal regeneration but criticized their articles of faith and their practice of having sponsors in baptism. Moreover, he asserted that Episcopalians "discouraged and condemned revivals" and were enemies of many doctrines loved by the Presbyterians. He further condemned them for admitting to the Lord's Supper those who had been baptized as infants and who had only to "learn the catecism in order to be confirmed and admitted to the sacramental table." He accused Episcopalians of admitting to the Lord's Supper, drunkards, sabbath-breakers, and profane swearers. One of his most stinging indictments was that Episcopalians observed the Lord's Supper on tables where members had played cards and in rooms where dances had been held. These remarks were qualified in a footnote: "This is not intended," he exclaimed, "as a declaration that Episcopalians actually do dance and play cards where they receive this sacrament. But it is well known that the generality of them insist that there is no evil in these amusements."[31] Nevertheless, the charges had been made; and a field of battle had been formed.

After reading Bacon's controversial work which had been authorized for publication by the presbytery, members of dif-

---

[30]Onderdonk, *An Appeal to the Religious Public,* 59-60.
[31]Bacon, *op. cit.,* 18-20.

ferent denominations living in the Finger Lake country took their pens in hand and returned fire. John Nicholas referred to Bacon's character as "malignant" and said that Presbyterians portrayed the role of a Pharisee who could claim credit for nothing but the boldness of his attempt. This "depraved," "deluded," minister, he added, is perpetuating innumerable "falsehoods" about the Episcopal church.[32]

Meanwhile, David Hudson, who testified that he was not an Episcopalian, responded to Bacon's published sermon by saying that the reverend was "a man of intemperate zeal, prompted by sectarian pride," who with "sophistry and slander" was misleading the minds of men. Hudson further referred to his remarks as "chicken from Satan's egg," and of Bacon's "own hatching."[33]

Another who entered into the controversy was Reverend Orin Clark, rector of the Trinity church at Geneva. Clark considered the sermon extraordinary for "boldness of assertion, grossness of misrepresentation, virulence of abuse, and arrogance in assailing and condemning sentiments which" promote piety. The work, he continued, was a compilation of inconsistencies and errors and "a virulent attempt to excite odium against the Episcopal Church."[34]

After examining Bacon's remarks, Reverend Henry Onderdonk added his indictments against this work:[35]

> That gentleman has so completely over charged his accusations that they fall, self-refuted, to the ground. He has exhibited such egotism, such weakness in his arguments, and saucy boyish incivility in his personal remarks, that his pamphlet is not worthy of the time and labor necessary for an appeal to the public.

---

[32][John Nicholas], *A Letter, Addressed to the Episcopalians, and other Religiously Disposed Persons in Waterloo and its Vicinity* (Geneva, 1818), 3, 6-7.

[33][David Hudson], *A Review of a Sermon, Delivered at Waterloo. May 10, 1818* (Geneva, 1818), 3-5.

[34]Orin Clark, *The Character and Principles of the Protestant Episcopal Church Vindicated; in a Letter Addressed to Rev. W. Bacon* (Geneva, 1818), 3, 7, 27.

[35]Onderdonk, *An Appeal to the Religious Public*, 3.

Although Onderdonk admitted that Bacon's work was not worthy of reply, he published not one but two tracts defending the Episcopalians against the "ludicrous" statements proclaimed by the Presbyterian minister of Waterloo.

Persecution During an Age of Confrontation

During this era of religious discord, a number of Yankee settlers living in the Genesee country experienced the sting of oppression. For a variety of reasons related to theological differences, individuals were socially ostracized, were driven from their homes by irate parents, or were threatened by crowds. James Erwin, for example, stated that after he joined the Methodist society in the 1820's, he was forced from his home in New York by a father who was then serving as a Presbyterian minister. "The Methodists," Erwin recalled, "were looked upon as a deluded and fanatical sect, and their preaching of a *free* and *full* salvation, the witness of the Spirit, and the possibility of a falling from grace, was so unlike the Calvinistic dogmas that they were made the butt of ridicule, and were everywhere evil spoken of." For three-and-a-half years after his conversion, Erwin stated, he "suffered very bitter persecution on account of" his Methodist connection.[36]

Another contemporary of the Prophet who described the "sectarian bigotry" which existed in western New York and other parts of the new nation was David Marks. In July, 1819, the teen-age boy traveled eighteen miles from his father's farm in Junius to attend a conference held in Phelps and during this quarterly meeting was baptized and became a member of the Freewill Baptist society. Less than two years later, early in 1821, the young man declared that he felt an "impulse from Heaven," saying to him, "Go thou and preach the gospel." Convinced that he had received an inward call from God to preach, the sixteen-year-old farm boy, who had attended school for about ten months, left home and commenced telling others about what he called the "pearl of great price."[37]

---

[36]James Erwin, *Reminiscences of Early Circuit Life* (Toledo, Ohio, 1884), 6.

[37]Marilla Marks, ed., *Memoirs of the Life of David Marks* (Dover, N.H., 1846), 17, 25-29.

Although the boy preacher, as he was sometimes called, met no serious opposition in most communities of the Genesee country, there were occasions when David Marks experienced cruel treatment from others. At times he was greeted with "contempt" and was sometimes mocked by others. Some of his most energetic and vicious critics lived in the neighborhood where his family had settled. After returning from one of his first itinerant crusades in 1821, he delivered a series of talks in Junius. "I spent about three weeks" there, David reported, "and met with considerable opposition. My trials were great. . . . One man gave notice that he would provide a handful of whips at my next meeting, and would give a gallon of whisky to anyone that would wear them out on me." Even though the threat to whip the young preacher did not materialize, men continued to circulate "scandalous reports" concerning his character and ridiculed the religion which he espoused.[38]

Another American who reported conditions existing in western New York at the time of the First Vision was William Lewis, one of the agents of a Sunday School society, an organization designed to establish Sabbath schools in the new nation. This agent asserted in 1828 that "ignorance and error prevailed to an alarming extent" in Monroe County and assumed that if he had not traveled in broad daylight to conduct his business, he would have been attacked.[39]

Not only was there contention among members of different denominations, but occasionally vehement debates occurred among members of the same congregation. For instance, in 1822 a controversy concerning whether or not it was proper to share communion with believers of other faiths became such a critical issue in a Calvinist Baptist society of western New York that the minister resigned.[40] Moreover, in the early 1820's the subject of Masonry also became a thorny problem

---

[38]*Ibid.*, 32, 36, 50-51, 56.

[39]William Lewis to Martin Townesend, June 3, 1828, located in the Presbyterian Historical Society, Philadelphia, Pennsylvania.

[40]Benjamin Lane, March 28, 1822, manuscript located in the Syracuse University Library.

among the Methodists. After gathering in Niagara, Methodists of the Genesee Conference agreed, in 1821, that it was improper for members of their faith to attend Masonic meetings. Members were warned that they should shun even the appearance of evil. And traveling preachers, they resolved, who attached themselves or persisted to attend "Lodges" were to be dealt with "as in other cases of imprudent conduct."[41]

A Momentous Decision

The ecclesiastical strife which periodically erupted in that age is further reflected by an event which took place within a few miles of the place where The Church of Jesus Christ of Latter-day Saints was later organized. After the Episcopalian congregation had been formed in Waterloo in 1818, Reverend William Bacon mounted his Presbyterian pulpit and offered the following advice to his congregation:[42]

> The question should not be whether some of the denomination [Episcopalians] are not pious and orthodox but whether the most of them are so; for there are probably some pious people in the most corrupt denomination of christians. Enquire then which denomination comes nearest to what you esteem right doctrine, and in which the most have what you call real religious exercises; and that is the denomination with which you should unite. In this enquiry, take nothing on my declaration. Look for yourselves. I do not wish you to trust my declaration, that the Episcopalian church is corrupt. I only wish you to look and judge for yourselves.

Bacon then counseled his congregation that all he feared was that they would not examine other churches thoroughly. "I beseech you by the mercies of God," he pleaded,[43]

> to be faithful in this respect. Consequences of the utmost importance may rest on your decision. If you

---

[41]Journal of the Genesee Conference, 1810 to 1828, 90, located in the Wyoming Seminary, Kingston, Pennsylvania, microfilm copy located in the Brigham Young University Library.

[42]Bacon, op. cit., 19.

[43]Ibid.

embrace wrong doctrines, and unite with a corrupt church, you may expect coldness and darkness all your lives; and as you will thus build with much hay, wood and stubble, which must be purged away at last, by the purifying flame—though saved, you will be saved so as by fire! and thus will "suffer loss." Besides this you will influence others, perhaps, to embrace the same errors, who will also suffer loss, and in their turn will influence others, until many may be led from the truth, and thereby the cause of religion may suffer immensely through your present decision.

Since Bacon insisted that the two religious societies in Waterloo were so different that they could not live in union, he prayed, "May God direct you to the choice of that which will be best for your own souls, and for the cause of Christ."[44]

Joseph Smith also aptly described the animosity which existed in the Genesee country during an era in which many settlers were engaged in a quest for religious truth. The Prophet wrote:[45]

Notwithstanding the great love which the converts to these different faiths expressed at the time of their conversion, and the great zeal manifested by the respective clergy, who were active in getting up and promoting this extraordinary scene of religious feeling, in order to have everybody converted, as they were pleased to call it, let them join what sect they pleased; yet when the converts began to file off, some to one party and some to another, it was seen that the seemingly good feelings of both the priests and the converts were more pretended than real; for a scene of great confusion and bad feelings ensued—priest contending against priest, and convert against convert; so that all their good feelings one for another, if they ever had any, were entirely lost in a strife of words and a contest about opinions.

It is not surprising that in the midst of this theological confusion, indeed "in the midst of this war of words and

---

[44]*Ibid.*, 20.
[45]Pearl of Great Price, 46-47.

tumult of opinions," Joseph was perplexed. "I often said to myself," Joseph explained, "What is to be done? Who of all these parties are right; or, are they all wrong together? If any one of them be right, which is it, and how shall I know it?"[46]

While Joseph was "laboring under the extreme difficulties caused by the contests of these parties of religionists," he read in the Epistle of James, "If any of you lack wisdom, let him ask of God, that giveth to all men liberally, and upbraideth not; and it shall be given him."[47]

Joseph decided that he lacked wisdom. After seeking, studying, investigating, and learning innumerable conflicting philosophies, the young man determined to seek assistance from another source. Joseph turned to the Father of Light for illumination.

---

[46]*Ibid.*, 47.
[47]*Ibid.*

CHAPTER 5

Recitals of the First Vision

In the spring of 1820, a young man walked from a beautiful grove located in the Genesee country to a small log cabin, entered his home, and leaned against the fireplace. His mother, detecting that something unusual had happened, asked: "What is the matter, Joseph?" "Never mind, mother," the boy replied, "All is well . . . I have learned for myself that Presbyterianism is not true."[1]

Persecution of a Young Prophet

A few days later, Joseph "happened to be in" the company of one of the Methodist preachers who had been an active participant in the "religious excitement" that had commenced, and the fourteen-year-old boy explained to him the events that had occurred in the grove. After hearing the boy's account of his vision, the minister became indignant and treated Joseph's "communication not only lightly, but with great contempt, saying it was all of the devil; that there was no such thing as visions or revelations in these days; that all such things had ceased with the apostles, and that there would never be any more of them." According to Joseph, other "professors of religion" also excited a great deal of "prejudice" against him; and as the months and years passed, persecution increased. It was difficult for young Joseph to understand the reasons for such bitter oppression, for he was an "obscure boy," only between fourteen and fifteen years of age, and his "circumstances in life" were such that under normal conditions

---

[1]Joseph Smith, History of the Church, Note B, 132, LDS Church Historian's Office. See also Appendix C.

he would not have become the subject of such scorn. Yet, individuals "of high standing" took sufficient notice "to excite the public mind against" him.[2]

While the boy could not comprehend the reasons for the opposition and continued to endure persecution, he refused to deny his testimony. It was a fact, he declared unrelentingly, that he had beheld a vision. "I have thought since," he later observed,[3]

> that I felt much like Paul, when he made his defense before King Agrippa, and related the account of the vision he had when he saw a light, and heard a voice; but still there were but few who believed him; some said he was dishonest, others said he was mad; and he was ridiculed and reviled. But all this did not destroy the reality of his vision. He had seen a vision, he knew he had, and all the persecution under heaven could not make it otherwise; and though they should persecute him unto death, yet he knew, and would know to his latest breath, that he had both seen a light and heard a voice speaking unto him, and all the world could not make him think or believe otherwise. So it was with me. I had actually seen a light, and in the midst of that light, I saw two Personages, and they did in reality speak to me; and though I was hated and persecuted for saying that I had seen a vision, yet it was true.

In the midst of oppression, Joseph continued to ask,

> Why persecute me for telling the truth? . . . Or why does the world think to make me deny what I have actually seen? For I had seen a vision; I knew it, and I knew that God knew it, and I could not deny it, neither dared I do it.

---

[2]Lucy Mack Smith, *History of Joseph Smith* (Salt Lake City: Bookcraft, 1958), 72-73; Joseph Smith, "History of Joseph Smith," *Times and Seasons* (Nauvoo), April 1, 1842, 748-49.

[3]The Pearl of Great Price (Salt Lake City: Church of Jesus Christ of Latter-day Saints, 1952), 49-50. See also Lucy Mack Smith, *op. cit.,* 72-74; Joseph Smith "History," *Times and Seasons,* April 1, 1842, 748-49.

Since Joseph was persecuted for telling others of his vision, the young man was cautious concerning who should be informed of this event. It was a most sacred experience; and consequently the lad probably instructed his family not to publicize it at that time. A few years later, after Joseph had been visited by an angelic messenger and learned the location of an ancient religious history, he instructed his family that they should not mention to others that which he unfolded to them. The world is so wicked, Joseph explained, that when others come to a "knowledge of these things" some will "try to take our lives." The seventeen-year-old further predicted that he and other members of the family would be regarded as "evil" individuals by people throughout the world. Hence Joseph advised that there was a "necessity of suppressing these things as much as possible, until the time should come for them to go forth to the world."[4]

Evidence of Oppression

The fact that Joseph and his family endured bitter persecution in the 1820's is evident not only from the writings of members of the Smith family but also from various non-Mormon sources. Lucy Smith recorded in her biography of the Prophet that when Joseph was fourteen he was returning home from an errand and as he passed through the dooryard, someone fired across his path, with the "evident intention" of killing the boy. Joseph sprang to the door, she added, much frightened. "We immediately went in search of the assassin, but could find no trace of him that evening," Lucy continued. "The next morning we found his tracks under a wagon where he lay when he fired, and the following day we found the balls which were discharged from the gun, lodged in the head and neck of a cow that was standing opposite the wagon in a dark corner."[5]

After the death of Joseph's brother, Alvin, who died November 19, 1823, someone circulated the rumor that Alvin's

---

[4]Lucy Mack Smith, *op. cit.*, 82.
[5]*Ibid.*, 67-68.

body had been "removed from the place of his interment and dissected." In an attempt to ascertain the truth of this report, Joseph Smith, Sr., along with neighbors gathered at the grave, removed the earth, and found the body undisturbed. To correct the fabrication, designed in the opinion of Joseph's father to injure the reputation of the Smith family, Joseph, Sr., placed in the *Wayne Sentinel* (which appeared on successive Wednesdays from September 30 to November 3, 1824) a public notice reciting his findings that the body was undisturbed.

Upon learning of Joseph's visions, settlers in Palmyra and vicinity branded the Prophet's testimony as a lie and a vicious falsehood. In derision, the myth-makers labeled Joseph as a visionary boy and circulated the rumor that Joseph was "lazy," "illiterate," "superstitious," "disorderly," "a drunkard," "an imposter," and "addicted to vice and the grossest immoralities."[6] Individuals spread flagrantly exaggerated statements such as "not one of the male members of the Smith family were entitled to any credit whatsoever,"[7] that Joseph and his father were "entirely destitute of moral character and addicted to vicious habits;"[8] and that "digging for money was their principal employment."[9]

In one of the most frequently cited non-Mormon accounts, a contemporary of the Smith family, Orsamus Turner, referred to the "elder Smith" as a "great babbler, credulous, not especially industrious, a money digger, prone to the marvellous; and withal, a little given to difficulties with neighbors, and petty law-suits." Lucy Smith was branded by this author as "a woman of strong uncultivated intellect; artful and cunning; imbued with an illy regulated religious enthusiasm." And "Jo. Smith" was judged as "lounging, idle; (not to say vicious,) and possessed of less than ordinary intellect." While summarizing his impressions of the Smith family, this same contemporary assumed that the "primitive designs of Mrs. Smith, her husband, Jo and Cowdery, was money making; blended

[6]E. D. Howe, *Mormonism Unvailed* (Painesville, 1834), 249, 259.
[7]*Ibid.*, 248.
[8]*Ibid.*, 261.
[9]*Ibid.*, 248-49.

with which perhaps, was a desire for notoriety, to be obtained by a cheat and a fraud."[10]

Analysis of the Charges

It is not surprising that during an era of theological warfare, when men were engaged in vehement debates and were misrepresenting others' characters and beliefs, suspicious, sensitive critics reacted to Joseph's testimony by manufacturing a variety of preposterous myths. Contemporaries of Joseph, especially individuals living in the area where he resided, created stories which were compounded as they were embellished by a second and third generation of critics. As with many other prophets, Joseph Smith was "not without honour, save in his own country." (Matt. 13:57.)

From an examination of the various primary sources available, it is evident that most of the men who circulated tales about Joseph and his family were but casual acquaintances of the Smiths. Many of the derogatory character references were gathered by D. P. Hurlbut, who was excommunicated from the Restored Church for immorality and traveled throughout the town of Palmyra in the early 1830's gathering disparaging statements about the Smith family.[11] Although those who purportedly signed affidavits, many of which Hurlbut evidently wrote, constituted a very small percentage of the settlers in Palmyra, it is questionable whether any one of these men could be classified as an authority on the character of members of the Smith family. During most of their residence in western New York, the Smiths lived in a sparsely settled section of the Genesee country. While they periodically traveled to Palmyra village, most inhabitants probably gained an acquaintance with the family by seeing them travel to town or observing the brothers secure supplies from one

---

[10]O. Turner, *History of the Pioneer Settlement of Phelps and Gorham's Purchase, and Morris' Reserve* (Rochester, 1852), 213-14.

[11]Joseph Smith, *History of the Church of Jesus Christ of Latter-day Saints,* ed. B. H. Roberts (2d ed. rev.; Salt Lake City: Deseret Book Co., 1959-60), I, 355, hereafter cited as *DHC*. Hurlbut also spelled his name Hurlburt but preferred the spelling used in the text.

of the local merchants. After Joseph announced his experience in the grove, in all probability the number who could be classified as intimate friends or acquaintances diminished; and many who met the Prophet after 1820 had previously formulated opinions concerning his character based on false rumors that had been circulated. The affidavits gathered by Hurlbut, therefore, serve as evidence of the "evil" stories which were circulated about the Smiths rather than as reliable assessments of their character. Neither is there evidence that Orsamus Turner was in a position to become a competent witness of the character or intentions of the Smith family.[12]

A legalistic investigation of the accusations made by settlers living in Palmyra further reflects the inconsistencies of their sworn statements. In nearly every instance the accusations were vague and were not documented with essential details or specific examples. For example, while Joseph and other members of his family were called liars and frauds, the critics failed to substantiate their charges with any proof. They relied on hearsay evidence or, on occasion, assumed he was a fraud because Joseph informed them of his visions. Joseph was also accused of being immoral, but again the muckrakers failed to cite facts which would satisfy a reasonable, objective appraisal. Such a charge conflicts with the teachings reflected in a work which was published under Joseph's jurisdiction, the Book of Mormon. This ancient scripture clearly identifies adultery and fornication as among the most serious sins which men and women can commit — "Yea, most abominable above all sins save it be the shedding of innocent blood or denying the Holy Ghost." (Alma 39:5.) Furthermore Orsamus Turner, who charged that Joseph was lazy and was possessed of less than ordinary intellect, contradicts himself by stating that young Joseph, along with other members of the family and possibly Oliver Cowdery, wrote the Book of Mormon.[13]

---

[12]For additional information on this subject see Richard Lloyd Anderson, "Joseph Smith's New York Reputation Reappraised," *BYU Studies,* X (Spring, 1970), 283-314, and Hugh Nibley, *The Myth Makers* (Salt Lake City: Bookcraft, 1961).

[13]Turner, *op. cit.,* 214.

Critics of the Smith family also failed to produce evidence
that Joseph was an alcoholic. It was reported, for example,
in a Michigan newspaper that an acquaintance of Joseph
Smith, a Mr. Bryant, had declared that this young man was
"a lazy, drinking fellow, loose in his habits every way." When
a William Bryant was interviewed shortly after this account
was published, he admitted that he had seen "Joe Smith once
or twice," and answered the question, "Were they (the Smiths)
drunkards," by replying, "Everybody drank whiskey in them
times," but denied that he had uttered the statement which
had been attributed to him.[14]

During an interview, Ezra Pierce, another of Joseph's
contemporaries, was asked if he knew the Prophet. Although
he was born in 1806, one year after Joseph's birth, and lived
about three miles from the Smith family, Pierce admitted
that he was not very well acquainted with these people, but
could recognize members of the family. "Did young Joe Smith
drink?" he was asked. "Everybody drank in them times,"
was the response. After admitting that he had never seen
Joseph inebriated, he reminisced that "it was customary in
those days for everybody to drink, more or less. They would
have it at huskings, and in the harvest field, and places of
gathering."[15]

One of the most absurd stories gathered and circulated
by Hurlbut was one purportedly related by William Stafford,
who lived about a mile from the Smith residence. According
to this story, Joseph had discovered a valuable treasure which
could be procured in only one way. A black sheep was to be
taken to where the treasure was concealed, its throat was
to be cut and, while bleeding, the animal was to be led around
in a circle. After this action was taken the supposed wrath
of an evil spirit would be appeased and the treasure could be
obtained. According to this myth, Stafford gave Joseph a

---

[14]Wm. H. Kelley, "The Hill Cumorah, and the Book of Mormon . . .
from late interviews," *The Saints Herald* (Plano, Illinois), June 1, 1881,
162.

[15]*Ibid.*, 163.

sheep, but later learned that the animal was killed, but the death did not "have the desired effect."[16]

When the physician son of William Stafford, Dr. John Stafford, was interviewed in his retirement in Rochester, he was asked about the "black sheep" story. Since John was about the same age as Joseph and was in a position to know whether or not the incident occurred, or at least to know if such a story was being circulated by his father, his reply is revealing. "I don't think it is true," Dr. Stafford said, "for I would have heard more about it." He further stated, "I have heard that story but don't think my father was there at the time they say Smith got the sheep" from him. "I don't know anything about it."[17]

Another contemporary who refuted some of the remarks perpetuated by the enemies of the Prophet, Thomas H. Taylor of Manchester, was asked, "What did the Smiths do that the people abused them so?" "They did not do anything," he observed.[18]

> Why! these rascals at one time took Joseph Smith and ducked him in the pond that you see over there, just because he preached what he believed and for nothing else. And if Jesus Christ had been there, they would have done the same to him. Now I don't believe like he did; but every man has a right to his religious opinions, and to advocate his views, too; if people don't like it, let them come out and meet him on the stand, and show his error. Smith was always ready to exchange views with the best men they had.

Orlando Saunders, who also lived in the neighborhood where Joseph resided, declared:[19]

> Yes, sir; I knew all the Smith family well; there were six boys; Alvin, Hyrum, Joseph, Harrison, William, and Carlos, and there were two girls; the old man was a

---

[16]Howe, *op. cit.*, 239.
[17]Kelley, *op. cit.*, 167.
[18]*Ibid.*, 163.
[19]*Ibid.*, 165.

cooper; they have all worked for me many a day; they
were very good people; Young Joe, (as we called him
then), has worked for me, and he was a good worker;
they all were. I did not consider them good managers
about business, but they were poor people; the old man
had a large family.

While many people continued to circulate the story that
the principal occupation of the Smiths was money-digging, the
accusers failed to assert that they witnessed the family continually engaging in this economic pursuit. One man suggested that evidence of their activity was found in the fact
that there were holes in the ground, and another who insisted
that this was their general employment said that he "always
declined being one of their number."[20] This accusation, like
many others, was not based on what people saw but what
they heard.

If the belittling statements by men who supposedly were
acquainted with the Smith family were correct, and if members of the family had been liars, immoral, and "addicted to
vicious habits," Lucy, Hyrum and Samuel would have been
unable to retain their membership in the Western Presbyterian Church until 1830. In that era excommunications were
frequent in most congregations, including the Presbyterian
society of Palmyra. Individuals judged guilty of immorality,
profanity, lying, drunkenness, gambling, and other such sins
were excommunicated from this society.[21] The reason members of the Smith family were dismissed from the Lord's Supper in the spring of 1830 was not because of any of the above
charges but only because they desired to withdraw their membership and had neglected to attend church for a year and
a half.[22]

Joseph Smith was not the only religious leader living in
western New York whose character was assailed by the circulation of vicious lies. The biographer of Jemima Wilkinson,

---

[20]*Ibid.*, 166; Howe, *op. cit.*, 232.
[21]Session Records, Western Presbyterian Church, II, 34, 36, 39, 42.
[22]*Ibid.*, 11-13. See Appendix K.

Herbert A. Wisbey, Jr., concluded in his life of the Public Universal Friend that "derogatory stories" were "circulated about Jemima Wilkinson," causing "her followers and their descendants to develop a hypersensitivity about" this woman. Although attempts were made "to correct" the rumors which had been formulated, Wisbey added that "the legendary anecdotes" were "much more entertaining than the actual facts." Consequently, fictitious accounts continued to be "circulated unchecked, acquiring new details as they were told and retold," sustaining the popular rumor that the Universal Friend was "a shrewd, unscrupulous imposter whose tricks won her fleeting notoriety but whose false pretentions ultimately brought on her downfall."[23]

As in the case of Jemima Wilkinson, innumerable imaginary tales were perpetuated about Joseph Smith. But the men and women who followed the Prophet from New York and lived near this resolute leader in Ohio, Missouri, and Illinois were in a much better position to judge his character than those who had only a casual acquaintance with Joseph while he resided on a farm located adjacent to the border dividing the towns of Palmyra and Manchester. Innumerable character references published by the men and women who knew Joseph best (samples of which appear in chapter 6) provide evidence that countless lies were created by the mythmakers who defamed the Prophet, as enunciated in Joseph's history of the Church.

Unfolding of Joseph's Testimony

While Joseph, particularly in the early years, was careful about who he told of his experience in the grove, he periodically informed others of this vision. In addition to unfolding the event of 1820 to his mother, a Methodist preacher, and a few other inhabitants of the Genesee country, Joseph occasionally informed Church members and nonmembers of his experience in the sacred grove. Many who heard Joseph bear his testimony recorded that which he related to them. Three of the

---

[23]Herbert A. Wisbey, Jr., *Pioneer Prophetess* (Ithaca: Cornell University Press, 1964), 181-82.

recorders, Frederick G. Williams, Warren Cowdery, and James Mulholland, were scribes hired by the Prophet and wrote that which was dictated to them by Joseph. Other accounts were written by individuals after they had listened to the Prophet testify of his experience. For example, Orson Pratt, one of the early converts to the Church, wrote the first account of Joseph's initial communication with God that was published, his tract being printed in Edinburgh in 1840 and in New York in 1841. In 1842, Orson Hyde published in Frankfurt, Germany, an account of the early history of the Church including the visitation of "two glorious personages" to Joseph Smith. The editor of the *Pittsburgh Gazette* also published a brief description of this vision after interviewing the Mormon Prophet in Illinois; and Alexander Neibaur, Edward Stevenson, John Taylor, and other contemporaries of the Prophet testified that Joseph informed them of his initial communication with God.[24]

While non-Mormon newspapers of 1830 and later make references to Joseph's claim that he had been visited by God, the earliest recorded recital of the First Vision that has been preserved and explains the event in some detail was dictated by Joseph to his scribe, Frederick G. Williams, between July 20, 1832 and November of that year.[25] Prior to that date, Joseph had been engaged in many other projects. In addition

---

[24]Orson Pratt, *An Interesting Account of Several Remarkable Visions* (Edinburgh, 1840), See Appendix E; Orson Hyde, *A Cry From the Wilderness, A Voice From the Dust of the Earth* (Frankfurt, Germany, 1842), see Appendix F; *New York Spectator,* September 23, 1843, see Appendix G; Alexander Neibaur, Journal, May 24, 1844, LDS Church Historian's Office, see Appendix H; Edward Stevenson, "The Life and History, Elder Edward Stevenson," 19-23, LDS Church Historian's Office; Edward Stevenson, *Reminiscences of Joseph, The Prophet, and the Coming Forth of the Book of Mormon* (Salt Lake City, 1893), 4, see Appendix I; and John Irvine, reporter, *Journal of Discourses,* XXI (London, 1881), 161-63, see Appendix J. For an analysis of the recitals of the First Vision, see Paul R. Cheesman, "An Analysis of the Accounts Relating Joseph Smith's Early Visions," (Master's thesis, Brigham Young University, 1965); Dean C. Jessee, "The Early Accounts of Joseph Smith's First Vision," *BYU Studies,* IX (Spring, 1969), 275-94; and James B. Allen, "Eight Contemporary Accounts of Joseph Smith's First Vision," *The Improvement Era* (April, 1970), 4-13.

[25]Frederick G. Williams, Papers, LDS Church Historian's Office; Jessee, *op. cit.,* 277-78.

FIG. 16. CONTEMPORARIES OF JOSEPH SMITH WHO RECORDED
OR RELATED ACCOUNTS OF THE FIRST VISION

A. Frederick G. Williams   C. Orson Hyde
B. Orson Pratt   D. President John Taylor

to preparing himself to translate the Book of Mormon and working on the translation of this early American religious history, the Prophet had traveled frequently between Harmony, Pennsylvania (where he moved after his marriage) and the Finger Lake country; had organized The Church of Jesus Christ of Latter-day Saints; had established branches of the Church; had moved the headquarters of the Church from New York to Kirtland, Ohio; had initiated a second gathering of the saints in Independence, Missouri; and had begun an inspired revision of the Bible. Also, prior to 1832, Joseph had appointed Oliver Cowdery and then John Whitmer to serve as Church Historian, but these men were not qualified to write a comprehensive history of the events which had occurred in the life of Joseph Smith. Only the Prophet could accurately describe the many significant developments which had occurred. Recognizing the priceless value of an accurate history, Joseph commenced preparing his history.

Recital of 1832

This account of 1832 was recorded as a rough draft, the style was not polished, nor was it published by the Prophet. It is possible that after dictating the account, Joseph recognized the desirability of modifying certain statements or correcting concepts not accurately written by an untrained scribe. Often when people record biographical sketches or historical incidents, they write and rewrite until their ideas are clearly expressed.

Although this account of 1832 is not as well written nor as comprehensive as later recitals, Joseph revealed one concept in this version which sheds some light on the historical setting of the First Vision. Since the Prophet stated that for two or three years he had been engaged in a quest for religious truth, it is apparent that his search for God's true church was not a sudden impulse. During his investigation, he became confused. There were occasions when he reflected on the possibility that an apostasy had occurred and that "there was no society or denomination that built upon the Gospel of Jesus Christ as recorded in the New Testament." Nevertheless, the young man continued to examine the religious societies constituted in the place where he lived and possibly desired to learn what Christians in other parts of the world believed.[26] In a later recital, the Prophet indicated his bewilderment when he said, "Who of all these parties are right? Or are they all wrong together? And if any one of them be right which is it? And how shall I know it?"[27]

An 1835 Account

The shortest known recital of the First Vision which was dictated by Joseph to a scribe occurred in 1835. This account, recorded by Warren Cowdery, was included as part of a conversation between Joseph Smith and Robert Matthias, who had adopted the priestly name of Joshua. Joseph explained his first communication to this visitor. After mentioning that a personage appeared in the midst of a pillar of fire, he said that another personage soon appeared like unto the first and informed Joseph that his sins had been forgiven. Then Joseph said, according to this account, "I saw many angels in this vision."[28]

Recital of 1838

The most comprehensive account of the First Vision was prepared for publication as part of Joseph's multi-volume *History of the Church* and was originally dictated by the Prophet in 1838. This recital was undoubtedly carefully recorded and might have undergone several revisions to improve the style and wording. The version of this account which has been preserved is in the handwriting of James Mulholland, who served as scribe for the Prophet in 1839, indicating that the recital was rewritten after its initial recording.[29]

---

[26]Joseph Smith, "Kirtland Letter Book," 1829-1835, 1-6, LDS Church Historian's Office. A Copy of the Recital of 1832 is found in Appendix A.

[27]Joseph Smith, "History," *Times and Seasons,* March 14, 1842, 727.

[28]Jessee, *op. cit.,* 283; Joseph Smith, "History," A-1, 120-22, LDS Church Historian's Office. See Appendix B.

[29]Jessee, *op. cit.,* 286-87. See Appendix C.

The Wentworth Letter

A second account which was prepared for publication was written for nonmembers of the Church in 1841. At the request of John Wentworth, editor of the *Chicago Democrat,* Joseph was asked to prepare a brief history of the church which he had founded. Joseph complied, and added to the history thirteen unnumbered statements of belief which are widely known today as the Articles of Faith.[30]

TRUTHS REVEALED IN 1820

In only one of the known accounts which resulted from Joseph's dictating to a scribe did the Prophet identify the two personages who appeared to him. In the 1832 recital the Prophet had mentioned one of the beings as Jesus Christ; and then in the 1838 version, Joseph informed us that the Father and Son appeared to him by stating that one personage pointed to the other and said, "This is My Beloved Son. Hear Him!" This 1838 account was also the only recital in which Joseph described the religious excitement which commenced in the place where he lived immediately prior to the First Vision. It was originally written, Joseph said, to correct the "many reports" which had been circulated "by evil-disposed and designing persons, in relation to the rise and progress of the Church of Jesus Christ of Latter-day Saints." Since this account was also the most complete description of what took place in the sacred grove, we can learn from this history many of the truths which were unfolded to the fourteen-year-old boy during his first direct communication with God. Let us examine this history as originally published in the *Times and Seasons* (Nauvoo) in March and April, 1842.[31]

It was on the morning of a beautiful clear day, early in the spring of eighteen hundred and twenty. It was the first time in my life that I had made such an attempt,

---

[30]Joseph Smith, "Church History," *Times and Seasons,* March 1, 1842, 706.

[31]See Appendix C for a copy of this account as it appears in Joseph's Manuscript history.

for amidst all my anxieties I had never as yet made the attempt to pray vocally.

After I had retired into the place where I had previously designed to go, having looked around me and finding myself alone, I kneeled down and began to offer up the desires of my heart to God. I had scarcely done so when immediately I was seized upon by some power which entirely overcome me, and had such astonishing influence over me as to bind my tongue so that I could not speak. Thick darkness gathered around me and it seemed to me for a time as if I were doomed to sudden destruction. But exerting all my powers to call upon God to deliver me out of the power of this enemy which had seized upon me, and at the very moment when I was ready to sink into despair and abandon myself to destruction, not to an imaginary ruin, but to the power of some actual being from the unseen world who had such a marvelous power as I had never before felt in any being. Just at this moment of great alarm, I saw a pillar of light exactly over my head, above the brightness of the sun; which descended gradually until it fell upon me. It no sooner appeared than I found myself delivered from the enemy which held me bound. When the light rested upon me I saw two personages (whose brightness and glory defy all description) standing above me in the air. One of them spake unto me, calling me by name, and said, (pointing to the other.) "This is my beloved Son, hear him."

My object in going to enquire of the Lord was to know which of all the sects was right that I might know which to join. No sooner therefore did I get possession of myself, so as to be able to speak, than I asked the personages who stood above me in the light, which of all the sects was right, (for at this time it had never entered into my heart that all were wrong,) and which I should join. I was answered that I must join none of them, for they were all wrong, and the personage who addressed me said that all their creeds were an abomination in his sight; that those professors were all corrupt, "they draw near to me with their lips, but their hearts are far from me; they teach for doctrine the commandments of men, having a form of godliness, but they deny the power thereof." He again forbade me to join with any of them: and many other things did he say unto me which I cannot write at this time. When I came to myself again I found myself lying on my back, looking up into heaven.

In contrast to this rather detailed description of the First Vision, the account which was sent to several non-Mormon authors and published in their religious works was very concise. In the account of 1841, which was originally published on March 1, 1842, two weeks before the 1838 version initially appeared in print, Joseph testified:[32]

I retired to a secret place in a grove and began to call upon the Lord, while fervently engaged in supplication my mind was taken away from the objects with which I was surrounded, and I was enwrapped in a heavenly vision and saw two glorious personages who exactly resembled each other in features, and likeness, surrounded with a brilliant light which eclipsed the sun at noon-day. They told me that all religious denominations were believing in incorrect doctrines, and that none of them was acknowledged of God as his church and kingdom. And I was expressly commanded to "go not after them," at the same time receiving a promise that the fulness of the gospel should at some future time be made known unto me.

In this account written for nonmembers, known as the Wentworth letter, Joseph did not identify either of the personages who appeared in the grove and tactfully adopted the expression that all religious denominations were believing in incorrect doctrines, rather than stating that "all their creeds

[32]Joseph Smith, "Church History," *Times and Seasons*, March 1, 1842, 706-07. Joseph's account prepared for nonmembers was published by I. Daniel Rupp, *An Original History of the Religious Denominations at Present Existing in the United States* (Philadelphia, 1844), 404-410 and by John Hayward, *The Book of Religions* (Portland, 1853), 260-66, but Hayward excluded the portion of the history describing the First Vision.

were an abomination in his [the Lord's] sight." One concept included in this recital but not mentioned in the other published
version was that Joseph learned that "at some future time"
the fulness of the everlasting gospel would be revealed to him.[33]

Satan's Power

A review of the various recitals of the First Vision reveals
many of the truths unfolded to Joseph Smith in the spring
of 1820. After kneeling in prayer, the first religious concept
which Joseph learned was that the power of Satan is real
and strong. Joseph said that he was "seized upon by some
power which entirely" overcame him and "had such astonishing influence" as to bind his tongue so that he could not
speak. It seemed to him that he was "doomed to sudden
destruction."

We are living in an era in which many Christians, ministers and laity, are challenging the historical authenticity of
innumerable events included in the New Testament. Among
the traditional Christian beliefs which are currently being
reinterpreted is the reality of Satan and his followers. A poll
was conducted in 1929 by George Herbert Betts, in which
five hundred ministers and two hundred theological students
were asked, "Do you believe that the devil exists as an actual
being?" Thirty percent of the ministers and 91 percent of the
students answered this question, "No" or "Undecided."[34]

Protestants are currently debating the subject of Satan
and his influence, but Joseph experienced the powerful force
of evil, learning that biblical accounts of devils and exorcism
are not romanticisms or legends. The first miracle performed
in the current dispensation of the gospel was the casting out
of an evil spirit from the body of Newel Knight. After recognizing that he had fallen under the influence of the devil,
Newel requested the latter-day Prophet to cast out the power
which was afflicting his body. Joseph responded by saying,

---

[33]*Ibid.*, 707.
[34]George Herbert Betts, *The Beliefs of 700 Ministers* (New York, 1929),
52-56.

"If you know that I can, it shall be done." Then in the name of Jesus Christ, the Prophet rebuked the evil spirit. Immediately Newel cried that he witnessed the entity depart from him and vanish. This early convert became normal, his bodily distortions ceased, and peace was restored to his soul.[35]

God's Transcendent Power and Wisdom

While Joseph discovered that the power of evil is genuine, he further learned in 1820 that the power of God is stronger than that exerted by Satan and his hosts. As Joseph looked into heaven, he witnessed a pillar of light which descended upon him; and "it no sooner appeared" than he found himself "delivered from the enemy which" had seized him. While translating the Book of Mormon, the Prophet learned that in order for man to progress he must have the opportunity of choice, which means that two forces are realities during man's journey through life. "For it must needs be," the Book of Mormon states, "that there is an opposition in all things. If not so ... righteousness could not be brought to pass, neither wickedness, neither holiness nor misery, neither good nor bad."[36] This concept is further expressed in the description of the Fall found in this record, which is a doctrine different from the beliefs included in the creeds of Christendom and the teachings of the various denominations existing in 1820.[37]

> And now, behold, if Adam had not transgressed he would not have fallen, but he would have remained in the garden of Eden. And all things which were created must have remained in the same state in which they were after they were created; and they must have remained forever, and had no end.
>
> And they would have had no children; wherefore they would have remained in a state of innocence, having no joy, for they knew no misery; doing no good, for they knew no sin.

---

[35]*DHC*, I, 82-83.
[36]2 Nephi 2:11.
[37]2 Nephi 2:22-26.

But behold, all things have been done in the wisdom of him who knoweth all things.

Adam fell that men might be; and men are, that they might have joy.

And the Messiah cometh in the fulness of time, that he may redeem the children of men from the fall. And because that they are redeemed from the fall they have become free forever, knowing good from evil.

The Father and Son, Distinct Personages Interested in Mankind

Many important concepts relating to Deity were unfolded to Joseph in 1820. He learned in the sacred grove that God lives, that Jesus is the Christ and the Son of God, that God is interested in his children, that he hears and answers prayers, and intervenes in the affairs of men. He further learned that the Father and Son are separate and distinct personages. In a sermon delivered one year before his martyrdom, Joseph described the Godhead when he declared: "The teachers of the day say that the Father is God, the Son is God, and the Holy Ghost is God, and they are all in one body and one God. . . . If I were to testify," Joseph continued, "that the Christian world were wrong on this point, my testimony would be true. . . . Any person that had seen the heavens opened knows that there are three personages in the heavens who hold the keys of power, and one presides over all."[38] On another occasion, the Prophet asserted that whenever he had spoken on the subject of the Godhead he had taught the plurality of Gods. "It has been preached by the Elders for fifteen years," he added. "I have always declared God to be a distinct personage, Jesus Christ a separate and distinct personage from God the Father, and that the Holy Ghost was a distinct personage and a Spirit; and these three constitute three distinct personages and three Gods."[39]

---

[38]*DHC*, V, 426.
[39]*Ibid.*, VI, 473-74.

A Direct Knowledge of God

When Joseph walked from the sacred grove, he knew more about God than any other mortal. Others were seeking to learn about the Father and Jesus Christ by reflecting upon passages included in the Bible or by studying the works of countless theologians. Joseph's knowledge was not based on his personal interpretation of the scriptures nor his capacity to reason, but was the result of a direct visitation to him by the Father and the Son. Many creedal statements of that age were ambiguous and unintelligible expressions about God which were masked with statements that God was a mystery not to be understood by man. Joseph introduced clarity into this situation with a "sureness of experience." When Joseph emerged from the sacred grove, there was no need for him to argue for a theory — he knew God. His Father appeared in the form like that of a man. He looked upon Joseph, and spoke to him as one man speaks to another. His Son was similar in appearance to the Father and was not one in essence with him. In obedience to his Father's will, Christ also acted as the mediator between God and man. As one of the twentieth century leaders of the Restored Church, Elder Stephen L Richards, aptly explained, "The presumption of God as a mere essence or principle of power and force in the universe was for all time exploded." Joseph's testimony was direct, positive, and irrefutable. "Many have not believed but no one has ever had the knowledge to disprove it."[40]

At some time during the life of the Prophet (we do not know the precise incident) Joseph Smith also learned about the nature of God's physical body. "The Father," Joseph declared in 1843, "has a body of flesh and bones as tangible as man's; the Son also; but the Holy Ghost . . . is a personage of Spirit."[41] This doctrine of God's character was another unique theological contribution of Joseph Smith. The knowledge of a literal creation of man in the image of God does

---

[40]Stephen L Richards, *Contributions of Joseph Smith* (n.p., n.d.), 1.

[41]The Doctrine and Covenants (Salt Lake City: The Church of Jesus Christ of Latter-day Saints, 1952), 130:22; hereafter cited as D&C; *DHC*, V, 325.

not conflict with the biblical statement that God is a spirit. Joseph learned that all spirit is matter, but is more refined than many other forms of matter. He further taught that the resurrected body is a spiritual body, for spirit not blood flows through these beings.[42] In other words, Joseph learned that after his ascension, Christ retained his body of flesh and bones, that the Savior is in the express image of his Father, and that all men will be resurrected like unto Christ's glorious body.

The Need for a Restoration

After asking the Savior which church he should join, the young man learned that the apostasy of Christ's original Church was a reality and that resolute reformers had not succeeded in restoring the fulness of the gospel. This does not mean that Joseph taught that Mormons had a monopoly on truth, for truth is a common right of all mankind. "Have the Presbyterians any truth?" asked Joseph on one occasion. "Yes," he answered. "They all have a little truth mixed with error. We should gather all the good and true principles in the world and treasure them up, or we shall not come out true 'Mormons.' "[43]

It is clear that, while ministers of the early Republic were proclaiming true concepts, they were also preaching incorrect doctrines. The Savior expressed to Joseph in 1820 that the professors of religion taught doctrines which were the "commandments of men, having a form of godliness," but denying "the power thereof." The truth of this assertion is evident from the fact that virtually all ministers of the new nation insisted that visions and revelations had ceased with the death of the apostles, a concept by which they limited the power of God. (Some appeared to believe that with God all things were possible — except his appearing to Joseph Smith.) Moreover, at the time of the First Vision, the priesthood, the power and authority to act in God's name, was not upon the earth. Joseph learned more about God's delegated power on May 15,

---

[42]D&C 131:7; *DHC,* IV, 575.
[43]*DHC,* V, 517.

FIG. 17. RESTORATION OF GOD'S AUTHORITY TO ACT IN HIS NAME
(Photographs of sculptures by Avard Fairbanks)

A. John the Baptist restores the Aaronic Priesthood
B. Peter, James, and John restore the Melchizedek Priesthood

1829, when John the Baptist restored the authority to baptize. Shortly thereafter, Peter, James, and John conferred on Joseph the right to bestow upon others the gift of the Holy Ghost. Joseph expressed in part what he eventually learned concerning this doctrine when he wrote in the Wentworth letter: "We believe that a man must be called of God, by prophecy and by the laying on of hands, by those who are in authority to preach the Gospel and administer in the ordinances thereof." Undoubtedly, one of the most significant contributions of the Prophet was to serve as God's instrument through whom was restored the power and authority to act in God's name.

Restoration of the Fulness of the Gospel

Although there is no way of determining through historical investigation the many "other things" which Joseph said he learned during the First Vision, he was informed that if he remained true and faithful the beauties of the everlasting gospel would be unfolded to him. Following his experience in the sacred grove, Joseph received many other visions and revelations. Principles of the gospel were gradually unfolded to him and were periodically revealed to the world by the latter-day Prophet. Joseph thereby learned many truths which had been lost as a result of the disruption of the Primitive Church. By communicating with an angelic messenger, Joseph learned the location in the Hill Cumorah of an ancient record engraven on golden plates; and through the gift and power of God, the Prophet translated this priceless history. This record contains an account of the visitation of the resurrected Christ to his other sheep living on the American continent and unfolds the teachings conveyed by the Savior and his prophets to America's early inhabitants. After translating this scripture, Joseph published the Book of Mormon, providing mankind with a precise description of the principles of salvation and exaltation.

As a result of receiving the priesthood and many visitations from heavenly beings, of serving as God's instrument in bringing forth the Book of Mormon, and of recording many revelations, the Prophet Joseph succeeded in restoring the fulness of the gospel of Jesus Christ. He learned the answers to the questions: Where did we come from? Why are we here? Where are we going? He learned unique truths, ideas that were not taught by his generation, concerning the Fall and the atonement. He was instructed by heavenly messengers concerning the function of temples, and received revelation concerning marriage for time and all eternity. Through direct communication with God, Joseph also received information concerning the pattern of Church government, and established a Church built upon the foundation of apostles and prophets.[44] Thus the First Vision was the important beginning of the restoration of the everlasting gospel with all its truths, blessings and powers.

Today millions testify that Joseph Smith was the servant called by God to usher in the gospel dispensation of the fulness of times. Following the martyrdom of the Prophet, a fitting tribute was prepared which is now included as part of a work which Latter-day Saints regard as modern scripture:[45]

> Joseph Smith, the Prophet and Seer of the Lord, has done more, save Jesus only, for the salvation of men in this world, than any other man that ever lived in it. In the short space of twenty years, he has brought forth the Book of Mormon, which he translated by the gift and power of God, and has been the means of publishing it on two continents; has sent the fulness of the everlasting gospel, which it contained, to the four quarters of the earth; has brought forth the revelations and commandments which compose this book of Doctrine and Covenants, and many other wise documents and instruc-

---

[44]For additional information on the distinct theological contributions of Joseph Smith, see Milton V. Backman, Jr., *American Religions and the Rise of Mormonism* (2nd ed., Salt Lake City: Deseret Book Co., 1970), 329-50; and Milton V. Backman, Jr., *A Distinct Theology: A Description of Mormon Beliefs in the Light of Other Patterns of Christian Thought* (Salt Lake City: Deseret Book Co., 1968).

[45]D&C 135:3.

tions for the benefit of the children of men; gathered many thousands of the Latter-day Saints, founded a great city, and left a fame and name that cannot be slain. He lived great, and he died great in the eyes of God and his people; and like most of the Lord's anointed in ancient times, has sealed his mission and his works with his own blood.

CHAPTER 6

Witnesses to the Restoration

Professors of Revelation

In the latter half of the eighteenth century, an eccentric woman emerged from a prison in England and announced: "I am Ann the Word. I feel the blood of Christ running through my soul and body." While she had been imprisoned, this woman continued, Christ appeared and commissioned her to preach the everlasting gospel to others. During her life, Mother Ann Lee claimed many other visions and revelations; and selections from her writings were regarded by disciples as the words of God. After migrating to America, this unusual leader founded a religious community, the United Society of Believers in Christ's Second Appearing; and her followers became known as the Shakers or Shaking Quakers.

The Shakers were not the only early Americans who believed that their leader was a spokesman of God. Members of the Jerusalem Community held that Jemima Wilkinson declared the words of God to all mankind; the Rappites believed that their leader, George Rapp, was instructed by God; and converts to the True Inspiration Society or Amana Community declared that their prophet, Christian Metz, was God's instrument in revealing the will of God to mankind. Likewise one of the early leaders of the Seventh-day Adventist faith, Ellen G. White, professed numerous visions and revelations. In fact, present-day custodians of her estate claim that this prophetess received at least two thousand visions.

Since many early Americans claimed latter-day revelations but issued conflicting statements, not all of their instructions could have emanated from God. Christ foresaw the appearance in society of many deceived or deluded individuals and warned the apostles to beware of false prophets. Our Savior, however, did not maintain that all future prophets would be counterfeits. Instead, Christ advised, "By their fruits ye shall know them."[1] He instructed his servants to examine carefully the accomplishments and the tangible effects of the teachings of those claiming latter-day revelations, after which they were to judge whether or not the professed prophet was a spokeman of God.

After reading a brief history of the rise of The Church of Jesus Christ of Latter-day Saints, many earnest seekers have cautiously questioned the testimony recorded by Joseph Smith and have asked, "What evidence exists that support the claims of this religious leader? Many other people have claimed vision and revelations. Not all alleged prophets can be ambassadors of the Lord. In what respects does Joseph Smith's testimony differ from the reports of others who have claimed latter-day revelation?"

DISTINCT EVIDENCES OF A LATTER-DAY PROPHET

There are a number of significant external evidences supporting the claims of Joseph Smith. An example of a distinct type of historical evidence produced by this prophet that has not been duplicated by any other individual claiming latter-day revelation is that an imposing group of witnesses verified the reality of many visions received by the Mormon leader.

Today all people accept as truth many facts which they have not personally observed or proven. Historians, for instance, attempt to reconstruct the past by relying heavily upon the testimonies of others. A task of the historian is to determine events of history by critically analyzing and judging accounts recorded by observers, especially those judged as competent witnesses. When historians locate one, two, or three competent witnesses who describe the same event and do not discover conflicting reports of that incident, they generally conclude that the event occurred. If one placed no

---

[1]Matthew 7:15-20.

faith in the testimonies of others, he would reject nearly all the statements recorded in the histories of mankind. Such a critic could not endorse statements of discovery announced by reputable scholars in scientific fields. Much of what all men believe is based upon testimonies of reliable witnesses.

Four Confirming Witnesses of Joseph's Visions

Joseph Smith occupies a unique position in the annals of religious history in that on six different occasions the Mormon Prophet beheld visions while he was in the company of friends, and these men beheld the same visions Joseph witnessed.

During four of the six visions, Oliver Cowdery was in the company of Joseph Smith. Oliver was present with the Mormon Prophet when John the Baptist restored the lesser priesthood; when Peter, James and John restored the higher priesthood; when an angel showed the Book of Mormon plates to him and his friend David Whitmer; and when Christ, Moses, Elias, and Elijah appeared in a Latter-day Saint temple constructed in Kirtland, Ohio. The heavenly messengers did not appear while the men were unconscious or dreaming, nor did the angels appear in a distant field or high above the ground. On all of these occasions the witnesses stood adjacent to the heavenly personages and listened to distinct messages. While perceiving by the sense of sight and hearing, they experienced, in most instances, the sense of touch. During three of the visions, Joseph and Oliver received special authority from God through the laying on of hands by resurrected beings and felt the hands of angelic messengers. On another occasion, Oliver Cowdery handled the golden plates employed by Joseph to translate the Book of Mormon.

Oliver Cowdery and David Whitmer were not the only men who claimed that they were in the presence of Joseph Smith when an angel appeared and showed them the plates. Martin Harris, a prominent farmer residing in Palmyra, New York, was another adult who witnessed a vision similar to that which Oliver and David beheld. Martin Harris also testified that he saw an angel, that he handled the plates, and that he heard a voice from heaven verifying the correct translation of the sacred record.

A fourth witness of the visions of Joseph Smith was Sidney Rigdon. This former Campbellite minister was present with Joseph when they saw Jesus Christ, standing on the right hand of the Father. These two men also saw "holy angels worshipping God and the Lamb" and learned many truths regarding life beyond the grave.

All of the three witnesses of the plates of the Book of Mormon were excommunicated from the Church. It is evident that they were not willing to abide by all the commandments of God which Latter-day Saints were expected to live. Although they fell into temporary disrepute among the membership of the Church, these witnesses did not deny their testimonies regarding that which they had experienced; and during their estrangement, all bore record of the reality of visions they had beheld in the presence of the Prophet Joseph Smith. Two of the three witnesses, Oliver Cowdery and Martin Harris, repented and returned to the Church, after which they bore additional testimonies.

The testimonies of the witnesses of the visions of Joseph Smith are enhanced by the fact that descriptions of three of the six visions were written and published less than one year after the visions took place. Approximately nine months after the two visions occurred in which they viewed the golden plates, the four participants — Joseph Smith, Oliver Cowdery, David Whitmer, and Martin Harris — published a description of their experience in the first edition of the Book of Mormon. "We declare with words of soberness," the men asserted, "that an angel of God came down from heaven, and he brought and laid before our eyes, that we beheld and saw the plates, and the engravings thereon." They further testified that they knew that the record had been translated by the gift and power of God, for they added: "His voice hath declared it unto us; wherefore we know of a surety that the work is true." Joseph Smith and Sidney Rigdon also published a description

FIG. 18. FOUR WITNESSES OF JOSEPH SMITH'S VISIONS

A. Oliver Cowdery   C. Martin Harris
B. David Whitmer   D. Sidney Rigdon

of their marvelous vision within a few months after the event occurred.[2]

Several accounts of the restoration of the lesser and higher priesthood were written and published less than six years after the events occurred. In an article appearing in a Mormon newspaper, *Messenger and Advocate* (October, 1834), Oliver Cowdery revealed his impressions of the visitation of John the Baptist:[3]

> The voice of the Redeemer spoke peace to us, while the veil was parted and the angel of God came down clothed with glory, and delivered an anxiously looked for message, and the keys of the gospel of repentance! . . . We listened — we gazed — we admired! 'Twas the voice of the angel from glory — 'twas a message from the Most High! . . . Where was room for doubt? Nowhere: uncertainty had fled, doubt had sunk, no more to rise. . . . What joy filled our hearts . . . when we received under his hand the holy priesthood, as he said, "Upon you my fellow servants, in the name of Messiah I confer this priesthood and this authority."

In addition to writing and publishing accounts of the visions which they beheld, the witnesses periodically related to others their memorable experiences and many contemporaries recorded their testimonies. All of the three witnesses of the Book of Mormon plates, for example, were asked repeatedly by earnest investigators if they really saw the angel and the plates, and these men again and again confirmed the statements they had earlier published. During Oliver Cowdery's estrangement from the Church, one of the Mormon pioneers, Reuben Miller, recorded some of the remarks delivered by the former official at a conference held in Council Bluffs, Iowa. According to this report, Oliver said:[4]

---

[2]The Book of Mormon (New York, 1830); *The Evening and Morning Star* (Independence, Missouri), July 1832.

[3]*Messenger and Advocate* (Kirtland, Ohio), October, 1834.

[4]Journal of Reuben Miller, located in LDS Church Historian's Office.

I beheld with my eyes, and handled with my hands the gold plates from which it was translated. I also beheld the Interpreters. That book is true. Sidney Rigdon did not write it. Mr. Spaulding did not write it. I wrote it myself as it fell from the lips of the prophet. . . . I was present with Joseph when a holy angel from God came down from heaven and conferred, or restored the Aaronic priesthood. . . . I was also present with Joseph when the Melchesideck [sic] priesthood was conferred by holy angels of God.

Many years after his excommunication, David Whitmer testified to James H. Moyle that "he saw the plates from which the Book of Mormon was translated, . . . and that he did hear the voice of God declare that the plates were correctly translated."[5] When David Whitmer was asked by another contemporary, Orson Pratt, if he saw the angel when he beheld the plates, David replied: "Yes; he stood before us. Our testimony as recorded in the Book of Mormon is strictly and absolutely true, just as it is there written."[6] And Martin Harris told a young missionary traveling east, "As many of the plates as Joseph Smith translated I handled with my hands, plate after plate."[7] On another occasion this same witness informed a friend: "Yes, I did see the plates on which the Book of Mormon was written: I did see the angel; I did hear the voice of God; and I do know that Joseph Smith is a Prophet of God, holding the keys of the Holy Priesthood."[8]

The three witnesses of the Book of Mormon plates also summoned friends to their bedsides shortly before their death, at which time all three men independently proclaimed a dying testimony to the world. It is clear then that throughout their lives the witnesses conveyed to others accounts verifying the

---

[5]Gordon B. Hinckley, *James Henry Moyle* (Salt Lake City: Deseret Book Co., 1951), 366-67.

[6]Orson Pratt and Joseph F. Smith to John Taylor and the Council of the Twelve, September 17, 1878, quoted in the *Millennial Star,* XL (December, 1878), 769-74.

[7]*Millennial Star,* XXI (August, 1859), 545.

[8]William Homer, "The Passing of Martin Harris," *The Improvement Era,* XXIX (March, 1926), 470-72.

original published versions of the visions they had experienced in the company of the Prophet Joseph Smith.

All the individuals who experienced remarkable manifestations in the presence of Joseph Smith were capable of accurately describing events. They were honest, intelligent persons. It is not surprising that, after these men informed others of their miraculous experiences, skeptics accused the witnesses of malicious lying and attempted to defame their characters. But an examination of descriptions of their characters recorded by many of their closest associates reveals that they were truthworthy individuals. Throughout his life, David Whitmer was regarded by virtually everyone who knew him as an honorable, competent farmer and citizen. Moreover, Oliver Cowdery was a conscientious, candid school teacher who served as a self-supporting missionary and as an unsalaried administrator in the Church he helped organize. During his estrangement, he practiced law; and when he returned to the Church, he sought no position but that of a lay member rendering service to others. Martin Harris was also an unselfish, virtuous citizen. He mortgaged part of his farm to help pay for the publication of the Book of Mormon, and sold his property in New York at the request of Joseph Smith to help the New York saints relocate their homes in Ohio. A number of years later, Martin Harris traveled to the Great Basin. While residing in Utah, he spoke to many individuals and groups. Many members of the Church became acquainted with him during these years, and subsequently several individuals described his character and activities. These accounts substantiate earlier records revealing that Martin Harris was a reliable witness.[9]

---

[9]For additional information on the three witnesses see the Master's theses which have been written on each of these men — Stanley R. Gunn, "Olivery Cowdery: Second Elder of The Church of Jesus Christ of Latter-day Saints," (Master's thesis, Brigham Young University, 1942); Ebbie L. V. Richardson, "David Whitmer, A Witness to the Divine Authenticity of The Book of Mormon," (Master's thesis, Brigham Young University, 1952); and Wayne Cutler Gunnell, "Martin Harris — Witness and Benefactor to The Book of Mormon," (Master's thesis, Brigham Young University, 1955). See also the exceptional series on the witnesses written by Richard L. Anderson, "New Evidence from Modern Witnesses," appearing in *The Improvement Era*, LXXI-LXXII (August, 1968-August, 1969).

The fourth witness of the visions of Joseph Smith was also a man of high moral standards. Before being contacted by Mormon missionaries, Sidney Rigdon labored as an influential Campbellite preacher, organizing many farmers in Ohio into a movement seeking a restoration of the gospel of Jesus Christ. After joining the Church, he served in many capacities of responsibility. His reputation as a scholar and success as a preacher provide evidence that he was another individual who was capable at the time of his vision of accurately reporting what he had experienced.

Eight Additional Witnesses

Another group of witnesses supporting the claims of the Mormon prophet were the eight men who testified that they were shown the plates by Joseph Smith. These men averred that the plates "have the appearance of gold; and as many of the leaves as the said Smith has translated we did handle with our hands; and we also saw the engravings thereon, all of which has the appearance of ancient work, and of curious workmanship." Although no heavenly messenger appeared on this occasion and no voice was heard verifying the correct translation of the record, after this experience all these men were convinced that Joseph Smith was a man called by God to restore the fulness of the gospel. All these men were also reliable witnesses. Although three of the eight were excommunicated from the Church, as were the three witnesses, none of the men denied their testimonies at any time, and periodically the eight men reaffirmed the testimony which they had published in the first edition of the Book of Mormon.

Joseph Smith a Reliable Witness

The most competent witness of the restoration was the man selected by God to restore the everlasting gospel — Joseph Smith. In addition to the testimony of the witnesses of the visions and of the golden plates, one of the strongest external evidences supporting the claims of the latter-day prophet is the Book of Mormon. No other religious leader has claimed that an angel delivered to him valuable records

FIG. 19. THE EIGHT WITNESSES

A sculpture depicting the eight witnesses viewing and handling the plates
from which the Book of Mormon was translated.

and that through the gift and power of God he succeeded in
translating an ancient history. Joseph Smith could not have
been deceived regarding the golden plates. He claimed that the
metallic records were in his possession for nearly two years
and that he translated most or all of the Book of Mormon
during a period of approximately three months.

The Book of Mormon an Evidence of the Restoration

The contents of the Book of Mormon are perhaps the most
powerful and valid witness of the divine calling of Joseph
Smith. This work accurately describes the history of several

cultures transplanted from the Old World to what is known as the New World, and relates the rise and progress of several different American civilizations. Although the limited vocabulary employed in this religious history reveals that the work was not the product of an educated scholar, the proper nouns, the phrases, and sentence structures indicate that this new witness for Christ is a translation from an ancient language. No linguistic mistakes have been detected in this large volume, and many names in the work have been substantiated in recent years as genuine Hebrew and Egyptian words. Many unusual customs described in the record have also been verified in recent years by scholars as correct reflections of the society from which the Book of Mormon civilizations emerged. Even though the plots of the book are complex, there is an internal consistency in the volume — it is void of conflicting incidents.[10] Many Indian beliefs and traditions also support the history described in this record, and archaeologists have located much evidence supporting the Book of Mormon description of a high order of civilization existing in early America. Moreover, the coming forth of the Book of Mormon fulfills a number of biblical prophecies and provides a key revealing clearly the meaning of many scriptures on which religious leaders have offered many conflicting interpretations.[11]

Testimonies of Dependable Contemporaries

Numerous character references recorded by men who were best acquainted with the Prophet and by a number of unbiased non-Mormon contemporaries show that Joseph Smith was a man of integrity. His brother, William Smith, aptly described his impressions of the latter-day Prophet by asserting: [12]

---

[10]Hugh Nibley, "New Approaches to Book of Mormon Study," *The Improvement Era,* LVI-LVII (November, 1953-July, 1954).

[11]Compare Genesis 49:22-26 in the Bible with 2 Nephi 3:3-5 in the Book of Mormon; Isaiah 29:4, 9-11, 13-14 with 2 Nephi 26:1-35; Ezekiel 37:15-20 with 2 Nephi 3:12; and John 10:15-16 with 3 Nephi 15:11-24.

[12]William Smith, Notes on "Chambers' Life of Joseph Smith," 1875, LDS Church Historian's Office; *Deseret News* (Salt Lake City, Utah), January 20, 1894.

Joseph Smith, at the age of seventeen years, with the moral training he had received from strictly pious and religious parents, could not have conceived the idea in his mind of palming off a fabulous story, such as seeing angels, etc. . . .

There was not a single member of the family of sufficient age to know right from wrong but what had implicit confidence in the statements made by my brother Joseph concerning his vision and the knowledge he thereby obtained concerning the plates.

Father and mother believed him; why should not the children? I suppose if he had told crooked stories about other things, we might have doubted his word about the plates, but Joseph was a truthful boy. That father and mother believed his report and suffered persecution for that belief shows that he was truthful.

After James Gordon Bennett, the editor of the New York *Herald*, visited Nauvoo, Illinois, in 1842, and became acquainted with the latter-day Prophet, he concluded that Joseph was "one of the most accomplished and powerful chiefs of the age." This correspondent further wrote a more detailed account of the Mormon leader which was later substantiated by one of Joseph's intimate friends, Helen Mar Whitney, as a "truthful description."[13]

Joseph Smith, the President of the Church, Prophet, Seer, and Revelator, is thirty-six years of age, six feet high in pumps, weighing two hundred and twelve pounds. He is a man of the highest order of talent and great independence of character, firm in his integrity, and devoted to his religion. . . . As a public speaker, he is bold, powerful, and convincing; . . . as a leader, wise and prudent, yet fearless; as a military commander, brave and determined; and, as a citizen, worthy, affable, and kind — bland in his manners, and of noble bearing.

---

[13]*New York Herald,* February 19, 1842; Helen Mar Whitney, "Scenes and Incidents in Nauvoo," *Woman's Exponent,* X (December 1, 1881), 97-98.

Fig. 20. Joseph Smith
From an early painting (about 1842)

Another individual who was well qualified to assess the character of the Prophet Joseph Smith was Orson Pratt. In a sermon delivered in the tabernacle in Salt Lake City on July 10, 1859, Orson Pratt declared: [14]

> I then [1830] became intimately acquainted with the Prophet Joseph Smith, and continued intimately acquainted with him until the day of his death. I had the great privilege, when I was in from my missions, of boarding . . . most of the time at his house, so that I not only knew him as a public teacher, but as a private citizen, as a husband and father. I witnessed his earnest and humble devotions both morning and evening in his family. I heard the words of eternal life flowing from his mouth, nourishing, soothing, and comforting his family, neighbours, and friends. I saw his countenance lighted up as the inspiration of the Holy Ghost rested upon him, dictating the great and most precious revelations now printed for our guide. . . .
>
> And what now is my testimony concerning that man, founded upon my own personal observations? It is the same to-day as it was when I first received the testimony that he was a Prophet. I knew that he was a man of God. It was not a matter of opinion with me, for I received a testimony from the heavens concerning that matter; and without such a testimony it is difficult for us always to judge; for no man can know the things of God but by the Spirit of God.

In addition to possessing qualities of honesty, genuineness, and leadership, Joseph Smith demonstrated many other capabilities possessed by prophets of old. He served as God's instrument in casting out devils and, on many occasions, instantly restoring the sick to normal health. He possessed the gifts of tongues and of the interpretation of tongues and, in the opinion of this writer, uttered more remarkable prophecies that have been fulfilled than any other person in modern history.

---

[14]*Journal of Discourses* (London, 1860), VII, 176-77.

Faith a Gift of God

Although other external evidences might be cited, the fact remains that faith is a combination of conscientious, prayerful investigation on the part of man and a divine influence radiating from God. We read in the Old Testament: "Trust in the Lord with all thine heart; and lean not unto thine own understanding. In all thy ways acknowledge him, and he shall direct thy paths."[15] An early American spokesman of God elaborated on this idea when he issued a challenge to those who desire to gain wisdom and to secure unlimited opportunities in the eternities. This prophet advised,[16]

> When ye shall read these things [the Book of Mormon], . . . I would exhort you that ye would ask God, the Eternal Father, in the name of Christ, if these things are not true; and if ye shall ask with a sincere heart, with real intent, having faith in Christ, he will manifest the truth of it unto you, by the power of the Holy Ghost. And by the power of the Holy Ghost ye may know the truth of all things.

Every year many thousands meet this challenge and receive their personal witness. Every year these thousands joyously link their lives with The Church of Jesus Christ of Latter-day Saints — the divinely restored Church which, with the Book of Mormon and other latter-day miracles, had its beginning in that glorious event of 1820: Joseph Smith's First Vision.

15Proverbs 3:5-6.

16The Book of Mormon (Salt Lake City: The Church of Jesus Christ of Latter-day Saints, 1950), 520.

Appendixes

APPENDIX A

1832 Recital of the First Vision

This 1832 account is the earliest known recital of the First Vision which was dictated by the Prophet Joseph Smith to a scribe and recorded and preserved. The Prophet dictated it to Frederick G. Williams between the summer of 1832 and the end of November of that year, and the handwriting has been identified as Williams' by Dean C. Jessee, a member of the staff at the LDS Church Historian's Office.[1]

A History of the life of Joseph Smith Jr an account of his marvilous experience and of all the mighty acts which he doeth in the name of Jesus Chist the son of the living God of whom he beareth record and also an account of the rise of the church of Christ in the eve of time according as the Lord brought forth and established by his hand firstly he receiving the testamony from on high secondly the ministering of Angels thirdly the reception of the holy Priesthood by the ministring of Aangels to adminster the letter of the Gospel – the Law and commandments as they were given unto him – and the ordinencs, forthly a confirmation and reception of the high Priesthood after the holy order of the son of the living God power and ordinence from on high to preach the Gospel in the administration and demonstration of the spirit the Kees of the Kingdom of God confered upon him and the continuation of the blessings of God to him &c-------- I was born in the town of Charon in the State of Vermont North America on the twenty third day of December A D 1805 of goodly Parents who spared no pains to instructing me in the christian religion at the age of about ten years my Father Joseph Smith Siegnior moved to Palmyra Ontario County in the State of New York

---

[1]*Note*: Errors, deletions and insertions are reproduced in Appendixes A-C as in the original manuscripts.

and being in indigent circumstances were obliged to labour hard
for the Support of a large Family having nine children and as it
required the exertions of all that were able to render any assistance
for the Support of the Family therefore we were deprived of the
bennifit of an education Suffice it to Say I was mearly instructed
in reading ~~and~~ writing and the ground ^{rules} of Arithmatic which
constuted my whole literary acquirements. At about the age of
twelve years my mind became seriously imprest with regard to
the all importent concerns for the wellfare of my immortal Soul
which led me to Searching the Scriptures believeing as I was
taught, that they contained the word of God thus applying myself
to them and my intimate acquaintance with those of differant
denominations led me to marvel excedingly for I discovered
that ^{they did not adorn} ~~instead~~ of ~~adorning~~ their profession by a holy
walk and Godly conversation agreeable to what I found contained
in that Sacred depository this was a grief to my Soul thus from
the age of twelve years to fifteen I pondered many things in my
heart concerning the sittuation of the world of mankind the
contentions and divions the wickeness and abominations and
the darkness which pervaded the ~~of the~~ minds of mankind my
mind become excedingly distressed for I became convicted of
my Sins and by Searching the Scriptures I found that ~~mand~~
^{mankind} did not come unto the Lord but that they had apostatised
from the true and liveing faith and there was no society or
denomination that built upon the Gospel of Jesus Christ as
recorded in the new testament and I felt to mourn for my own
Sins and for the Sins of the world for I learned in the Scriptures
that God was the same yesterday to day and forever that he
was no respecter to persons for he was God for I looked upon
the sun the glorious luminary of the earth and also the moon
rolling in their magesty through the heavens and also the Stars
Shining in their courses and the earth also upon which I stood
and the beast of the field and the fowls of heaven and the fish
of the waters and also man walking forth upon the face of the
earth in magesty and in the Strength of beauty whose power
and intiligence in governing the things which are so exceding
great and marvilous even in the likeness of him who created ~~him~~
^{them} and when I considered upon these things my heart exclaimed
well hath the wise man Said ~~the~~ ^{it is a} fool ^{that} Saith in his heart
there is no God my heart exclained all all these bear testimony
and bespeak an omnipotent and omnipreasant power a being

who makith Laws and decreeeth and bindeth all things in their bounds who filleth Eternity who was and is and will be fron all Eternity to Eternity and when I considered all these things and that ^{that} being Seeketh such to worship him as worship him in spirit and in truth therefore I cried unto the Lord for mercy for there was none else to whom I could go and ~~to~~ obtain mercy and the Lord heard my cry in the wilderness and while in ^{the} attitude of calling upon the Lord ^{in the 16th year of my age2} a pillar of ~~fire~~ light above the brightness of the Sun at noon day come down from above and rested upon me and I was filld with the Spirit of God and the ^{Lord} opened the heavens upon me and I Saw the Lord and he Spake unto me Saying Joseph ^{my} ^{Son} thy Sins are forgiven thee. go thy ^{way} walk in my Statutes and keep my commandments behold I am the Lord of glory I was crucifyed for the world that all those who believe on my name may have Eternal life ^{behold} the world lieth in sin ~~and~~ at this time and none doeth good no not one they have turned asside from the Gospel and keep not ^{my} commandments they draw near to me with their lips while their hearts are far from me and mine anger is kindling against the inhabitants of the earth to visit them acording to this ungodliness and to bring to pass that which ^{hath} been spoken by the mouth of the prophets and Apostles behold and lo I come quickly as it written of me in the cloud ^{clothed} in the glory of my Father and my Soul was filled with love and for many days I could rejoice with great joy and the Lord was with me but could find none that would believe the hevenly vision. . . .

    Nevertheless I fell into transgression and sinned in many things which brought wound upon my Soul and there were many things which transpired that cannot be writen and my Fathers family have suffered many persecutions and afflictions.

---

[2]Although the age recorded in the manuscript appears to be 16 the 6 was not clearly written in the document and might have been written as a 5.

1835 Recital of the First Vision

In 1835 Joseph Smith related his experience in the grove to a visitor to Kirtland, a man named Matthias. This account was recorded by Warren Cowdery.

Monday Nov. 9th. . . While sitting in his house this morning between the hours of ten an eleven a man came in and introduced himself to him calling himself Joshua the Jewish Minister. His appearance was something singular, having a beard about three inches in length which is quite grey, his hair was also long and considerably silvered with age. He had the appearance of a man about 50 or 55 years old. He was tall and straight, slender frame, blue eyes, thin visage, and fair complexion. He wore a green frock coat and pantaloons of the same color. He had on a black fur hat with a narrow brim. When speaking he frequently shuts his eyes and exhibits a kind of scowl upon his countenance. He (Joseph) made some inquiry after his name, but received no definite answer. The conversation soon turned upon the subject of Religion, and after the subject of this narrative had made some remarks concerning the bible, he commenced giving him a relation of the circumstances, connected with the coming forth of the Book of Mormon, which were nearly as follows. Being wrought up in my mind respecting the subject of Religion, and looking at the different systems taught the children of men, I knew not who was right or who was wrong, but considered it of the first importance to me that I should be right, in matters of so much moment, matter involving eternal consequences. Being thus perplexed in mind I retired to the silent grove and there bowed down before the Lord, under a realizing sense (if the bible be true) ask and you shall receive, knock and it shall be opened, seek and you shall find, and again, if any man lack wisdom, let of God who giveth to all men liberally & upbraideth not.

Information was what I most desired at this time, and with a fixed determination to obtain it, I called on the Lord for the first time in the place above stated, or in other words, I made a fruitless attempt to pray My tongue seemed to be swoolen in my mouth, so that I could not utter, I heard a noise behind me like some one walking towards me. I strove again to pray, but could not; the noise of walking seemed to draw nearer, I sprang upon my feet and looked round, but saw no person or thing that was calculated to produce the noise of walking. I kneeled again, my mouth was opened and my tongue loosed; I called on the Lord in mighty prayer. A pillar of fire appeared above my head; which presently rested down upon me, and filled me with un-speakable joy. A personage appeared in the midst of this pillar of flame, which was spread all around and yet nothing con-sumed. Another personage soon appeared like unto the first: he said unto me thy sins are forgiven thee. He testified also unto me that Jesus Christ is the son of God. I saw many angels in this vision. I was about 14 years old when I received this first communication. . .

1838 Recital of the First Vision

The account of the early history of the Church, including a description of the First Vision, which appears in the Pearl of Great Price was originally dictated by the Prophet Joseph Smith in 1838. The manuscript copy located in the Church Historian's Office is in the hand-writing of James Mulholland, who was Joseph's scribe in 1839.

Owing to the many reports which have been put in circulation by evil disposed and designing persons in relation to the rise and progress of the Church of ^{Jesus Christ of} Latter day Saints, all of which have been designed by the authors thereof to militate against its Character as a Church, and its progress in the world I have been induced to write this history so as to disabuse the publick mind, and put all enquirers after truth into possession of the facts as they have transpired in relation both to myself and the Church as far as I have such facts in possession.

In this history I will present the various events in relation to this Church in truth and righteousness as they have transpired, or as they at present exist, being now the eighth year since the organisation of said Church. I was born in the year of our Lord One thousand Eight hundred and five, on the twenty third day of December, in the town of Sharon, Windsor County, State of Vermont. ^{Note A 131} My father Joseph Smith Senior ^{See note E page 2.} ^{adenda. My Father} left the State of Vermont and moved to Palmyra, Ontario, (now Wayne) County, in the State of New York when I was in my tenth year. or ^{thereabout.}

In about four years after my father's arrival at Palmyra, he moved with his family into Manchester in the same County of Ontario. His family consisting of eleven souls, namely, My Father

Joseph Smith, My Mother Lucy Smith whose name previous to her marriage was Mack, daughter of Solomon Mack, my brothers Alvin (who is now dead) died Nov 19th 1823 in the 25 year of his age Hyrum, Myself, Samuel-Harrison, William, Don Carloss, and my Sisters Sophonia, Cathrine and Lucy. Sometime in the second year after our removal to Manchester, there was in the place where we lived an unusual excitement on the subject of religion. It commenced with the Methodists, but soon became general among all the sects in that region of country, indeed the whole district of Country seemed affected by it and great multitudes united themselves to the different religious parties, which Created no Small stir and division among the people, Some Crying, "Lo here" and some Lo there. Some were contending for the Methodist faith, Some for the Presbyterian, and some for the Baptist, for notwithstanding the great love which the Converts to these different faiths expressed at the time of their conversion, and the great Zeal manifested by the respective Clergy who were active in getting up and promoting this extraordinary scene of religious feeling, in order to have everybody converted as they were pleased to Call it, let them join what sect they pleased. Yet when the Converts began to file off some to one party and some to another, it was seen that the seemingly good feelings of both the Priests and the Converts were more pretended more pretended than real, for a scene of great confusion and bad feeling ensued, Priest contending against priest, and convert against convert So that all their good feelings one for another (if they ever had any) were entirely lost in a strife of words and a contest about opinions.

I was at this time in my fifteenth year. My Fathers family was ere proselyted to the Presbyterian faith and four of them joined that Church, Namely, My Mother Lucy, My Brothers Hyrum, Samuel Harrison, and my Sister Sophonia.

During this time of great excitement my mind was called up to serious reflection and great uneasiness, but though my feelings were deep and often pungent, still I kept myself aloof from all these parties though I attended their several meetings as often as occasion would permit. But in process of time my mind became somewhat partial to the Methodist sect, and I felt some desire to be united with them, but so great was the confusion and strife amongst the different denominations that it was impossible for a person young as I was and so unacquainted with men and things to come to any certain conclusion who was right and who was wrong. My mind at different times was greatly excited for the cry and tumult were so great and incessant. The Presbyterians were most decided against the Baptists and Methodists and used all their powers of either reason or sophistry to prove their errors, or at least to make the people think they were in error. On the other hand the Baptists and the Methodists in their turn were equally Zealous in endeavoring to establish their own tenets and disprove all others.

In the midst of this war of words, and tumult of opinions, I often said to myself, what is to be done? Who of all these parties are right? Or are they all wrong together? And if any one of them be right which is it? And how shall I know it? While I was laboring under the extreme difficulties caused by the contests of these parties of religionists, I was one day reading the Epistle of James, First Chapter and fifth verse which reads, "If any of you lack wisdom, let him ask of God, that giveth to all men liberally and upbraideth not, and it shall be given him. Never did any passage of scripture come with more power to the heart of man that this did at this time to mine. It seemed to enter with great force into every feeling of my heart. I reflected on it again and again, knowing that if any person needed wisdom from God, I did, for how to act I did not know and unless I could get more wisdom than I then had, would never know, for the teachers of religion of the different sects understood the same passage of Scripture so differently as to destroy all confidence in settling the question by an appeal to the Bible. At length I came to the conclusion that I must either remain in darkness and confusion or else I must do as James directs, that is, Ask of God. I at last came to the determination to ask of God, Concluding that if he gave wisdom to them that lacked wisdom, and would give liberally and not upbraid, I might venture. So in accordance with this my determination to ask of God, I retired to the woods to make the attempt. It was on the morning of a beautiful clear day early in the spring of Eighteen hundred and twenty. It was the first time in my life that I had made such an attempt, for amidst all my anxieties I had never as yet made the attempt to pray vocally.

After I had retired into the place where I had previously designed to go, having looked around me and finding myself alone, I kneeled down and began to offer up the desires of my heart to God, I had scarcely done so, when immediately I was seized upon by some power which entirely overcame me and had such astonishing influence over me as to bind my tongue So that I could not speak. Thick darkness gathered around me and it seemed to me for a time as if I were doomed to sudden destruction. But exerting all my powers to call upon God to deliver me out of the power of this enemy which had siezed upon me, and at the very moment when I was ready to sink into despair and abandon myself to destruction, not to an imaginary ruin but to the power of some actual being from the unseen world who had such a marvelous power as I had never before felt in any being. Just at this moment of great alarm I saw a pillar of light exactly over my head above the brightness of the sun, which descended gracefully gradually untill it fell upon me. It no sooner appeared than I found myself delivered from the enemy which held me bound. When the light rested upon me I saw two personages (whose brightness and glory defy all description) standing above me in the air. One of them spake unto me calling me by name and said (pointing to the other) "This is my beloved Son, Hear him." My object in going to enquire of the Lord was to know which of all the sects was right, that I might know which to join. No sooner therefore did I get possession of myself so as to be able to speak, than I asked the personages who stood above me in the light, which of all the sects was right, (for at this time it had never entered into my heart that all were wrong) and which I should join. I was answered that I must join none of them, for they were all wrong, and the Personage who addressed me said that all their Creeds were an abomination in his sight, that those professors were all corrupt, that "they draw near to me with their lips but their hearts are far from me; They teach for doctrines the commandments of men, having a form of Godliness but they deny the power thereof." He again forbade me to join with any of them and many other things did he say unto me which I cannot write at this time. When I came to myself again I found myself lying on my back looking up into Heaven. B Note P 132 Some few days after I had this vision I happened to be in company with one of the Methodist Preachers who was very active in the before mentioned religious excitement and conversing with him on the subject of religion I took occasion to give him an account of the vision which I had had. I was greatly surprised at his behavior, he treated my communication not only lightly but with great contempt, Saying it was all of the Devil, that there was no such thing as visions of revelations in these days, that all such things had ceased with the Apostles and that there never would be any more of them. I soon found however that my telling the story had excited a great deal of prejudice against me among professors of religion and was the Cause of great persecution which continued to increase and though I was an obscure boy only between fourteen and fifteen years of age ^{or thereabouts} and my circumstances in life such as to make a boy of no consequence in the world, Yet men of high standing would take notice sufficiently to excite the public mind against me and create a hot persecution, and this was common ^{among} all the Sects: all united to persecute me. It has often caused me serious reflection both then and since, how very strange it was that an obscure boy of a little over fourteen years of age and one too who was doomed to the necessity of obtaining a scanty maintainance by his daily labor should be thought a character of sufficient importance to attract the attention of the great ones of the most popular sects of the day so as to create in them a spirit of the bitterest persecution and reviling. But strange or not, so it was, and was often cause of great sorrow to myself. However it was nevertheless a fact, that I had had a Vision. I have thought since that I felt much like Paul ~~did~~ when he made his defence before King Aggrippa and related the account of the vision he had when he saw a light and heard a voice, but still there were but few who beleived him, Some Said he was dishonest, others said he was mad, and he was ridiculed and reviled, But all this did not destroy the reality of his vision. He had seen a vision he knew he had, and ^{all} the persecution under Heaven could not make it otherwise, and though they should persecute him unto death Yet he knew and would know to his latest breath that he had both seen a light and heard a voice speaking unto him and all the world could not make him think or believe otherwise. So it was with me, I had actualy seen a light and in the midst of that light I saw two personages, and they did in reality speak ^{un} to me, or one of them did, And though I was hated and persecuted for saying that I had seen a vision, Yet it was true and while they were persecuting me reviling me and speaking all manner of evil against me falsely for so saying, I was led to say in my heart why persecute ^{me} for telling the truth? I have actually seen a vision, "and who am I that I can withstand God" or why does the world think to make me deny what I have actually seen, for I had seen a vision, I knew it, and I knew that God knew it, and I could not deny it, neither dare I do it, at least I knew that by so doing I would offend God and come under condemnation. I had now got my mind satisfied so far as the Sectarian world was concerned, that it was not my duty to join with any of them, but continue as I was untill futher directed, for I had found the testimony of James to be true, that a man who lacked wisdom might ask of God, and obtain and not be upbraided. . . .

NOTE A

When I was 5 years old or thereabouts I was attacked with the Typhus Fever, and at one time, during my sickness, my father despaired of my life. The Doctors broke the fever, after which it settled under my shoulder and The Dr. Dr. Parker called it a sprained shoulder and anointed it with bone ointment, and freely applied the hot shovel, when it proved to be a swelling under the arm which opened, and discharged freely, after which the disease removed and descended into my left Leg and ancle and terminated in a fever Sore of the worst kind, and I endured the most acute suffering for a long time under the care of Drs. Smith, Stone and Perkins, of Hanover.

At one time eleven doctors came from Dartmouth Medical College, at Hanover, New Hampshire, for the purpose of amputation, but young as I was, I utterly refused to give my assent to the operation, but I consented to their Trying an experiment by removing a large portion of the bone from my left leg, which they did. & fourteen additional peices of bone afterwards worked out before my leg healed, during which time I was reduced so very low that my mother could carry me with ease. & after I began to get about, I went on crutches till I started for the state of New York where he my father had gone for the purpose of preparing a place for the removal of his family, which he affected by sending a man after us by the name of Caleb Howard, who, after he had got started on the Journey with my mother and family spent the money he had received of my father by drinking and Gambling etc.—We fell in with a family by the name of Gates who were travelling west, and Howard drove me from the waggon and made me travel in my weak state through the snow 40 miles per day for several days, during which time I suffered the most excrutiating weariness and pain, and all this that Mr. Howard might enjoy the Society of two of Mr. Gates Daughters which he took in the waggon where I should have Rode, and thus he continued to do day day [*sic*] after day through the Journey and when my brothers remonstrated with Mr. Howard for his treatment to me, he would knock them down with the but of his whip.—When we arrived at Utica, N. York, Howard threw the goods out of the waggon into the Street and attempted to run away with the Horses and waggon, but my mother seized the horses by the reign, and calling witnesses forbid his taking them away as they were her property. On our way from Utica, I was left to ride on the last Sleigh in the company, (the Gates family were in sleighs) but when that came up I was knocked down by the driver, one of Gate's Sons, and left to wollow in my blood until a stranger came along, picked me up, and carried me to the Town of Palmyra.—Howard having spent all our funds My Mother was compelled to pay our landlords bills from Utica to Palmyra, in bits of cloth, clothing etc., the last payment being made with the drops [earrings] taken from Sister Sophronia's ears for that purpose. Although the snow was generally deep through the country during this Journey we performed the whole on wheels, except the first two days when we were accompanied by my mother's mother, grandmother, Lydia Mack who was injured by the upsetting of the sleigh. & not wishing to accompany her friends west, tarried by the way with her friends in Vermont, and we soon after heard of her death supposing that she never recovered from the injury received by the overturn of the Sleigh.

NOTE B

When the light had departed I had no strength, but soon recovering in some degree, I went home. & as I leaned up to the fire piece, Mother enquired what the matter was. I replied never mind all is well.—I am well enough off. I then told my Mother I have learned for myself that Presbyterranism is not True. It seems as though the adversary was aware at a very early period of my Life that I was destined to prove a disturbance & annoyer of his kingdom, or else why should the powers of Darkness combine against me, why the oppression & persecution that arose against me, almost in my infancy?

NOTE C

In making this confession no one need suppose Me guilty of any great or malignant Sins: a disposition to commit such was never in My nature; but I was guilty of Levity, and sometimes associated with Jovial company, &c, not consistent with that character which ought to be maintained by one who was called of God as I had been, but this will not seem very strange to any one who recollects My youth & is acquainted with my native cheerly Temperment.

APPENDIX D

Extract from Wentworth Letter

A selection from Joseph Smith's' history prepared for non-Mormons and known as the Wentworth Letter.

At the request of Mr. John Wentworth, Editor, and Proprietor of the "Chicago Democrat," I have written the following sketch of the rise, progress, persecution, and faith of the Latter-Day Saints, of which I have the honor, under God, of being the founder. Mr. Wentworth says, that he wishes to furnish Mr. Bastow [George Barstow], a friend of his, who is writing the history of New Hampshire, with this document. As Mr. Bastow has taken the proper steps to obtain correct information all that I shall ask at his hands, is, that he publish the account entire, ungarnished, and without misrepresentation.

I was born in the town of Sharon Windsor co., Vermont, on the 23d of December, A. D. 1805. When ten years old my parents removed to Palmyra New York, where we resided about four years, and from thence we removed to the town of Manchester.

My father was a farmer and taught me the art of husbandry. When about fourteen years of age I began to reflect upon the importance of being prepared for a future state, and upon enquiring the plan of salvation I found that there was a great clash in religious sentiment; if I went to one society they referred me to one plan, and another to another; each one pointing to his own particular creed as the summum bonum of perfection: considering that all could not be right, and that God could not be the author of so much confusion I determined to investigate the subject more fully, believing that if God had a church it would not be split up into factions, and that if he taught one society to worship one way, and administer in one set of ordinances, he would not teach another principles which were diametrically opposed. Believing the word of God I had confidence in the declaration of James; "If any man lack wisdom let him ask of God who giveth all men liberally and upbraideth not and it shall be given him," I retired to a secret place in a grove and began to call upon the Lord, while fervently engaged in supplication my mind was taken away from the objects with which I was surrounded, and I was enwrapped in a heavenly vision and saw two glorious personages who exactly resembled each other in features, and likeness, surrounded with a brilliant light which eclipsed the sun at noon-day. They told me that all religious denominations were believing in incorrect doctrines, and that none of them was acknowledged of God as his church and kingdom. And I was expressly commanded to "go not after them," at the same time receiving a promise that the fulness of the gospel should at some future time be made known unto me.

Orson Pratt's Account of the First Vision

A selection from Orson Pratt's An Interesting Account of Several Remarkable Visions, *1840, the first known publication of the First Vision.*

Mr. Joseph Smith, jun. who made the following important discovery, was born in the town of Sharon, Windsor county, Vermont, on the 23d December, A.D. 1805. When ten years old, his parents, with their family, moved to Palmyra, New York; in the vicinity of which he resided for about eleven years, the latter part in the town of Manchester. Cultivating the earth for a livelihood was his occupation, in which he employed the most of his time. His advantages for acquiring literary knowledge, were exceedingly small; hence, his education was limited to a slight acquaintance, with two or three of the common branches of learning. He could read without much difficulty, and write a very imperfect hand; and had a very limited understanding of the ground rules of arithmetic. These were his highest and only attainments; while the rest of those branches, so universally taught in the common schools, throughout the United States, were entirely unknown to him. When somewhere about fourteen or fifteen years old, he began seriously to reflect upon the necessity of being prepared for a future state of existence; but how, or in what way, to prepare himself, was a question, as yet, undetermined in his own mind. He perceived that it was a question of infinite importance, and that the salvation of his soul depended upon a correct understanding of the same. He saw, that if he understood not the way, it would be impossible to walk in it, except by chance; and the thought of resting his hopes of eternal life upon chance, or uncertainties, was more than he could endure. If he went to the religious denominations to seek information, each one pointed to its particular tenets, saying—"This is the way, walk ye in it;" while, at the same time, the doctrines of each were in many respects, in direct opposition to one another. It also occurred to his mind that God was the author of but one doctrine, and therefore could acknowledge but one denomination as his church, and that such denomination must be a people who believe and teach that one doctrine, (whatever it may be,) and build upon the same. He then reflected upon the immense number of doctrines, now in the world, which had given rise to many hundreds of different denominations. The great question to be decided in his mind, was—if any one of these denominations be the Church of Christ, which one is it? Until he could become satisfied in relations to this question, he could not rest contented. To trust to the decisions of fallible man, and build his hopes upon the same, without any certainty, and knowledge of his own, would not satisfy the anxious desires that pervaded his breast. To decide, without any positive and definite evidence, on which he could rely, upon a subject involving the future welfare of his soul, was revolting to his feelings. The only alternative, that seemed to be left him was to read the Scriptures, and endeavor to follow their directions. He, accordingly commenced persuing the sacred pages of the Bible, with sincerity, believing the things that he read. His mind soon caught hold of the following passage:—"If any of you lack wisdom let him ask of God, that giveth to all men liberally, and upbraideth not; and it shall be given him."—James 1:5. From this promise he learned, that it was the privilege of all men to ask God for wisdom, with the sure and certain expectation of receiving liberally; without being upbraided for so doing. This was cheering information to him; tidings that gave him great joy. It was like a light shinning forth in a dark place, to guide him to the path in which he should walk. He now saw that if he inquired of God, there was not only a possibility, but a probability; yea, more, a certainty, that he should obtain a knowledge, which, of all the doctrines, was the doctrine of Christ; and, which of all the churches, was the church of Christ. He therefore, retired to a secret place in a grove, but a short distance from his father's house, and knelt down, and began to call upon the Lord. At first, he was severely tempted by the powers of darkness, which endeavored to overcome him; but he continued to seek for deliverance, until darkness gave way from his mind, and he was enabled to pray in feverency of the spirit, and in faith. And while thus pouring out his soul, anxiously desiring an answer from God, he at length, saw a very bright and glorious light in the heavens above; which, at first, seemed to be a considerable distance. He continued praying, while the light appeared to be gradually descending towards him; and as it drew nearer, it increased in brightness and magnitude, so that, by the time that it reached the tops of the trees, the whole wilderness, for some distance around was illuminated in a most glorious and brilliant manner. He expected to have seen the leaves and boughs of the trees consumed, as soon as the light came in contact with them; but perceiving that it did not produce that effect, he was encouraged with the hope of being able to endure its presence. It continued descending slowly, until it rested upon the earth, and he was enveloped in the midst of it. When it first came upon him, it produced a peculiar sensation throughout his whole system; and immediately, his mind was caught away, from the natural objects with which he was surrounded; and he was enwapped in a heavenly vision, and saw two glorious personages, who exactly resembled each other in their features or likeness. He was informed that his sins were forgiven. He was also informed upon the subjects, which had for some time previously agitated his mind, viz.—that all the religious denominations were believing in incorrect doctrines; and consequently, that none of them was acknowledged of God, as his church and kingdom. And he was expressly commanded, to go not after them; and he received a promise that the true doctrine—the fulness of the gospel, should, at some future time, be made known to him; after which, the vision withdrew, leaving his mind in a state of calmness and peace, indescribable.

Orson Hyde's Account
of the First Vision

A selection from A Cry From the Wilderness, A
Voice From the Dust of the Earth, *written by Orson
Hyde and published in Frankfurt, Germany, in 1842.
Elder Hyde was called on a mission to Jerusalem in 1840
to dedicate that land for the return of the Jews, leaving
New York City in February, 1841. After accomplishing
his mission in Jerusalem, he traveled to Germany where
he published an account of the First Vision in the German language. The translation below was made by Justus Ernst in 1960 and is located in the LDS Church
Historian's Office.*

Joseph Smith, Jr., to whom the angel of the Lord was sent
first, was born in the town of Sharon, Windsor County, Vermont,
on the 23rd of December, 1805.

When ten years old, his parents with their family, moved to
Palmyra, New York, in the vicinity of which he resided for about
eleven years, the latter part in the town of Manchester. His
only activity was to plow and cultivate the fields. As his parents
were poor and had to take care of a large family, his education
was very limited. He could read without much difficulty, and
write a very imperfect hand; and had a very limited understanding of the elementary rules of arithmetic. These were his highest
and only attainments; while the rest of those branches, so universally taught in the common schools throughout the United
States, were entirely unknown to him.

When somewhere about fourteen or fifteen years old, he
began seriously to reflect upon the necessity of being prepared
for a future state of existence; but how, or in what way to pre-

pare himself, was a question, as yet, undetermined in his own mind; he perceived that it was a question of infinite importance. He saw, that if he understood not the way, it would be impossible to walk in it, except by chance; and the thought of resting his hopes of eternal life upon chance or uncertainties, was more than he could endure.

He discovered a religious world working under numerous errors, which through their contradicting nature and principles, gave cause to the organization of so many different sects and parties, and whose feelings against each other were poisoned through hate, envy, malice and rage. He felt that there should be only one truth, and that those who would understand it correctly, would understand it in the same manner. Nature had gifted him with a strong, discerning mind and so he looked through the glass of soberness and good sense upon these religious systems which all were so different; but nevertheless all drawn from the scripture of truth.

After he had sufficiently assured himself to his own satisfaction that darkness was covering the earth, and gross darkness the minds of the people, he gave up hope ever to find a sect or party that was in the possession of the pure and unadulterated truth.

He accordingly commenced persuing the sacred pages of the Bible with sincerity, believing the things that he read. His mind soon caught hold of the following passage—"If any of you lack wisdom, let him ask of God, that giveth to all men liberally and upbraideth not; and it shall be given him."—James I:5. From this promise he learned that it was the privilege of all men to ask God for wisdom, with the sure and certain expectation of receiving liberally, without being upbraided for so doing. And thus he started to send the burning desires of his soul with a faithful determination. He, therefore, retired to a secret place, in a grove, but a short distance from his father's house, and knelt down and began to call upon the Lord. At first, he was severely tempted by the powers of darkness, which endeavoured to overcome him. The adversary benighted his mind with doubts, and brought to his soul all kinds of improper pictures and tried to hinder him in his efforts and the accomplishment of his goal. However, the overflowing mercy of God came to buoy him up, and gave new impulse and momentum to his dwindling strength. Soon the dark clouds disappeared, and light and peace filled his troubled heart. And again he called upon the Lord with renewed faith and spiritual strength. At this sacred moment his mind was caught away from the natural objects with which he was surrounded, and he was enwrapped in a heavenly vision, and saw two glorious personages, who exactly resembled each other in their features or likeness. They told him that his prayers had been answered, and that the Lord had decided to grant him a special blessing.

He was told not to join any of the religious sects or any party, as they were all wrong in their doctrines and none of them was recognized by God as His Church and kingdom. He received a promise that the true doctrine—the fulness of the gospel—should, at some future time, be made known to him; after which, the vision withdrew, leaving his mind in a state of calmness and peace indescribable.

Non-Mormon Editor's Account of the First Vision

An early non-Mormon publication of the First Vision based on an interview with Joseph Smith by the editor of the Pittsburg Gazette *who visited Nauvoo in 1843. This account was published in the* New York Spectator, *September 23, 1843.*

[According to the editor of the *Pittsburg Gazette*, Joseph Smith said]:

The Lord does reveal himself to me. I know it. He revealed himself first to me when I was about fourteen years old, a mere boy. I will tell you about it. There was a reformation among the different religious denominations in the neighborhood where I lived, and I became serious, and was desirous to know what Church to join.

While thinking of this matter, I opened the Testament promiscuously on these words, in James, Ask of the Lord who giveth to all men liberally and upbraideth not. I just determined I'd ask him. I immediately went out into the woods where my father had a clearing, and went to the stump where I had stuck my axe when I had quit work, and I kneeled down, and prayed, saying, O Lord, what Church shall I join? Directly I saw a light, and then a glorious personage in the light, and then another personage, and the first personage said to the second, Behold my beloved Son, hear him.—I then addressed this second person, saying, O Lord, what Church shall I join? He replied, "don't join any of them, they are all corrupt." The vision then vanished, and when I came to myself, I was sprawling on my back and it was some time before my strength returned.

When I went home and told the people that I had a revelation, and that all the churches were corrupt, they persecuted me, and they have persecuted me ever since.

Alexander Neibaur's Recording of Joseph Smith's Testimony

On May 24, 1844, shortly before the death of the Prophet, Alexander Neibaur heard Joseph relate his experience in the sacred grove and recorded in his journal his impressions of what Joseph said on that occasion.

After Dinner . . . called at BR. J.S. met Mr. Bonnie. Br. Joseph tolt us the first call he had a Revival Meeting, his Mother, Br. and Sisters got Religion. He wanted to get Religion too, wanted to feel and shout like the rest but could feel nothing, opened his Bible of the first Passage that struck him was if any man lack wisdom let him ask of God who giveth to all men liberallity & upbraideth not. Went into the Wood to pray, kneels himself Down, his tongue was closet cleaveh to his roof—could utter not a word, felt easier after awhile—saw a fire toward heaven came near and nearer; saw a personage in the fire, light complexion, blue eyes, a piece of white cloth Drawn over his shoulders his right arm bear after a while a other person came to the side of the first. Mr. Smith then asked, must I join the Methodist Church. No, they are not my People, have gone astray There is none that Doeth good, not one, but this is my Beloved Son harken ye him, the fire drew nigher, Rested upon the tree, enveloped him comforted I endeavored to arise but felt uncomen feeble—got into the house told the Methodist priest, said this was not a age for God to Reveal himself in Vision Revelation has ceased with the New Testament.

Selections from the Writings of Edward Stevenson

One of the early converts who heard Joseph Smith bear his testimony concerning the appearance of the Father and Son and who listened to the three witnesses preach that an angel showed to them the plates from which the Book of Mormon was translated was Edward Stevenson. The following two accounts were recorded by Stevenson in the early 1890's. The first appeared in his manuscript, "The Life and History, Elder Edward Stevenson," 19-23, located in the Church Historian's Office; and the second reference is quoted from his Reminiscences of Joseph, The Prophet, and the Coming Forth of the Book of Mormon *(Salt Lake City, 1893), 4.*

The following year after the organization of the Pontiac [Michigan] Branch of the Church of Jesus Christ of L. D. Saints, in 1834, we had the pleasure of having a visit from the Prophet Joseph Smith: a plain but noble looking man, of large frame and about 6 feet high. With him was his Father, Joseph Smith, and Oliver Cowdery, David Whitmer and Martin Harris, whose sister Sophia Kellog lived in our settlement. A great stir was made in this settlement at so distinguished visitors. The meetings held were crowded to see and hear the testimonies given which were very powerful. I will here relate my own experience on the occasion of a meeting in our log School House. The Prophet stood at a table for the pulpit where he began relateing his vision and before he got through he was in the midst of the congregation with up lifted hand. I do not believe that there was not one person present who did at the time being, or who was not convicted of the truth of his vision, of an Angel to him his countance seemed to me to assume heavenly whiteness, and his voice was so peirseing and forcible for my part it so impressed me as to become indellibly imprinted on my mind. . . In those meetings, the Prophet said the gifts and signs should follow believers now as they did the ancient Saints in the days of our Saviours administration, and said he by this shall ye prove me to be a true Prophet . . . The 3 witnesses bore their testamonies as to seeing the Angle, and hearing his voice. Their were many who were baptized. . . The visit of this man of God to our house and the testimonies of the 3 witnesses left a lasting remembrance with us and will stand as a witness against those who were so favoured above many.

* * * * * * * *

In that same year, 1834, in the midst of many large congregations, the Prophet testified with great power concerning the visit of the Father and the Son, and the conersation he had with them. Never before did I feel such power as was manifested on these occasions.

APPENDIX J

John Taylor's Testimony
of Joseph Smith's Visions

*In a discourse delivered in Salt Lake City on De-
cember 7, 1879, John Taylor testified that Joseph informed him of the appearance of the Father and Son
and of the visitation of the Angel Moroni, Nephi, and
other heavenly messengers. See John Irvine, reporter,*
Journal of Discourses, *XXI (London, 1881), 161-63,
from which the following selection has been taken. Italics
inserted by the present author.*

Now, we will come to other events, of later date; events
with which we are associated—I refer now to the time that
Joseph Smith came among men. What was his position? and
how was he situated? *I can tell you what he told me about it.*
He said that he was very ignorant of the ways, designs and purposes of God, and knew nothing about them; he was a youth
unacquainted with religious matters or the systems and theories
of the day. He went to the Lord, having read James' statement,
that "If any of you lack wisdom let him ask of God that giveth
to all men liberally and upbraideth not; and it shall be given
him." He believed that statement and went to the Lord and
asked him, *and the Lord revealed himself to him together with
his Son Jesus,* and, pointing to the latter, said: "This is my
beloved Son, hear him." He then asked in regard to the various
religions with which he was surrounded. He enquired which of
them was right. for he wanted to know the right way and to walk
in it. He was told that none of them was right, that they had
all departed from the right way. that they had forsaken God
the fountain of living waters, and hewed them out cisterns, broken
cisterns, that could hold no water. *Afterwards the Angel Moroni*

come to him and revealed to him the Book of Mormon, with the history of which you are generally familiar, and also with the statements that I am now making pertaining to these things. *And then came Nephi,* one of the ancient prophets, that had lived upon this continent, who had an interest in the welfare of the people that he had lived amongst in those days.

APPENDIX K

Smith Family Members—
Withdrawal from Presbyterian Church

A selection from the "Records of the Session of the Presbyterian Church in Palmyra," Vol. II, 11-13, located in the Western Presbyterian Church, Palmyra, New York.

(March 10, 1830)

The committee appointed to visit Hiram Smith Lucy Smith and Samuel Harrison Smith reported that they had visited them and received no satisfaction. They acknowledged that they had entirely neglected the ordinances of the church for the last eighteen months and that they did not wish to unite with us any more.

Whereupon Resolved that they be cited to appear before the Session on the 24th day of March inst. at 2 Oclk P.M. at the Meeting House to answer to the following charge to wit Neglect of public worship and the Sacrament of the Lord's Supper for the last eighteen months—

Witnesses   Henry Jessup   James Robinson
               Harvey Shel   Robert W. Smith
               Levi Dagget   Fri U. Sheffield

Closed with prayer—adjourned to 24 inst 2 Oclk P.M.
Records from the minutes of the moderator

                           Geo. N. Williams Clk.

. . . .
(March 29, 1830)

The persons before cited to wit. Hiram Smith Lucy Smith and Samuel Harrison Smith not appearing and the Session having satisfactory evidence that the citations were duly served Resolved that they be censured for their contumacy. Resolved that George

Beckwith manage their defence—The charge in the above case being fully sustained by the testimony of Henry Jessup Harvey Shel Robert W. Smith and Frederick U. Sheffield (in minutes of testimony on file with the clerk) the Session after duly considering the matter were unanimously of opinion that Hiram Smith Lucy Smith and Samuel Harrison Smith ought to be Suspended. Resolved that Hiram Smith Lucy Smith and Samuel Harrison Smith be and they are hereby suspended from the Sacrament of the Lord's Supper.

APPENDIX L

Palmyra in 1812

A selection from History of Wayne County, New York *(Philadelphia, 1877), p. 142.*

We have seen the origin of Palmyra, twenty years before Rochester began to have an existence. In 1812, the village consisted of Main street, east and west, with a cross-street, which was known south of Main as Canandaigua, and north as Church street. At the corners stood the Ensworth tavern. [Azel Ensworth owned the property on the southwest corner where the Baptist church is currently located.] A low, wet ground on the northeast corner was unoccupied. East of this was the office of Abner Cole, and next beyond was the dwelling of Ezra Shepardson. Eliphalet Rowe, the Presbyterian minister, occupied the only house which stood on Canandaigua street. On Church street there were two residences—that of James Benson and "Washington Hall," a two-story house, occupied below by George Beckwith, above for societies. On the cemetery lot stood the old church. Down Main street the eye rested upon small one-story frame houses, with a few two-story exceptions. There were no log houses—their day was past. There were spacious lots fenced with pickets and board fences. Sidewalks were of rude character, and a row of poplars extended from the present Palmyra Hotel westward to Canandaigua street, with a break in front of the stores. North along Main street, from the west, in order, were the drug-store of Dr. Gain Robinson, a story-and-a-half frame; a large low building occupied by William Jackway, Platt Williams, and Zebulon Williams; and a dwelling occupied by William P. Wilson, the tanner. On the next lot were a house and a blacksmith shop. Levi daggett later occupied both. A daughter of Daggett, Sarah, married Henry Wells, prominent in connection with the express business.

Next stood the Hurlbut property. Here was a distillery—a favorite resort. A story-and-a-half dwelling, occupied by Benjamin, brother of Abner Cole, was adjacent the property, and eastward lived the Blackmans, on the grounds now the property of Mrs. Beckwith. On the Lilley lot was the blacksmith shop of [Zachariah] Blackman, and east of it was a long shed for shelter to the teams, whose drivers had business in the coffee-house. Before this house the militia were wont to parade for "convenience sake." Some distance below Shepardson's was the store of N. H. & G. [Nathaniel H. and George] Beckwith, the tailor-shop of A. H. Reed, the saddlery of Abraham Shattock, the drugstore of McIntyre, and the house and shop of John B. Robson. A daughter of Robson married L. B. Tousley, the well-known Sabbath-school worker and eloquent speaker. Admirers in large cities asked him of what institution he was a graduate. "Deacon Jessup's tannery, Palmyra," was the reply.

The store of Nathan Thayer came next, then the dwelling of Levi Thayer, and Colt's store. East of Market street of to-day was the store of Samuel Wagstaff, and then that of O'Rourke. The house of Peleg Holmes, afterwards occupied by General Rogers, came next. At the foot of the street was the residence of Swift, and below were the Durfee mill and dwelling.

Returning westward, the first improvements were [Henry] Jessup's residence and tannery, William Cooks' cooper-shop and dwelling, known as the "Long House," the house of Stephen Skellinger, and the "Democratic" school-house. Farther on stood the dwelling of William T. Hussy, and adjoining was the house of Samuel Jennings, the store-keeper, and beside him was Johnson, the tailor.

There was no other dwelling till that of Dr. Robinson, previously inhabited by Ira Selby, and by Rev. Jesse Townsend. Then came the Phelps tavern, and beyond was the store building of Selby & Phelps. The house of Joseph Colt, a large flat-roofed structure, stood next west, then the residence, office, and store of William Howe Cuyler. The Franklin House, owned by S. Hathaway, a saddler and harness-shop; and on the site of the Episcopal church was the clothiery of Andrew G. Howe. Passing the brick store of the Whites and the residence of Dyer Ensworth, we find the house of Silas Hart, and above him the Tice and the Shutliff places. Isolated upon the hill north of Main street was the residence of John Russel, conspicuous both as to location and architecture. The house stands on Canal street, in the rear of its former location. Such is an outline of residence, shop, store, and tavern which made up the Palmyra of 1812.

APPENDIX M

Palmyra in the Early 1820's

A selection from Horatio Gates Spafford, A Gazetteer of the State of New York *(Albany, 1824), pp. 400-01.*

Palmyra, a Post-Township of Ontario County, 15 miles N. of Canandaigua, and 220 from Albany; bounded N. by Ontario and Williamson, E. by Lyons, S. by Manchester and Farmington, W. by Perrinton of Monroe County. It comprises 2 townships of Phelps and Gorham's Purchase, being No. 12, in the 2d and 3d ranges. This town has Mud Creek running eastward through its whole length, a little S. of the center. This creek affords fine advantages for mills, and is of some little use for navigation. The soil is of a superior quality, and the settlements of a date to give much of farming ease and independence to the inhabitants. There is a large meeting of Quakers, and there is one Episcopal, and 1 Presbyterian Church, with 25 common school-houses and schools. A road, from Canandaigua to Sodus bay, leads across the E. part, and there are many other roads, in various directions. This Town is 12 miles long, E. and W., and 6 miles wide. Besides Mud Creek, the W. township has Red Creek, from Perrinton, and the Erie Canal extends through the whole length, E. and W., passing through the Village of Palmyra. As it is a good Town, and enjoys the navigation of this Canal, its population will probably increase pretty rapidly, and it may soon be divided, into two towns. At no distant day, it is not improbable that a new County may be erected, from the N. end of Ontario, when the steeples of its Capital may rise somewhere along here, on the banks of the Canal. Public convenience may call for this, by and by, but the thirst for office, and the intrigues and designs of self-interest, and party-policy, will hardly wait so long. The roads are numerous and good, and the Canal navigation is here in full activity, August 1822. Population, 3724: 748 persons engaged in agriculture, 190 in manufactures, and 18 in commerce; 9 foreigners not naturalized; 46 free blacks; no slaves: taxable property, $486001; Electors, 841; 16292 acres of improved land; 3402 cattle, 793 horses, 7734 sheep; 43830 yards of cloth made in 1821; 10 grist mills, 17 saw mills, 2 fulling mills, 2 carding machines, 1 iron works, 6 distilleries, and 2 asheries; school districts, 25; schools kept 5 months; $498.53 public monies; 1048 children; 1253 taught in the schools in 1821. The Village, or Borough of Palmyra, where is the Post Office, is on Mud Creek, in the E. township, and has the Erie Canal along the N., and across the E. part of the village. It has long been a place of very considerable business, and is the third in rank in this County, and increasing rapidly. Several large stores and store houses, for the Canal trade, are erected and erecting here, and a regular line of two Canal Packets, for passengers, have been running through the season of 1822, between Pittsford of Monroe Co., this place and Utica. . . . This Village is incorporated, and ought to be called a Borough, for reasons assigned under Ithaca, and many other places. It has 1 Presbyterian, 1 Methodist, and 1 Baptist Church, an academy, 2 or 3 school-houses, 13 dry good stores, 3 druggist shops, 3 inns, 2 tanneries, one of which is so extensive as to employ 40 hands, and a number of other mechanical establishments. It has 3 capacious basins, on the Canal, one of which has a dry dock. Mud creek runs eastward, 40 rods N. of the main street, which is one mile in length, and the Erie Canal is between this street and the creek, except that near the east border of the Village, it crosses this street. At the W. extremity of the Village, the Canal comes within 2 rods of it, so that Palmyra may by-and-by look much more like a city of the Netherlands, than its great namesake, of ancient fame. There are many mills, close bordering, and some within the Village, which now contains 125 families, 85 dwelling houses, a printing office, post office, and about 1,000 inhabitants. A turnpike is nearly finished to Montezuma. Palmyra Village is situated 13 miles N. of Canandaigua, 22 E. of Rochester, 15 W. of Lyons, 16 S. of Pulteneyville, 12 NW. of Vienna V., and 22 from Geneva.

APPENDIX N

Manchester in the Early 1820's

A selection from Horatio Gates Spafford, A Gazetteer of the State of New York *(Albany, 1824), pp. 302-03.*

Manchester, a Post-Township of Ontario County, 10 miles N. of Canandaigua, (that is, its centre is 10 miles N. from Canandaigua Village.) bounded N. by Palmyra, E. by Phelps, S. by Hopewell, W. by Farmington, being T.11, in the 2d Range, 6 miles square. In the 1st edition of this Work, this was the easternmost of the 2 townships that then constituted the Town of Farmington. It was erected into a separate Town in 1821, and called Burt; and in April, 1822, received its present name, by another act of legislation. The surface is gently uneven or waving, and the soil good, without exception, with good proportions of arable and meadow land. It is all thickly settled, divided into small farms, owned in fee simple by their occupants. The Canandaigua outlet, as it is here called, runs SW. to NE. across this Town, forming many valuable mill-seats, well improved. The Ontario Manufacturing Co., had their works on this stream, and the loss of them is much regretted by the inhabitants. They were destroyed by fire, in the winter of 1821-2. Manchester Village, in the W. part, on the W. side of the C. outlet, (or the Clyde, or any thing that is short,) has some manufactures, a small collection of houses, the Post-Office, 'and elegant stone Church, with a bell.' This village is on the post-road from Canandaigua to Palmyra, Williamson, &c., 8 miles from Canandaigua.— About 1 mile southerly, or up-stream, is the Village called Shortsville, where there are mills of various kinds, a paper mill, furnace, and a great deal of business. It is 7 miles from Canandaigua. The Sulphurous Fountains in the SE. corner of this Town, have very justly attracted considerable notice. They are situated about 10 miles NE. of Canandaigua, and 12 NW. of Geneva, and have somehow obtained the name of Clifton Springs. The principal issues are in 3 large springs, and the rocks are calcareous, filled with impressions generally imputed to petrification of testaceous shells; and, as I apprehend, very erroneously in most instances. The waters are strongly impregnated with sulphur, at first perfectly transparent, becoming opaque, and changing to a yellowish cream color, as the precipitates form, which consist of a carbonate of lime, and of sulphur, in the state of brimstone. In this state they emit great quantities of sulphuretted hydrogen, which diffuses the scent to very considerable distances. Yet plants grow in these springs, though covered with the deposition of sulphurous and calcareous matter, as are the stones also, and every other body resting in the water; and cattle drink freely of them without injury, or any perceptible effects. Where one of these springs rises, is a spot of 5 or 6 rods diameter, completely covered with these mineral precipitates, principally sulphur, which is found to be in some places near 6 feet deep: and cart-loads of it may be collected in a few minutes, though mixed with every substance which chance has thrown into the mass. And yet abundant as it is, I do not learn that any attempts have been made to cleanse or manufacture any of it for use. The rocks of this region partake very abundantly of that peculiar fetor noticed under MINERALOGY. These Springs have become places of considerable resort, especially by persons afflicted with scrofulous affections, in which the use of these waters has been found highly beneficial. The Clifton Hotel has a small library, with good accommodations for visitants. For the number of inhabitants, &c., see FARMINGTON, less than half of which are supposed to be in this Town, which was unfortunately erected just after the 2 late Censuses, and before any of the returns as to schools, &c., now in my possession, were made.

Farmington in the Early 1820's

A selection from Horatio Gates Spafford, A Gazetteer of the State of New York *(Albany, 1824), pp. 170-71.*

Farmington, a Post-Township of Ontario County, 9 Miles N. of Canandaigua, bounded N. by Palmyra, E. by Manchester, S. by Canandaigua. W. by Victor, being T. 11, in the 3d Range of Phelps and Gorham's purchase, and 6 miles square. In the first edition of this work, Farmington comprised this Township, and that which is now Manchester, lately erected from the E. half, and since the 2 late Censuses. The surface in the N. is gently undulated, with a gravelly soil, and in the S. quite level, with a clayey or argillaceous soil, uniformly good for grain or grass. Nearly in the centre are extensive tracts of water limestone, 2 to 400 acres in extent, very near, and in some places on the very surface, circumstances that I note the more carefully, as an opinion has got abroad that this variety of limestone, by no means so rare as many imagine, is found only in soils of sterility and barrenness. The reverse is more probably the fact. This Town is settled principally by Friends, or 'Quakers,' who have 2 meeting houses, in one of which is held a Monthly meeting, and once in 6 months a Quarterly meeting: and though Dr. Morse might hardly admit it, they seem to be a religious people, who pay proper attention to the education of their children, and have, besides, a competent number of school houses. The lands are owned in fee simple, in small farms, well cultivated; and this Town will soon have one distillery, at least one too many. Mud Creek runs from the SW. corner along the W. line, and across the NW. corner, supplying mill seats, on which there are 2 grist mills, and 4 saw mills. The stage road, from Canandaigua to Rochester, leads across the SW. corner. The Post-office is kept in New-Salem Village, near the N. meeting house, where there is a small collection of houses, stores, &c., 11 miles from Canandaigua. There is a little Village on the W. border, called Browns-vill, where are some mills, on Mud Creek. My Correspondents differ in opinion as to the number of inhabitants in this Town and Manchester; and I presume the population stated below is about equally divided between the 2 Towns. The Sulphur Springs, are now in Manchester. A Correspondent writes me this town was settled by dairy farmers, from Cheshire, Massachusetts, and that they are still good dairy farmers.

Whole population, 4214: 929 farmers, 192 mechanics, and 3 traders, or engaged in commerce: 6 foreigners not naturalized: 23 free blacks; no slaves: taxable property, $437489; school districts, 21; schools kept 8 months; $350.48 public monies; 972 children between 5 and 15; 1051 received instruction in the schools in 1821: electors, 793; 18909 acres of improved land; 4690 cattle, 902 horses, 10208 sheep: 35319 yards of cloth made in families in 1821: 2 grist mills, 14 saw mills, 6 fulling mills, 8 carding machines, 2 cotton and woollen factories, 1 iron works, 5 distilleries, and 5 asheries.

APPENDIX P

Reports of Revivals Appearing in the Palmyra Register in 1820

The following selections from the Palmyra Register *describe the widespread nature of an 1819-1820 revival in the state of New York. These reports were available to Joseph Smith in 1820 and might have been one of the sources that helped the Prophet recognize that "great multitudes" were joining churches in "the whole district of country" at the time of the First Vision. The date on which the article appeared has been inserted in parentheses at the end of each selection.*

GREAT REVIVALS IN RELIGION

The religious excitement which has for some months prevailed in the towns of this vicinity (says the Ballston Watch-Tower, of May 17) has not yet wholly subsided. — The third communion season, which has been observed in Ballston, since the commencement of the work there, was witnessed on the last Lord's day, when *thirty* additional communicants were received — making the whole number added within three months, *one hundred and forty-five*. We have heard it asserted, on what we believe to be good authority, that the whole number, who have hopefully experienced a saving change, during the progress of the great work in the towns of Stillwater, Malta, Ballston, Schenectady, Amsterdam and Galway, is not less than *twelve hundred!* — This is the Lord's work alone, and it is marvellous in our eyes. This is a time the prophets desired to see, but they never saw it.

We are happy to learn that a connected narrative of the whole work, by the several clergymen particularly concerned, is contemplated for one of our religious periodical publications. Extracts from which will appear in this paper. (June 7, 1820)

Revival

A letter from Homer [N. Y.] dated May 29, received in this town, states, that 200 persons had been hopefully converted in that town since January first; 100 of whom had been added to the Baptist church. The work was still progressing. (August 16, 1820)

Revivals of Religion

Extract of a letter from Rev. Asahel Nettleton, to a gentleman in Boston, dated Nassau, May 8, 1820.

"The county of Saratoga, for a long time, has been as barren of revivals of religion, as perhaps any other part of this state. It has been like 'the mountains of Gilboa, on which were neither rain nor dew.' But the face of the country has been wonderfully changed of late. The little cloud made its first appearance at Saratoga Springs last summer. As the result of this revival about 40 have made a public profession of religion in Rev. Mr. Griswold's church.—Directly south in the town of Malta—I spent a few days preaching and visiting among them.—I had not proceeded far in my work before the attention became universal. They have had no Presbyterian church in that town for a number of years past. As the fruit of this revival a church has been recently organized, consisting of 105 members. A number more are rejoicing in hope, and some anxious for their souls. The attention there excited a deep interest in the surrounding region. The inhabitants are scattered over a large extent, and yet I do think I have seen more than 1400 people assembled at once to hear the gospel. Directly east, and adjoining Malta, is the town of Stillwater; here the revival, has been very powerful; about two hundred have become hopeful subjects; more than 160 of whom were added to the church at their two last communion sessions. The work there is still advancing. Directly west, and adjoining Malta, is the town of Ballston. This place has been visited with refreshing showers in years that are past. But the present far exceeds anything they have ever before witnessed. At their two last communion sessions 118 were added to that church, and a number more are rejoicing—and some yet anxious for their souls.—Directly north of Ballston is the town of Milton. A revival has just commenced there, and about 12 recently entertaining hope. Traveling north-west, and adjoining Milton, is East Galway. Here the work has been overwhelming. Within about two months, not less than 150 have become hopeful subjects of divine grace; and a number are still anxious for their

souls. Onward to south-west is Amsterdam. About fifty are there
hopeful subjects of divine grace. Adjoining this, is a very wicked
place called Tripes hill. About 50 are hopeful subjects of the same
glorious work, and the attention in both these places is still increasing. South-west from Malta is the city of Schenectady, and
Union College. At one of our communion sessions in Malta, the
Rev. Dr. M'Auley, from that College visited us in company with a
number of the students. Some of them have become anxious. . . .
And a number engaged to attend in the concerns of their souls on
earth. From that time a number began to enquire, 'What must I
do to be saved?' About thirty of the students are rejoicing in hope.
In the city of Schenectady the work has been very powerful. . . .
A revival has just commenced in the town of Nassau, a little east
of Albany. It has commenced in a very powerful manner. Within
less than 3 weeks past, more than 80 are rejoicing in hope in this
place, a number in deep distress. I have neither time nor room to
state particulars. My dear brother, we live in an interesting time
—'This is that which was spoken of by the prophet Joel.' '' (September 13, 1820)

FROM THE RELIGIOUS REMEMBRANCER
A SPIRITUAL HARVEST

Extract of a letter from a gentleman in Bloomingsgrove
(N. Y.) to his sister in Philadelphia, dated August 22, 1820.

"My Dear Sister,
    "I wish you could have been with us yesterday. I had the
pleasure to witness 80 persons receive the seal of the covenant, in
front of our Church. Soon after 135 persons, new members, were
received into full communion. All the first floor of the Church was
cleared; the seats and pews were all crowded with the members,
and after they had all partaken of the symbols, and gone through
with the ordinance, they were requested to leave their seats and
give room for those who had not yet partaken. The seats and pews
were re-occupied, and the most of the day taken up in celebrating
the Lord's Supper. About twelve more were taken under the
charge of the Church. Service was kept up the whole time out of
doors. Such a throng of people was hardly ever known here. I
think, my dear sister will now join me in prayer and thanksgiving
to our Heavenly Father for his special goodness." (October 4,
1820)

APPENDIX Q

A Reply to the Critics

Some critics have challenged the reliability of Joseph Smith's description of the historical setting of the First Vision, have expressed concern because of differences in the four accounts of the First Vision which were written or dictated by the Prophet, and have asked, "What evidence exists that Joseph Smith was actually persecuted following his sacred experience in 1820?" Although this book is not limited to refutation of charges which have been leveled against the Prophet's writings, it does contain information which substantiates Joseph Smith's historical accounts and provides confirming evidence of the divine calling of this latter-day prophet.

The Revival of 1819-1820

Recognizing that one can neither prove nor disprove a vision by using the secular tools of modern researchers, investigators have attempted to substantiate or invalidate such claims by examining the validity of contemporary historical references. The supposition is that if the details of the historical framework are found to be true or false, they will likewise reflect on claims, such as visions, which cannot be objectively evaluated. One investigator examined contemporary records and failed to locate any evidence of an 1820 revival in Palmyra that led to an increase in church membership. His conclusion was that since there was an "absence" of a revival in 1820 in the churches in Palmyra and vicinity, Joseph Smith's historical account of the First Vision was not accurate, and he inferred that the reliability of his description of the vision itself should thus be questioned.[1]

---

[1] Wesley P. Walters, "New Light on Mormon Origins from Palmyra (N.Y.) Revival," *Bulletin of the Evangelical Theological Society,* X (Fall, 1967), 228.

Before one can demonstrate that Joseph Smith's narrative of events which surrounded the First Vision is incorrect, however, he must determine what Joseph Smith meant by the statements he recorded. Reference to a revival at the time of the First Vision is made in the Prophet's history of the Church which he commenced in 1838. This account was written after the Prophet had traveled extensively from the eastern coast to the Missouri frontier and while he was living in western America. He was viewing an event in his life from a substantial distance in time and place, which makes plausible the assumption that such historical statements as he made in his account were of a more general nature. Joseph did not write in 1838 that great multitudes joined churches in Palmyra in 1820. Instead, the Prophet declared that in "the second year" after his "removal to Manchester, there was in the place where . . . [he] lived an unusual excitement on the subject of religion," and that "it commenced with the Methodists, but soon became general among all the sects in that region of country." Then he added that "great multitudes united themselves to the different religious parties" in "the whole district of country."[2] In this discussion, the Prophet did not describe what he meant by "religious excitement," "place where he lived," "whole district of country," and "great multitudes," nor did he identify a precise time period when all these events took place, or when or how he learned about these developments.[3]

Although Joseph Smith noted that the religious excitement was occurring in the area where he lived during his fifteenth year and that his vision took place in the spring of 1820, he did not necessarily state that the revival which he described was limited to a few months or to a particular year. In his 1832 autobiography, the Prophet declared that for three years, from the ages of twelve through fifteen, he was involved in serious religious reflections and from about 1818 to 1820 he was searching for religious truth and the right church. Based on this long quest, the 1838 history may imply a longer time span for the revival he referred to than is

---

[2]Joseph Smith 2:5; see also Joseph Smith, "History," *Times and Seasons*, April 1, 1842, 748-49.

[3]According to Richard L. Bushman, "At best, critics of Joseph's story can claim that there was not enough excitement close enough to Palmyra to satisfy them. But again that all depends on how near is near and big is big. I doubt very much that historical inquiry will ever settle that question to the satisfaction of all." Richard L. Bushman, "The First Vision Story Revived," *Dialogue: A Journal of Mormon Thought*, IV (Spring, 1969), 86, 90-91.

generally assumed, and possibly Joseph Smith did not "intend to portray all revival events as happening just before his vision." Although Joseph Smith stated that "an unusual excitement" was in evidence in the second year after his removal to Manchester, the results of this religious quickening might well have extended beyond Joseph Smith's sacred experience in the grove, thus expanding the possible time period for the revival which initiated such great events in his young life.[4]

It is also improper to assume that all religious excitement occurring in the early nineteenth century was associated with significant increases in church membership. There may or may not have been an increase in church membership in the neighborhood where Joseph lived at the time of the great religious excitement; membership reports do not always reflect accurately spiritual conditions within a congregation or community. Sometimes the first stage of a conversion process was the "awakening or conviction, when the preacher aroused fears in the prospective convert." During this experience, the awakened person often began worrying about pleasing God. Filled with anguish and concern, the awakened souls sometimes delayed joining a church. Others who were converted to the belief that Jesus was their Savior did not join a church because they were confused regarding which church they should join or because they felt that not all the churches in a particular area were patterned after New Testament Christianity. Consequently, increases in membership sometimes did not immediately follow mighty spiritual awakenings. Moreover, sometimes increases in membership resulted from families moving into a new region rather than from old residents being converted. At the same time, decreases in membership occurred because of the emigration of families or because of a redistribution of the boundaries of an ecclesiastical unit. In a year when there might be no reported increases in membership, there might be an increase from conversions that was not reflected because of the exodus of other families or of a reshuffling of ecclesiastical boundaries. Such circumstances indicate the possible inaccuracies caused by sole reliance on limited statistics.[5]

In addition to the problem of interpreting the writings of the past, another major challenge that hinders contemporary his-

---

[4]Richard Lloyd Anderson, "Circumstantial Confirmation of the First Vision Through Reminiscences," *BYU Studies*, IX (Spring, 1969), 375.

[5]Bushman, op. cit., 87-88.

torians from reconstructing past events is the absence of many
important records and the incomplete nature of the records that
have survived. This might be especially true of a religious quickening in a neighborhood at the time of the Second Great Awakening. Protracted religious meetings were so common during that
age that many were not reported in the newspapers and periodi-
cals. Brigham Young declared in 1860 that he had "been brought
up in the midst of those flaming, fiery reformations from his childhood."[6] Sometimes publishers did not report developments in their
local newspapers because they assumed that many residents knew
of the event; instead they concentrated on printing events
occurring in outlying regions. At the time of the First Vision there
was only one meetinghouse in Palmyra village, that of the
Western Presbyterian Church, and records of that church prior to
1828 have not been located. Similarly, records of the Methodists
of Palmyra and Manchester who were meeting in homes and outdoors are not available. Therefore the absence of records or reports
indicating no increases in membership does not necessarily mean
that there was not a great religious excitement in a community.

Although Joseph Smith wrote that the religious excitement
began with the Methodists and spread to other faiths in his neighborhood, he did not identify the gathering or gatherings that
initiated this religious quickening. Such a meeting or meetings
might have been generated by a traveling preacher in or near a
farmhouse in Manchester or Palmyra township. An awareness of
unusual religious excitement by the Prophet also might have
occurred while he was attending a camp meeting near Palmyra
village, in Manchester township, or in Phelps.

Many contemporary records confirm Joseph Smith's testimony of religious excitement in the place where he lived prior to
the First Vision. Methodists held camp meetings east of the Smith
farm, and many of these meetings could have been considered by
an earnest seeker after truth as ones which generated unusual
religious excitement. As described in this book, in the summer of
1819 Methodists of the Genesee Conference held an annual
meeting in Phelps (then Vienna), and more than one hundred
ministers, including the Reverend George Lane, attended this July
gathering.

Members of the Smith family could very likely have been

⁶*Deseret News*, April 11, 1860.

attracted to attend meetings held in that community in order to investigate Methodism, to socialize, and to sell goods which they had produced. One contemporary of Joseph Smith, Orsamus Turner, who resided in Palmyra for several years prior to 1822, wrote that "after catching a spark of Methodism in the camp meeting, away down in the woods, on the Vienna road, he [Joseph Smith] was a very passable exhorter in evening meetings."[7] Another contemporary who lived in Palmyra in 1820, Pomeroy Tucker, verified the religious excitement that was occurring in that part of America at the time of the First Vision. "Protracted revival meetings," he wrote,

> were customary in some of the churches, and Smith frequented those of different denominations, sometimes professing to participate in their devotional exercises. . . . At one time he joined the probationary class of the Methodist Church in Palmyra, . . . and he soon withdrew from the class. The final conclusion announced by him, was, that all sectarianism was fallacious.[8]

The Prophet's mother also confirmed portions of Joseph Smith's history when she inserted in her biography of the Prophet, *after* recording an event that took place in 1819, his most detailed account of the First Vision. Prior to her quoting from the Prophet's history of the First Vision as published in the *Times and Seasons*, Lucy Mack Smith wrote that "a great revival in religion" extended to "the surrounding country in which we resided." Moreover, the Prophet's mother declared that Joseph Smith refused to attend any meetings conducted during the religious excitement that was occurring following the death of her son, Alvin (November 19, 1823). She added that Joseph believed that none of the churches taught the pure gospel of Christ, but did not object to other members of the family worshipping in the churches of that day. Consequently, Lucy Mack Smith identified a widespread revival that was occurring about the time of the First Vision and a local revival that took place about 1824.[9]

---

[7]O. Turner, *History of the Pioneer Settlement of Phelps and Gorham's Purchase, and Morris' Reserve* (Rochester, 1852), 214.

[8]Pomeroy Tucker, *Origin, Rise, and Progress of Mormonism* (New York, 1867), 17-18.

[9]Lucy Mack Smith, *History of Joseph Smith* (Salt Lake City: Bookcraft, 1958), 68-69, 90-91. This information was also included in the first edition of this biography: *Biographical Sketches of Joseph Smith, the Prophet, and His Progenitors for Many Generations* (Liverpool, 1853), 74, 90-91.

Contemporary records further indicate that great multitudes were joining churches in the whole region of country during the months surrounding the First Vision. As explained in this book, various ecclesiastical records state that there were substantial increases in church membership in many sections of western and upstate New York in 1819 and 1820. There is not only evidence of religious excitement occurring in the area where Joseph Smith lived in 1820, but one can substantiate the Prophet's accounts of great multitudes joining churches in the whole district of country by defining "that district of country" as an area within twenty, fifty, or one hundred miles of the Smith farm. New York was an ecclesiastical storm center at the time of the First Vision, and national and regional membership records clearly reveal that during this great revival there were substantial increases in Methodist, Presbyterian, and Baptist congregations located in that state. Since Joseph Smith did not write the account of this revival until 1838, he might have learned about the extensive nature of this religious quickening months or years after the event occurred. Accounts of the enlivenments which occurred in New York in 1819 and 1820 were advertised in Palmyra, and the number of conversions occurring in the area east of Lake Cayuga and in the region of Albany was enumerated in the local newspaper, the *Palmyra Register*.[10]

Although some critics insist that the only proper interpretation of Joseph Smith's 1838 account of the background of the First Vision is that of a revival which led to a significant increase in church membership in Palmyra and vicinity, this limited view fails to consider that the Prophet might have associated great increases in church membership with a geographical region that extended beyond Palmyra and nearby villages. At least one contemporary of Joseph Smith, David Marks, who was approximately the same age as the Prophet, "ranged over a fairsized area in the process of participating in certain religious revivals" about 1820.[11] In 1821, for example, David Marks learned that a great revival was progressing in Brutus and Camillus, communities located from twenty to thirty miles from his father's home. Anxious to witness it, Marks left home and walked fifteen miles to Brutus, where he tarried with strangers. For approximately one month,

[10]See Chapter 3 and Appendix P.

[11]Peter Crawley, "A Comment on Joseph Smith's Account of His First Vision and the 1820 Revival," *Dialogue*, VI (Spring, 1971), 106-07.

Marks remained in that area, attending some forty-four meetings. When Marks later summarized his travels during his early years he wrote that they were "confined to a few towns in the vicinity of Junius."[12] Commenting on this narrative, which in some respects resembles writings of Joseph Smith, one Mormon scholar, Peter Crawley, wrote:

> Marks's narrative demonstrates ... the fallacy in dogmatically requiring Joseph Smith's "the place where we lived" [or whole district of country] to lie within 10 or 15 miles of the Smith farm. Marks, at least, in 1821 could refer to an area including towns 30 miles to the east and to the west of his home as "the vicinity of Junius."[13]

To recapitulate, sometimes when we write in general terms describing experiences of the past we are misunderstood by others. Information included in this book substantiates Joseph Smith's description of religious excitement in the neighborhood where he lived and provides evidence that there was a great revival which led to significant increases in church membership in many sections of western New York during the period surrounding the First Vision. Joseph Smith was a reliable historian. He not only wrote an accurate description of events that were occurring in New York at the time of the First Vision but prepared an accurate account of a remarkable vision that occurred in the tranquility of a grove in the spring of 1820.

Joseph Smith's Four Accounts

Critics have not only challenged the historical accuracy of Joseph Smith's description of the religious awakening which occurred at the time of his First Vision, but they have questioned the reliability of his writings because differences appear in his four descriptions of his 1820 vision. Some have suggested that if a person does not relate an experience in the same manner each time he discusses the event, then he is not to be considered a reliable witness. In an important way, however, the fact that the four recitals of the First Vision are different helps support the integrity of the Mormon Prophet. The variations indicate that Joseph Smith did not deliberately create a memorized version which he

---

[12]Marilla Marks, ed., *Memoirs of the Life of David Marks* (Dover, N.H., 1846), 29-32; David Marks, *The Life of David Marks* (Limerick, Maine, 1831), 39.
[13]Crawley, op. cit., 107.

related to everyone. In the legal profession, attorneys and judges recognize that if a witness repeats an incident by using precisely the same language, the court might seriously challenge the validity of such a statement. While the wording in Joseph's accounts are different, a number of basic truths are disclosed in each of his recitals, clearly indicating a rich harmony in many details.

As one considers the variations in the four accounts of the First Vision as written or dictated by Joseph Smith, he should remember that the accounts are of various lengths (from a few paragraphs to several pages) and were prepared under different circumstances, at different periods in the life of the Prophet (from 1832 to 1842), and for different audiences. It is not surprising, therefore, that each of them emphasizes different aspects of his experience. Today when Latter-day Saints explain this remarkable vision to others, their descriptions often vary according to the audience or circumstances that prompt such recitals. If one were relating the incident to a group of high priests, for example, he would undoubtedly tell it somewhat differently than he would to individuals who had never heard of Joseph Smith or the restoration of the gospel.

One can better understand and appreciate the different emphases in Joseph's four recitals of the First Vision by examining their individual historical settings, by considering Joseph's efforts to write history, and by noting his attempts to improve the form in which the basic message of the Restoration was conveyed to others.

In the 1832 account Joseph Smith emphasized his long quest for religious truth which emerged from his desire to secure a remission of sins. A concern for the welfare of his soul led him to an investigation of religious communities, and this investigation convinced the boy that religious leaders were teaching doctrines that did not harmonize with New Testament Christianity. In 1832 when the Prophet described what he learned during his vision, he emphasized that the Lord forgave him of his sins, instructed him concerning the Atonement, and said that others had turned aside from the gospel and were not keeping the Lord's commandments.[14]

Two accounts, the 1835 diary record and the brief history published in 1842 known as the Wentworth Letter, were directed

---

[14]See Appendix A.

to a non-Mormon audience. In these accounts the Prophet emphasized the confusion which developed in his mind because professors of religion proclaimed conflicting doctrines. In the 1835
recital the Prophet said:

> Being wrought up in my mind respecting the subject of
> Religion, and looking at the different systems taught the
> children of men, I knew not who was right or who was
> wrong, but considered it of the first importance to me
> that I should be right, in matters of so much moment,
> matters involving eternal consequences.[15]

A similar theme was included in the history which the Prophet
wrote in the early 1840s:

> Considering that all could not be right, and that God
> could not be the author of so much confusion I determined
> to investigate the subject more fully, believing that if God
> had a church it would not be split up into factions, and
> that if he taught one society to worship one way, and
> administer in one set of ordinances, he would not teach
> another principles which were diametrically opposed.[16]

After emphasizing in the two accounts addressed to non-
Mormons that he was perplexed because of the different religious
systems that were being advanced by others, he wrote that he
called upon the Lord in prayer. In the condensed version which
was based on a conversation between Joseph Smith and Matthias,
Joseph Smith's scribe recorded in the Prophet's diary that during
this first communication Joseph learned that his sins were forgiven and that Jesus Christ is the Son of God (two concepts that
were included in the 1832 autobiography). This account was not
written for publication, nor did the Prophet include it with many
other selections from his diary in his official history of the Church.
Joseph Smith prepared for publication two more detailed accounts
of this experience. Consequently, this 1835 diary entry mentioned
only a few truths which he learned when he was "about" fourteen
years old.[17]

Even though the summary included in the Wentworth Letter
of the truths which were unfolded in the 1820 vision was very

---

[15]See Appendix B.
[16]See Appendix D.
[17]See Appendix B.

different from the 1835 diary account, all except one concept disclosed in that account harmonized with details that had been included in the 1832 or the 1838 recital. After writing that he learned that all religious denominations believed in incorrect doctrines (a concept recorded in 1832 and 1838), Joseph added a concept that was not mentioned in any of the other accounts. He received the promise, he wrote, "that the fulness of the gospel should at some future time be made known unto me."[18]

Although the Prophet testified in the two accounts which were addressed to non-Mormons that two personages appeared to him, he did not identify these heavenly beings in those recitals. Joseph had experienced cruel persecution for claiming that he beheld visions, and perhaps he hesitated in revealing to some that he had been instructed by God Himself. The First Vision, along with many other visions received by the Prophet, was a sacred experience. Perhaps the Prophet decided in some instances not to broadcast the fact that he had seen the Father and the Son, especially to individuals who might have said that with God all things were possible except appearing to a young boy in the new nation, ridiculing an experience that Joseph cherished because of its sacredness. According to the Prophet, one reason he commenced writing a history in 1838 was to correct many false reports that had been circulated regarding his religious experiences. He was the only one who knew many details concerning his remarkable visions. Therefore, he decided to write about many events in his life so that a reliable history would be available for earnest inquirers.

In the official history of the Church which he commenced in 1838, Joseph Smith identified the two personages as the Father and the Son. This history was the most carefully prepared account and contains many details not included in other records. This was the only account in which Joseph described in detail the religious awakenings and war of words which occurred at the time of the First Vision. It was also the only account in which Joseph Smith specified that during the vision he was told that the professors of religion had a form of godliness but denied "the power thereof."[19] Meanwhile, other individuals, members and non-members, who were close associates of the Prophet or who interviewed the Mormon leader, wrote descriptions of the First Vision based on

[18]See Appendix D.
[19]See Appendix C.

what they had learned from Joseph Smith, and they reported that he testified that during his First Vision he beheld the Father and the Son.[20]

Joseph Smith did not mention in his 1832 account the appearance of the Father nor of angels. He emphasized instead the truths conveyed to him by the Lord. Such an omission, however, does not preclude the fact that the Father appeared to the fourteen-year-old boy. After Joseph Smith wrote the account of this vision which was published in the official history of the Church, he prepared the Wentworth Letter, which, as previously explained, did not identify the personages who appeared to him. None of the accounts written by Joseph Smith are complete descriptions of this remarkable vision. In Joseph Smith's most extensive account, the 1838 history, the Prophet concluded by writing that during his First Vision he learned many other things. By examining the other three accounts we can learn some of the other truths which were unfolded in 1820, but probably not all. The experience in the Sacred Grove was undoubtedly so glorious that the Prophet found it difficult to explain in human language his innermost feelings and to delineate many concepts which he learned during this visitation of the Father and the Son.

Some critics have suggested that there was an evolutionary development in Joseph Smith's descriptions of his First Vision and that as the years passed the Mormon Prophet extended his claims concerning that which he learned in the Sacred Grove. Such a charge does not seem justified by a careful comparison of the four recitals. All emphasize different themes. The first two recorded accounts state, for example, that during his First Vision Joseph was told he was forgiven of his sins. All except the 1835 recital emphasize that during this vision he was instructed to join none of the churches. All except the 1832 account reported that two personages appeared, and in the 1835 diary report Joseph Smith stated that he saw many angels during this vision. The 1835 and 1838 accounts refer to the presence of an evil power prior to his visitation from the two glorious personages. All except the 1832 autobiography refer to his reading the admonition of James regarding prayer prior to his petitioning his Heavenly Father. The variations of the accounts, therefore, do not follow a particular pattern.

---

[20]See Appendixes C, I and J.

Harmony of Eight Contemporary Accounts of the First Vision

Instead of an evolutionary development, the following summary reflects the harmony and also the different emphases appearing in the four recitals prepared by the Prophet (and his contemporaries).[21] The dates in the first set of parentheses refer to the approximate date when Joseph Smith wrote the account, and the letters in the second set of parentheses refer to four other accounts written or published by contemporaries before 1844: Orson Pratt's *Several Remarkable Visions* (1840, identified as P); Orson Hyde's *A Cry from the Wilderness* (1842, identified as H); an account written by a non-Mormon and printed in the New York *Spectator*, September 23, 1843 (identified as S); and an account recorded in the diary of Alexander Neibaur (identified as N). (See Appendixes A-H.)

THE HISTORICAL SETTING

Joseph's quest for forgiveness of his sins, his concern for his soul and/or his preparation for a future estate.	(1832, 1835, 1842) (P, H)
Joseph's concern for mankind in general.	(1832) (P, H)
Joseph's investigation of various faiths.	(1832, 1835, 1838, 1842) (P, H)
Joseph's concern because faiths proclaimed conflicting doctrines.	(1838, 1842) (P, H)
Joseph's desire to know which church to join or his desire to join Christ's church.	(1832, 1835, 1838, 1842) (P, H, S)
Joseph's quest continued for several years.	(1832)

---

[21]See Appendixes A-D. There are not only variations in the accounts written by Joseph Smith but in accounts written by Joseph Smith's contemporaries as they recorded what they learned from the Prophet. "In the case of versions written by others," it is not surprising that people were impressed with different concepts and therefore recorded accounts differently, using their language and emphasizing points that most impressed them. James B. Allen, "Eight Contemporary Accounts of Joseph Smith's First Vision," *The Improvement Era*, LXXIII (April, 1970), 6.

Unusual religious excitement in the area.	(1838) (N)
Contention among the faiths.	(1838, 1842) (P, H)
Joseph's searching the scriptures (Bible).	(1832, 1835, 1838, 1842) (P, H, S, N)
Joseph's reading James 1:5.	(1835, 1838, 1842) (P, H, S, N)
Joseph's seeking an answer through prayer.	(1832, 1835, 1838, 1842) (P, H, S, N)
Vision occurred when he was about fourteen or fifteen.	(1832, 1835, 1838, 1842) (P, H, S, N)
Vision occurred in the spring of 1820.	(1838)

THE VISION
(Truths revealed and descriptions of what Joseph beheld)

God hears and answers prayers and intervenes in the affairs of men.	(1832, 1835, 1838, 1842) (P, H, S, N)
The power of evil is real and strong.	(1835, 1838) (P, H)
The power of God is stronger than the influence of evil.	(1835, 1838) (P, H)
Joseph was enwrapped in a pillar of light and/or filled with unspeakable joy (or the Spirit of God).	(1832, 1835, 1838) (P, H)
Joseph beheld two personages.	(1835, 1838, 1842) (P, H, S, N)
The two personages resembled each other in features and likeness.	(1835, 1838, 1842) (P, H)
The two personages were identified as the Father and the Son, and man was created in the image of God.	(1838) (S)
Joseph saw many angels.	(1835)

THE MESSAGE

Jesus Christ is the Son of God.	(1835, 1838) (S)

The Lord was crucified for the world, and all who believe in him will have eternal life.	(1832)
The Second Coming of Christ is imminent.	(1832)
Joseph was forgiven of his transgressions.	(1832, 1835) (P, N)
God's true church was not upon the earth in 1820.	(1832, 1838, 1842) (P, H, N)
Professors of religion taught incorrect doctrines.	(1832, 1838, 1842) (P, H, N)
Professors of religion denied the power of God.	(1838)
The fulness of the gospel would be revealed to Joseph.	(1842) (P, H)
Joseph learned many other truths.	(1838)

AFTERMATH

Joseph rejoiced, for he was filled with peace and love.	(1832) (P, H)
Joseph's unsuccessful attempt to convince ministers and others outside his family of his vision.	(1838) (N)
Joseph persecuted after reporting his vision.	(1832, 1838) (S)

(For additional references, by contemporaries, of Joseph Smith's testimony that he beheld the Father and the Son during his First Vision and reports of what he learned during this vision see Appendixes I-J. See also various accounts related by Orson Pratt in the *Journal of Discourses*, 12:353-55; 13:65-67; 14:140-41; 22:29.)

Early Persecution

Another question that has been raised about the accuracy of Joseph's writings pertains to the availability of evidence that Joseph Smith was persecuted in the early 1820s. In the 1838 recital of the First Vision, Joseph Smith declared that a "few days" after his experience in the Sacred Grove he happened to be in the company of a Methodist minister, and while conversing with this preacher he informed the minister of his theophany. "I was greatly surprised at his behavior," Joseph declared;

> he treated my communication not only lightly but with great contempt, Saying it was all of the Devil, that there were no such things as visions or revelations in these days. . . . I soon found however that my telling the story had excited a great deal of prejudice against me among professors of religion and was the Cause of great persecution which continued to increase and though I was an obscure boy, only between fourteen and fifteen years of age . . . Yet men of high standing would take notice sufficient to excite the public mind against me and create a bitter persecution, and this was common among all the Sects: all united to persecute me.[22]

What evidence exists, some have asked, that Joseph Smith was persecuted during the months and years immediately following his First Vision? In responding to such a question, one needs to remember that, generally speaking, persecutors do not describe their acts of oppression. Intolerant acts usually are recorded by those who have been subjected to persecution. In addition to the testimony of Lucy Mack Smith that someone attempted to assassinate her son when he was about fourteen, circumstantial evidence confirms Joseph Smith's testimony that in the early 1820s he was persecuted. Others living in the Burned-over District endured a similar form of persecution; and the same kinds of historical sources available today to substantiate the non-Mormon oppression vindicate Joseph's testimony regarding the prejudices exerted against him.

This book includes many references to individuals who lived in western New York during the early nineteenth century (for example, James Erwin, David Marks, William Lewis and Jemima Wilkinson) who complained they experienced harsh treatment from others because of their expressions of religious conviction. Moreover, the Hurlbut affidavits illustrate the type of "evil" stories that were circulated about the Smiths in the neighborhood where they lived during the 1820s.

---

[22]See Appendix C.

Evidence of oppression experienced by various contemporaries of Joseph Smith who lived in the Burned-over District follows a common pattern. Many who endured the bigotry of that age complained in their writings that they were cruelly treated and misrepresented. Occasionally others bore witness that individuals of diverse religious and philosophical beliefs with whom they were acquainted were mistreated. Affidavits were sometimes circulated defaming men's characters; and writers published in their works, without restraint, exaggerated statements, unjustifiable opinions, and malicious lies denouncing individuals living in the Finger Lake country. These various forms of evidence tend to substantiate Joseph's testimony that, because of his unorthodox statements, others excited the public against him, and that people of various denominations united to persecute him.

Joseph Smith lived during an age of paradoxes. The early nineteenth century was an era when men boasted that freedom of conscience was one of man's inalienable rights but refused to extend this right to many with whom they disagreed. Like many other Christians of that age, Joseph Smith must have been continually perplexed as he endured bitter persecution throughout his life from his fellow citizens in a land built on the idea of individual liberty and freedom of conscience.

While tangible and circumstantial evidence confirms Joseph Smith's historical descriptions of events that occurred about the time of the First Vision, this evidence does not prove that he was visited by the Father and Son in a peaceful grove in upper New York in the spring of 1820. The only route by which earnest seekers after truth will learn of the reality of the Restoration is through the guidance and power of the Holy Ghost. Faith is a gift of God, and a conviction that one of the greatest visions in the history of the world occurred in 1820 is one important element of that gift.

When Joseph Smith walked from the Sacred Grove in 1820 he knew more about God and Christ and the conditions of the churches of that age than any other mortal soul, but that vision was merely the beginning. Other visions and revelations would follow that theophany, expanding, line upon line, Joseph's understanding of the connections between God and man. The young Joseph, filled with unspeakable joy and peace as he walked home from the grove that spring day, would usher in a new era in the religious history of mankind—the dispensation of the fulness of times.

Bibliography

GUIDES FOR RESEARCH

Brigham, Clarence S. *History and Bibliography of American Newspapers*, 1690-1820. 2 vols. Worchester: American Antiquarian Society, 1947.

Burr, Nelson, and others (editors). *A Critical Bibliography of Religion in America.* Vol. 4. Princeton: Princeton University Press, 1961.

Carman, Harry J., and Arthur W. Thompson. *A Guide to the Principal Source for American Civilization, 1800-1900, in the City of New York: Manuscripts.* New York: Columbia University Press, 1960.

Gregory, Winifred. *Union Lists of Serials.* New York: H. W. Wilson Co., 1943.

Hamer, Philip M. *A Guide to Archives and Manuscripts in the United States.* New Haven: Yale University Press, 1961.

Handlin, O., and others (editors). *Harvard Guide to American History.* Cambridge: Harvard University Press, 1954.

Kirkham, E. Kay. *A Survey of American Church Records, for the Period Before the Civil War, East of Mississippi River.* Salt Lake City: Deseret Book Co., 1959.

Mode, P. G. *Sourcebook and Bibliography Guide for American Church History.* J. S. Canner, 1964.

Roorbach, O. A. *Bibliotheca Americana: Catalogue of American Publications . . . 1820 to 1852.* New York: Peter Smith, 1939.

Shaw, Ralph R., and Shoemaker, Richard H. *American Bibliography: A Preliminary Checklist 1801 to 1819. Author Index.* New York: Scarecrow Press, 1966.

Shipton, Clifford K., and Mooney, James E. *National Index of American Imprints Through 1800: The Short-Title Evans.* 2 vols. Worchester: American Antiquarian Society, 1969.

Winchell, Constance M. *Guide to Reference Books.* Chicago: American Library Association, 1967.

PRIMARY SOURCES

Unpublished Sources

Albany Synod Records, 1812-1828. Presbyterian Historical Society, Philadelphia, Pennsylvania.

Benjamin Lane, March 28, 1822. MS in the Syracuse University Library.

Butler, Charles. Charles Butler Collection. MSS in the Library of Congress.

Farmington Monthly Meetings (Society of Friends). Pt. 9, 10, 11, 12, 17. Microfilm copy in Genealogical Society, Salt Lake City, Utah.

Journal of the Genesee Conference, 1810-1828. Wyoming Seminary, Kingston, Pennsylvania.

Journal of Reuben Miller. LDS Church Historian's Office, Salt Lake City, Utah.

Justice Records, 1828-1830. Town Clerk's Office, Clifton Springs, New York.

Neibaur, Alexander. Journal. LDS Church Historian's Office.

Populations Schedules of the Fourth Census of the United States, 1820. Washington: National Archives, 1959. Microfilm Roll 62, New York, Vol. I.

Public School Records. MSS in Town Clerk's Office, Clifton Springs, New York.

Records of the Bath Presbytery, 1817-1826. Presbyterian Historical Society, Philadelphia, Pennsylvania.

Records of the First Baptist Church of Farmington. American Baptist Historical Society, Rochester, New York.

Records of the First Baptist Church of Macedon. American Baptist Historical Society, Rochester, New York.

Records of the Genesee Presbytery, 1819-1826. Presbyterian Historical Society, Philadelphia, Pennsylvania.

Records of the Palmyra Schools. Public Library, Palmyra, New York.

Records of the Presbytery of Cayuga. Vol. I. Presbyterian Historical Society, Philadelphia, Pennsylvania.

Records of the Presbytery of Geneva. Presbyterian Historical Society, Philadelphia, Pennsylvania.

Records of the Sessions of the Presbyterian Church, Palmyra. Western Presbyterian Church, Palmyra, New York.

Records of the Synod of Genesee. Presbyterian Historical Society, Philadelphia, Pennsylvania.

Smith, Joseph. Kirtland Letter Book, 1829-1835. LDS Church Historian's Office.

——————. History of the Church, A-1, B-1, LDS Church Historian's Office.

Stevenson, Edward. The Life and History. MS in the LDS Church Historian's Office.

Wiles, Harriet M. (comp.). Church Records of the Presbyterian Church of East Palmyra, Wayne County, New York, 1933. Genealogical Society, Salt Lake City, Utah.

Williams, Frederick G. Papers. MSS in LDS Church Historian's Office, Salt Lake City, Utah.

Zion Episcopal Church Records, Palmyra, Wayne County. Copy located in New York Public Library.

Published Sources

Anabaptism Disproved. New York, 1818.

Armenius, Theophilus. "Account of the Rise and Progress of the Work of God in the Western Country," *Methodist Magazine,* II (1819), 272-74.

Bacon, William. *Regeneration, The New Birth. A Sermon delivered May 10th, 1818, at Waterloo.* Waterloo, 1818.

Barclay, Robert. *An Apology for the True Christian Divinity.* London, 1736.

Bell, Benjamin. *Strictures, upon the Doctrine and Discipline, of the Methodist Episcopal Church.* Utica, 1812.

Catlin, Jacob. *The Gentiles Inheritance of the Blessings of Abraham Through Jesus Christ. A Sermon Respecting Infant Baptism.* Canandaigua, 1799.

Chase, Abner. *Recollections of the Past.* New York, 1846.

Clark, Orin. *The Character and Principles of the Protestant Episcopal Church Vindicated; in a Letter Addressed to Rev. W. Bacon.* Geneva, 1818.

Coles, George. *My First Seven Years in America*. New York, 1854.

The Constitution of the State of New York. Fishkill, 1777.

Cooper, William. *Guide in the Wilderness*. New York, 1810.

Crowther, Jonathan. *A True and Complete Portraiture of Methodism*. New York, 1813.

Curtis, Lewis (ed.). *The General Conference of the Methodist Episcopal Church from 1792-1896*. Cincinnati, 1900.

Darby, William. *A Tour from City of New York to Detroit*. New York, 1819.

Duncan, John M. *Travels Through Part of the United States and Canada in 1818 and 1819*. New York, 1823.

Erwin, James. *Reminiscences of Early Circuit Life*. Toledo, Ohio, 1884.

Extracts from the Minutes of the General Assembly of the Presbyterian Church, Philadelphia, 1821.

"Genesee Conference," *Methodist Magazine*, IX (1826), 313-14.

Giles, Charles. *Pioneer: A Narrative of the Nativity, Experience, Travels and Ministerial Labours of Rev. Charles Giles*. New York, 1844.

Gill, John. *Infant-Baptism, A Part and Pillar of Popery*. Boston, 1805.

Hudson, David. *A Review of a Sermon, Delivered at Waterloo, May 10, 1818*, Geneva, 1818.

"Joseph Smith, the Prophet," *Young Woman's Journal*, 1905, XVI, 548-558.

Journals of the General Conventions of the Protestant Episcopal Church in the United States of America; From the Year 1784, to the Year 1814. Philadelphia, 1817.

Journal of the Proceedings of the Bishops, Clergy, and Laity of the Protestant Episcopal Church . . . 1820. Philadelphia, 1820.

Madden, Thomas. "Good Effects of Campmeetings," *Methodist Magazine*, I (1818), 152-53.

Marks, Marilla (ed.). *Memoirs of the Life of David Marks*. Dover, N.H., 1846.

Methodist Minutes, 1810-1830.

Millard, David. *The True Messiah Exalted, or Jesus Christ Really the Son of God, Vindicated; in Three Letters to a Presbyterian Minister.* Canandaigua, 1818.

Minutes of the Cayuga Baptist Association, 1820-1821.

Minutes of the Franklin Baptist Association, 1820.

Minutes of the General Assembly of the Presbyterian Church in the United States of America from its Organization A.D. 1789 to A.D. 1820.

Minutes of the Holland Purchase Baptist Association, 1820-21.

Minutes of the Madison Baptist Association, 1820.

Minutes of the Ontario Baptist Association, 1814-1890.

Minutes of the Oneida Baptist Association, 1820-21.

Minutes of the Otsega Baptist Association, 1820-1821.

Minutes of the Twenty-Sixth Anniversary of the Wayne Baptist Association, 1860.

A Narrative of the Revival of Religion within the Bounds of the Presbytery of Albany, in the Year 1820. Schenectady, 1821.

Neill, Wm. "Thoughts on Revivals of Religion," *The Christian Herald,* VII (1821), 708-11.

Nicholas, John. *A Letter, Addressed to the Episcopalians, and other Religiously Disposed Persons in Waterloo and its Vicinity.* Geneva, 1818.

O'Callaghan, E. B. (ed.). *The Documentary History of the State of New York.* 4 vols., Albany, 1849.

Onderdonk, Henry U. *An Appeal to the Religious Public, in Behalf of the Protestant Episcopal Church, against the Slanders and Sophistry Printed under the name of Rev. W. Bacon.* Canandaigua, 1818.

————. *Baptismal Regeneration: Briefly Defended and Explained.* Canandaigua, 1818.

Perry, William Stevens (ed.). *Journals of General Conventions of the Protestant Episcopal Church, in the United States, 1785-1835.* Claremont, N.H., 1874.

Proceedings of the Baptist General Convention in the United States, at their Second Triennial Meetings. Philadelphia, 1820.

"Revivals of Religion," *The Western New York Baptist Magazine,* III (1820), 90-94.

Ricketson, S. *An Account of the Times and Places of Holding the Meetings Constituting New York Yearly Meeting of Friends.* Poughkeepsie, 1821.

Rupp, I. Daniel (ed.). *An Original History of the Religious Denominations at Present Existing in the United States.* Philadelphia, 1844.

Smith, Eden. "Progress of the Work of God on Hudson-River District," *Methodist Magazine*, V (1822), 474-76.

Smith, Joseph. *History of the Church of Jesus Christ of Latter-day Saints*, ed. B. H. Roberts. 7 vols. 2nd ed. rev. Salt Lake City: Deseret Book Co., 1959-1960.

——— (trans.). The Book of Mormon. Salt Lake City: The Church of Jesus Christ of Latter-day Saints, 1950.

———. The Doctrine and Covenants. Salt Lake City: The Church of Jesus Christ of Latter-day Saints, 1921.

———. The Pearl of Great Price. Salt Lake City: The Church of Jesus Christ of Latter-day Saints, 1952.

Smith, Lucy Mack. *History of Joseph Smith*, ed. Preston Nibley. Salt Lake City: Bookcraft, 1958.

Smith, R. *Recollections of Nettleton, and the Great Revival of 1820.* Albany, 1848.

Spicer, T. "A Short Sketch of the Revival of Religion in the City of Troy, A.D. 1816," *Methodist Magazine*, I (1818), 152-54.

Stansbury, P. *A Pedestrian Tour of Two Thousand Three Hundred Miles, in North America.* New York, 1822.

Sweet, William Warren. *Religion on the American Frontier: A Collection of Source Materials.* 4 vols. New York-Chicago, 1931-1946.

Thacher, William. "A Sketch of the History and Present State of Methodism in Connecticut," *Methodist Magazine*, V (1822), 33-38.

Tuke, Henry. *The Principles of Religion, as Professed by the Society of Christians, Usually Called Quakers.* New York, 1837.

Wesley, John. *Sermons, on Several Occasions.* Hudson, 1810.

Winchester, Elhanan. *Lectures on the Prophecies.* Ballston Spa., New York, 1811.

NEWSPAPERS

The Evening and Morning Star (Independence, Missouri).

Geneva Gazette.

Messenger and Advocate (Kirtland, Ohio).

New York Herald.

New York Observer.

New York Spectator.

Ontario Messenger (Canandaigua, New York).

Ontario Repository (Canandaigua, New York).

The Palmyra Courier.

Palmyra Register.

The Palmyra Reflector.

Phelps Citizen.

The Saints' Herald.

Shortsville Enterprise.

Times and Seasons (Nauvoo, Illinois).

Wayne County Journal (Palmyra, New York).

The Wayne Sentinel (Palmyra, New York).

Weekly Herald (New York).

SECONDARY WORKS

Addison, James Thayer. *The Episcopal Church in the United States.* New York: Charles Scribner's Sons, 1951.

Allen, James B. "Eight Contemporary Accounts of Joseph Smith's First Vision," *The Improvement Era*, LXIII (1970), 4-13.

—————. "The Significance of Joseph Smith's 'First Vision' in Mormon Thought," *Dialogue: A Journal of Mormon Thought*, I (1966), 29-45.

Allen, James, and Arrington, Leonard J. "Mormon Origins in New York: An Introductory Analysis," *BYU Studies*, IX (1969), 241-74.

Anderson, Richard L. "Circumstantial Confirmation of the First Vision Through Reminiscences," *BYU Studies*, IX (1969), 373-404.

—————. "Joseph Smith's New York Reputation Reappraised," *BYU Studies*, X (1970), 283-314.

————. "New Evidence from Modern Witnesses," *The Improvement Era*, LXXI-LXXII (August, 1968-August, 1969).

Backman, Milton V., Jr. *American Religions and the Rise of Mormonism*. Salt Lake City: Deseret Book Co., 1970.

————. "Awakenings in the Burned-over District: New Light on the Historical Setting of the First Vision," *BYU Studies*, IX (1969), 301-20.

————. *A Distinct Theology: A Description of Mormon Beliefs in the Light of Other Patterns of Christian Thought*. Salt Lake City: Deseret Book Co., 1969.

Barber, John W., and Howe, Henry. *Historical Collections of the State of New York*. New York, 1841.

Bean, Willard W. *ABC History of Palmyra and the Beginnings of Mormonism*. Palmyra, 1938.

Betts, George Herbert. *The Beliefs of 700 Ministers*. New York, 1929.

Blakeslee, M. P. "Notes for a History of Methodism in Phelps, 1886." MS copy, Brigham Young University Library.

Bradley, Joshua. *Accounts of Religious Revivals in Many Parts of the U.S. from 1815-1818*. Albany, 1819.

Brown, Charles. "Manchester in the Early Days," *Shortsville Enterprise Press*, 1902-1903.

Burgess, G. A., and Ward, J. T. *Free Baptist Cyclopaedia*. Chicago, 1889.

Carman, Harry J., and Syrett, Harold C. *History of the American People*, New York: Alfred A. Knopf, 1959.

Carmer, Carl. *Genesee Fever*. New York: Farrar and Rinehart, Inc., 1941.

Carrie, John S. *Zion Episcopal Church*, Palmyra, New York, n.p., n.d.

Cheesman, Paul R. "An Analysis of the Accounts Relating Joseph Smith's Early Visions." Unpublished Master's thesis, Brigham Young University, 1965.

Child, Hamilton. *Gazetteer and Business Directory of Ontario County, New York, for 1867-8*. Syracuse, 1867.

Conable, F. W. *History of the Genesee Annual Conference of the Methodist Episcopal Church*. New York, 1885.

Cook, Thomas A. *Palmyra and Vicinity*. Palmyra, 1930.

Cross, Whitney R. *The Burned-over District*. Ithaca: Cornell University Press, 1950.

Dada, W. B. *A History of the Presbyterian Church of East Palmyra*. New York, 1876.

Dayton, Charles H., and Coleman, John Garth. *A Brief History of the Presbytery of Geneva and a Tribute to some Early Ministers*. Shortsville, New York: Geneva-Lyons Presbytery, 1955.

Dexter, Franklin Bowditch. *Biographical Sketches of the Graduates of Yale College with Annals of the College History*. New York, 1907.

Dubler, Alice M. *Manchester Through the Years*. Houghton, New York: Houghton College Press, 1954.

Eldredge, Mary Louise (comp.). *Pioneers of Macedon and other Papers of the Macedon Center Historical Society*. Macedon Center, 1912.

Ellis, David E., and others. *A Short History of New York State*. Ithaca: Cornell University Press, 1967.

Flick, Alexander C. (ed.). *History of the State of New York*. New York City: Columbia University Press, 1935.

Gaustad, Edwin Scott. *Historical Atlas of Religion in America*. New York: Harper and Row, 1962.

Goodykoontz, Colin B. *Home Missions on the American Frontier*. Caldwell, Idaho: Caxton Printers, 1939.

Gregg, Thomas. *The Prophet of Palmyra*. New York, 1890.

Gunn, Stanley R. "Oliver Cowdery: Second Elder of the Church of Jesus Christ of Latter-day Saints." Unpublished Master's thesis, Brigham Young University, 1942.

Gunnell, Wayne Cutler. "Martin Harris—Witness Benefactor to the Book of Mormon." Unpublished Master's thesis, Brigham Young University, 1955.

Hayes, Charles Wells. *The Diocese of Western New York*. Rochester, 1904.

Hayward, John (ed.). *The Book of Religions*. Portland, 1853.

Hedrick, Ulysses Prentiss. *A History of Agriculture in the State of New York*. New York: Hill and Wang, 1966.

Hibbard, F. G. *History of the Late East Genesee Conference of the Methodist Episcopal Church.* New York, 1887.

Hill, Marvin S. "The Role of Christian Primitivism in the Origin and Development of the Mormon Kingdom, 1830-1844." Unpublished Doctor's dissertation, University of Chicago, 1968.

Hinckley, Gordon B. *James Henry Moyle.* Salt Lake City: Deseret Book Co., 1951.

Homer, William. "The Passing of Martin Harris," *The Improvement Era*, XXIX (1926), 470-73.

Hotchkin, James H. *History of the Purchase and Settlement of Western New York, and of the Progress, and Present State of the Presbyterian Church in that Section.* New York, 1848.

Howe, E. D. *Mormonism Unvailed.* Painesville, 1834.

Hyde, Orson. *A Cry From the Wilderness, A Voice From the Dust of the Earth*, trans. Justus Ernst. Frankfurt, Germany, 1842.

Jessee, Dean C., "The Early Accounts of Joseph Smith's First Vision," *BYU Studies*, IX (1969), 275-94.

Katkamier, A. B. (ed.). *The History of the Township of Farmington, New York*, n.p., 1897.

Kelley, William H. "The Hill Cumorah, and the Book of Mormon," *The Saints' Herald*, XXVIII (1881), 161-68.

Kirkham, Francis W. *A New Witness for Christ in America.* 2 vols. Provo: Brigham Young University, 1960.

Lines, Sarah. *One Hundred and Twenty-five Years of the Western Presbyterian Church*, Palmyra, n.p., 1942.

McIntosh, W. H. (ed.). *History of Ontario County, New York.* Philadelphia, 1876.

————. *History of Wayne County, New York.* Philadelphia, 1877.

McNall, Neil Adams. *An Agricultural History of the Genesee Valley 1790-1860.* Philadelphia: University of Pennsylvania Press, 1952.

Milliken, Charles F. *A History of Ontario County, New York and Its People.* 2 vols. New York, 1911.

Nibley, Hugh. "New Approaches to Book of Mormon Study," *The Improvement Era*, LVI-LVII (November, 1953-July, 1954).

————. *The Myth Makers.* Salt Lake City: Bookcraft, 1961.

Nibley, Preston. *Joseph Smith The Prophet.* Deseret News Press: Salt Lake City, Utah, 1944.

Nicholas, Robert Hastings, and Nicholas, James Hastings. *Presbyterianism in New York State.* Philadelphia: Westminster Press, 1968.

Oaks, Mabel E. *History of Oaks Corners Church and Community.* Phelps, 1954.

"Orson Pratt and Joseph F. Smith to John Taylor and the Council of the Twelve," *Millennial Star,* XL (1878), 769-74.

Paddock, Zachariah. *Memoir of Rev. Benjamin G. Paddock.* New York, 1875.

Palmer, Louis De Forest. *Heroism and Romance: Early Methodism in Northeastern Pennsylvania,* n.p. 1950.

Palmyra, Wayne County, New York. Rochester: Woman's Society of the Western Presbyterian Church, 1907.

Parsons, Levi. *History of the Rochester Presbytery.* Rochester, 1889.

Peck, George. *Early Methodism within the Bounds of the Old Genesee Conference from 1788 to 1828.* New York, 1860.

Porter, J. Jemain. *History of the Presbytery of Geneva 1805-1889.* Geneva, 1889.

Porter, Larry C. "Reverend George Lane," *BYU Studies,* IX (1969), 321-40.

Pratt, John Webb. *Religion, Politics, and Diversity: The Church-State Theme in New York History.* Ithaca: Cornell University Press, 1967.

Pratt, Orson. *An Interesting Account of Several Remarkable Visions and of the Late Discovery of Ancient American Records.* New York, 1841.

Quincy, Josiah. *Figures of the Past.* Boston, 1883.

Reynolds, Fred G. *One Hundred Years' History of the First Baptist Church of Macedon, N.Y.* Macedon, n.d.

Richardson, Ebbie L.V. "David Whitmer, A Witness to the Divine Authenticity of the Book of Mormon." Unpublished Master's thesis, Brigham Young University, 1952.

Ridley, Helen Post. *When Phelps Was Young.* Phelps, 1939.

Roberts, B. H. *A Comprehensive History of the Church.* 6 vols. Salt Lake City, 1930.

Spafford, Horatio Gates. *A Gazetteer of the State of New York.* Albany, 1824.

Sprague, William B. *Annals of the American Methodist Pulpit.* New York, 1861.

Stevenson, Edward. *Reminiscences of Joseph, The Prophet, and the Coming Forth of the Book of Mormon.* Salt Lake City, 1891.

Tucker, Pomeroy. *Origin, Rise, and Progress of Mormonism.* New York, 1867.

Turner, O[rsamus]. *History of the Pioneer Settlement of Phelps and Gorham's Purchase, and Morris' Reserve.* Rochester, 1852.

Tuttle, G. A. "Historical Sketch of Palmyra Methodist Episcopal Church." Copy located in Palmyra Public Library.

Tyler, Alice Felt. *Freedom's Ferment.* Minneapolis, 1944.

White, W. Pierrepont. "Indian Possessions and Settled Areas in New York State from 1771 to 1820," *The Rochester Historical Society Publication Fund Series,* VII (1928), 225-33.

Whitney, Helen Mar. "Scenes and Incidents in Nauvoo," *Woman's Exponent,* X (1881), 97-98.

Whittemore, Charles P. *A General of the Revolution, John Sullivan of New Hampshire.* New York: Columbia University Press, 1961.

Willers, Diedrich, Jr. *The Centennial Celebration of General Sullivan's Campaign against the Iroquois, in 1779.* Waterloo, 1880.

Wisbey, Herbert A., Jr. *Pioneer Prophetess: Jemima Wilkinson, the Publick Universal Friend.* Ithaca: Cornell University Press, 1964.

Wissler, Clark. *Indians of the United States.* Garden City, New York: Doubleday, 1948.

Woods, James. *Facts and Observations Concerning the Organization and State of the Churches in the Three Synods of Western New York and the Synod of Western Reserve.* Saratoga Springs, 1837.

Index

Corrections

Page 29, line 30. Substitute the word *east* for *north*.

Page 81, lines 3-4. Substitute the wording "an area east of the Smith farm" for "in or near Phelps or in Oaks Corners, a small farming community situated southeast of Phelps village."

Page 51, line 18. Substitute the word *literary* for *literal*.

Page 88, lines 9-11. Amend sentence beginning "In 1820" to read: "Between 1820 and 1821 there was an increase of 1,885 members in that region, which was one of the largest increases reported at that time by this faith for any section of America."

Page 88, footnote 60. Delete footnote, and substitute: "*Methodist Minutes* (1820), 27-28; *Methodist Minutes* (1821), 27. In 1819 the Genesee District (an ecclesiastical unit containing circuits located in western New York between Lake Cayuga and Buffalo) was divided into two districts. The eastern part was called Ontario, and the western section, the area west of Rochester, retained the name Genesee. The 1820 reported membership in the combined districts was 5,683, and in 1821 it was 7,568, the latter figure representing an increase of 1,885 members between the summer of 1820 and the summer of 1821, with a 398 increase in the Ontario District and 1487 in the Genesee District."

Page 122, lines 21-22. Substitute the wording "written by Joseph Smith" for "dictated by Joseph to his scribe, Frederick G. Williams." (The first portion of this manuscript was dictated by Joseph to his scribe, Frederick G. Williams, but the portion relating to the First Vision was written by Joseph Smith. This is the only account of the First Vision that has been preserved that is in the handwriting of the Prophet. Most of the information recorded by the Prophet was dictated to scribes and therefore is in the handwriting of others. [Note: This affects also the introduction to Appendix A.])

Page 124, line 21. Substitute the word *recording* for *dictating*.

Page 126, line 3. Substitute the word *about* for *in*.

Page 128, line 11. Delete the words "of 1841."

Page 155, line 4. Add the following explanation: "(the portion, however, relating to the First Vision was written by Joseph Smith.)"